MW01038841

JUSTICE AND EMPATHY

ROBERT A. BURT

Justice and Empathy

Toward a Constitutional Ideal

EDITED AND INTRODUCED BY FRANK IACOBUCCI

FOREWORD BY ROBERT C. POST

Yale UNIVERSITY PRESS

NEW HAVEN AND LONDON

Published with assistance from the Ralph S. Brown
Memorial Publication Fund and from the foundation
established in memory of Philip Hamilton McMillan of the
Class of 1894, Yale College.

Yale University Press books may be purchased in quantity
for educational, business, or promotional use. For
information, please e-mail sales.press@yale.edu (U.S. office)
or sales@yaleup.co.uk (U.K. office).

Set in Janson type by IDS Infotech, Ltd.
Printed in the United States of America.

Library of Congress Control Number: 2017938418
ISBN 978-0-300-22426-9 (hardcover : alk. paper)

A catalogue record for this book is available from the
British Library.

This paper meets the requirements of ANSI/NISO Z39.48–
1992 (Permanence of Paper).

10 9 8 7 6 5 4 3 2 1

CONTENTS

FOREWORD

Robert C. Post

On a sunny morning in August of 2015, Bo Burt went swimming in a beloved pond in the Berkshires. He slipped beneath the surface and was suddenly and unaccountably gone. It was an incalculable loss to me personally and to American constitutional law scholarship generally. Bo was a dear friend and a remarkable scholar.

Bo was the last representative of a perspective, once strong at Yale in the work of Joseph Goldstein and Jay Katz, which sought to bring psychoanalytic insights to bear on the analysis of law. Most legal scholars believe that the purpose of law is to provide definitive rules and doctrine. They think of law as a dispute settlement mechanism. Generalizing from impersonal market relationships, they assume that clear and predictable guidelines will empower persons to organize their behavior in the most effective possible way.

Bo entirely rejected this picture of law. From the outset of his career he was fascinated by the governance of intimate rather than impersonal relationships. He realized that in such contexts law could not depend upon "clear-cut rules and . . . formal bureaucratized procedures."[1] It must instead respond to the complex dynamics of actual interpersonal relationships, where the stylized impersonal rationality ordinarily attributed to marketplace actors has little place. Bo explained intimate relationships in the nuanced and layered language of psychoanalysis.

Bo used this same perspective to reconceptualize questions of constitutional law. He argued that constitutional decision makers should not imagine themselves as settling disputes, as creating clear-cut rules that would control the actions of rational actors. Constitutional jurists should instead understand their role as dynamically shaping with the complex psychosocial forces that cause and characterize intergroup conflict.

When Bo died, he left a nearly finished manuscript that directly and beautifully addresses these issues and that has been brought to completion by Bo's dear friend Frank Iacobucci, a former justice of the Canadian Supreme Court. Now published as *Justice and Empathy: Toward a Constitutional Ideal*, the manuscript represents Bo's last and most fully realized defense of his distinctive perspective on constitutional law.

Bo composed the manuscript during his retirement, as the Alexander M. Bickel Professor Emeritus of Law. He was proud of his title. He had learned a great deal from Bickel, his distinguished Yale Law School predecessor. Bickel had taught that constitutionalism in the United States frequently involved fundamental controversies that could not be definitively settled by judges. He had argued that judges could not have the last and final word. He observed that "[v]irtually all important decisions of the Supreme Court are the beginnings of conversations between the Court and the people and their representatives. . . . [T]o say that the Supreme Court lays down the law of the land is to state the ultimate result, following upon a complex series of events. . . . The effectiveness of the judgment universalized depends on consent and administration.[2] Implicit in Bickel's view was a radical account of judicial decision making: "The Court is a leader of opinion, not a mere register of it, but it must lead opinion, not merely impose its own; and—the short of it is—it labors under the obligation to succeed."[3]

Bo became fascinated with the question of how courts might succeed in "leading" opinion. He wanted to know how they could shape public consent in the context of unforgiving and polarizing controversies that rage over issues like the death penalty, racial equality, same-sex marriage, and abortion. Bickel had focused largely on narrow techniques of judicial timing, but Bo wanted to push the issue much further, and in his posthumous book he bequeaths us his most explicit and complete response to this challenge.

Unlike Bickel, Bo offers an explicit theoretical account of the nature of social conflict. Bo begins with the insights of psychoanalysis. He believes that there is an intense and unending struggle within every person between a self that is independent and bounded and a self that is dependent and boundless. Often this struggle can prompt persons to project intolerable aspects of their own selves onto those around them. Persons can control their internal conflicts by subordinating and oppressing the objects of their own projections.

When persons in dominant groups project intolerable aspects of their own personalities onto members of subordinate groups, they frequently use these projections to justify the legal oppression of dominated groups. Bo seeks to explain how such projections ebb and flow in American history and how periods of emancipation are followed by periods of repression. He contends that these psychological mechanisms drive many of our most important constitutional controversies.

Short of reaching an impossible state of nirvana, persons cannot transcend their own intrapsychic conflicts. At most they can acknowledge and mediate these conflicts. This is because aspects of the self that are repressed tend to rebound and find expression in unconscious and therefore uncontrollable ways. *Justice and Empathy* argues that these same mechanisms characterize the psychology of social groups. Dominant groups suppress subordinate groups to ease their own intrapsychic tensions. These tensions cannot simply be erased; they must be acknowledged and mediated.

Building on the work of pioneering theorist Hans Loewald, Bo argues that a psychoanalyst's role is to moderate intrapsychic conflict by making patients aware of internal tensions and by creating "an intertwined equality of authority, between the conflicting forces in individuals' minds." In this way patients are encouraged to establish a "healthier . . . communication and interplay between the world of fantasy and the world of objectivity, between imagination and rationality." Patients who acknowledge the conflicting forces within their own psyches are less likely to act in unconscious and unconscionable ways. They are less likely to project onto others attributes they seek to repress in themselves.

Psychoanalysts seek to encourage such intrapsychic balance by creating a safe holding space for patients to explore the conflicting forces within themselves. Psychoanalysts cannot simply command patients to tolerate intolerable internal conflicts; psychic health is not ultimately a matter of will. Psychoanalysts instead attempt to facilitate psychological health by provoking forms of intrapsychic recognition that are mediated through interpretations continuously shared between therapists and patients. Patients who seek merely to censor uncomfortable aspects of their own personality will experience ever greater self-alienation and suffer from ever more uncontrollable unconscious projections. It is not for nothing that we fear the return of the repressed.

In *Justice and Empathy*, Bo explicitly compares judges to psychoanalysts. Parties involved in a constitutional conflict are typically not the impersonal, rational actors postulated in market transactions. Constitutional conflicts involve social groups struggling to realize their own distinct visions of communal political identity. A group's vision of political identity will reflect internal psychic tensions afflicting the group's members. Judges, like psychoanalysts, must create a safe space within which contending groups can examine the nature of their own internal conflicts. Groups must acknowledge and mediate these conflicts through a continuous public effort to interpret past and present events. Through their unique authority, courts can facilitate these interpretations and create a hope of future cooperation by easing the intrapsychic tension within groups.

If judges were to use mechanical rules to decide cases, one vision of political identity would triumph and the other would be excommunicated. The excommunicated group would be tempted to redouble its efforts to alter political identity outside courts, and its repression and projection might become ever more virulent. Bo observes that rule-bound, inflexible judicial decision making can be constitutionally counterproductive when it unleashes such effects:

> Courts today must guard against resurgence of the psychological forces that have repeatedly impelled subordination of vulnerable groups—not just blacks but women, LGBTQ people, people with disabilities, and convicted criminals. These psychological forces impel some people to protect themselves by inflicting degradation on others; they are powerful and often difficult to detect. If I believe I can affirm my sense of righteousness by projecting (without conscious awareness)

my destructive impulses onto someone else, it is easy for me to imagine myself as pure-hearted. After all, I am acting in compliance with the directive of my internal compass pointed toward righteousness. This self-justificatory attitude among oppressors is so common, so strong, and so much entangled with a conviction of goodness that it is very difficult for the oppressor to see his actions for what they truly are. Somehow the oppressor must be induced to see his mixture of motives, good and bad, honorable and dishonorable—and to accept full responsibility for what he is doing, one might say, with half his mind.

Just as a therapist helps a patient "to develop empathic relations among the conflicting rational and irrational forces in his mind," so an effective judicial remedy should "address hostile subordinating social relations by invoking empathic identification between the previously warring litigants." Judges in constitutional cases should strive to establish a relationship between contending parties in which each can acknowledge and respect the other, even though they may not agree.

Bo writes that judges should pursue this goal by "combining the psychotherapeutic and Socratic principles of pedagogy—by providing a safe space in which litigants are obliged to transform their hostile, disrespectful actions into a conversational interchange in a courtroom where the conflicting parties are required to treat one another with equal mutual respect." Judges should press "litigants to directly interact with one another rather than relating primarily to the judge," and to acknowledge "a shared rather than hierarchically opposed self-identity." The power of a court is "to force into conscious awareness aspects of our relationship to [other] groups that are easily shut away from acknowledgment, often because of unease and even guilt." Courts, like therapists, "must recognize their ultimate powerlessness to resolve the conflicts which appear before them, their dependence on the conflicted parties to take responsibility to forge relationships of mutual respect that supplant the previous hostilities between and within them."

This is, to say the least, a profoundly original and distinctive vision of American constitutional law. Most law professors, like Bo's treasured colleague Owen Fiss, hope that constitutional law will lay down explicit rules that embody "what justice requires, and then, even if the world must be turned upside down, . . . make certain that the dictates of justice become a living truth."[4] For Bo, by contrast, constitutional law concerned relationships rather than outcomes. "[D]emocratic equality is not so much an end state as measured by a judge and much more a relationship of mutual respect among people in conflict with one another. . . . [It] is not for the parties to satisfy the judge's conception of equality," they "must justify themselves to one another."

What was important for Bo was that constitutional litigation "promote empathy rather than confirming or intensifying antagonism between the parties in conflict." Courts should "guide hostile parties into egalitarian democratic interaction based on mutual respect for one another." Without such interaction, Bo believed, the attempted imposition of rules, no matter how ideal in theory, was a self-defeating enterprise. *Justice and Empathy* is about how courts might chart a course toward creating egalitarian democratic interaction. It contains extensive and lively discussions of the U.S. Supreme Court's death-penalty and same-sex-marriage jurisprudence, and more abbreviated comments on its jurisprudence of abortion and race relations.

One can only guess how Bo might have modified the manuscript had he emerged from the pond on that sunny August day. But if he had lived—and what a sad tearful phrase that is—I would have asked him two questions. The first concerns the analogy between the psychic tension that is the domain of psychoanalysis and the social conflict that is the domain of constitutional law. The object of the therapist's intervention is a patient's psychic health. The therapist cannot forcibly produce a patient's health; if therapy fails, the cost is borne entirely by the patient.

Matters seem quite otherwise with respect to a constitutional judge. With respect to the kinds of constitutional issues that concern Bo, the object of judicial intervention is the protection of subjugated groups from the predations of dominant groups. If judicial intervention fails, subjugated groups suffer. Although Bo convincingly establishes that explicit rules cannot heal the relationship between oppressed and oppressor, he does not ask whether such rules might protect the former from overt harm at the hands of the latter. I would have liked to ask Bo whether this difference might justify a greater role for constitutional rules than the analogy to psychotherapy might otherwise suggest. Might rules be necessary to guide judges in their use of judicial violence to protect vulnerable groups?

I would have liked to ask Bo a second question. Throughout *Justice and Empathy*, he eloquently invokes the value of "a democratic relationship of equality between . . . conflicting parties." He rejects the thought that constitutional law can be "nothing more than stylized violence," because that would be "inherently irreconcilable with democratic values." He advocates that constitutional law be understood as a set of "self-consciously adopted processes . . . [to] promote empathy rather than confirming or intensifying antagonism between the parties in conflict."

It is grievous that I can no longer ask Bo to clarify this concept of "democratic values." Throughout *Justice and Empathy*, he characterizes these values as analogous to a psychologically healthy person in which all dimensions of a personality are acknowledged, respected, and dynamically interconnected. So perhaps this image is the source of Bo's constitutional ideal, which suggests that for Bo constitutionalism ultimately rests on an analogy between individual psychological health and the social health of the body politic.

Yet sometimes Bo appeals to the concept of "democratic values" in a manner that reflects a different and more distinctively legal etiology. I have in mind a passage in his discussion of the Court's jurisprudence of same-sex marriage, when he suddenly and surprisingly asserts that despite the importance of "deliberative processes in the formulation of constitutional protections for vulnerable, subjugated groups," courts should nevertheless not "wait indefinitely for popular majorities to form." The thought that the constitutional "goal" of emancipation should override constitutional processes of deliberation is startling in light of the overall thesis of *Justice and Empathy*.

The anomaly suggests that Bo might be torn between a psychoanalytically oriented ideal of social health and a specifically legal ideal of harm prevention. Had Bo lived, this tension would no doubt have been the subject of long and illuminating discussions. When he was alive, we had many such intense and enlightening conversations. But, as matters stand, *Justice and Empathy* escorts us to the very verge of this deep and provocative question and leaves us with only tantalizing hints.

The prevention of harm is a traditional legal objective that justifies the prohibition of certain clearly defined behaviors. Social health, by contrast, is not a traditional legal objective; it is a large, diffuse, and positive aspiration that cannot be ascertained by definite metrics or guideposts. The prevention of harm and the aspiration to social health might actually be in tension with each other. The path to social health might require the temporary acceptance of harm; the premature prevention of harm might damage the ultimate achievement of social health. The most profound contribution of *Justice and Empathy* is the exploration of these uncomfortable tensions.

I can imagine Bo asking, for example, whether the holding of the Supreme Court in *Obergefell*, which forcibly suppresses bans against same-sex marriage, might have prompted the displacement of prejudice against LGBTQ people into the pervasive and increasingly powerful language of religious exceptionalism and conscientious objection. *Justice and Empathy* is unsettling because it asks whether categorical holdings like *Obergefell*, which avert obvious and immediate harm, might actually increase long-term injurious social conflict. Although *Justice and Empathy* is undeniably oriented toward long-term benefits, it never explicitly addresses the trade-off between preventing present harm and facilitating future health. Resolving such puzzles requires a clearer sense of the "democratic values" that ought to guide judicial decision making.

Justice and Empathy is written with Bo's usual verve and elegance. It is clear, original, and consequential. It is a hard book to put down. Every page yields lovely and characteristic insights. The book makes Bo's loss so palpable and consequential that it is difficult to bear.

I said at Bo's funeral that we were lucky to "still have with us Bo's remarkable texts to help us in the difficult task of acknowledging the ambiguous fullness of our own humanity."⁵ I did not know then about *Justice and Empathy*. This posthumous book is an unexpected gift from a departed friend. Reading it is like hearing Bo alive once again, summoning us to acknowledge and forgive our own frailties.

In death, as in life, Bo calls on us to appreciate the complex web of human relationships in which our constitutional values are necessarily embodied. Even the great ideal of justice cannot be separated from the human fragility of empathy.

INTRODUCTION

Frank Iacobucci

This book is unusual in a number of ways. Sadly, the manuscript is the last one Robert A. Burt (Bo) worked on before his sudden death.[1] Happily, we are blessed that he was able to complete what can be described as a triumphant valedictory addition to his research, scholarship, and teaching over some fifty years.

As a preliminary matter, I should explain why I refer to the author as "Bo." When I met him twenty years ago, he immediately instructed me to call him that. Since then he has been Bo, and I find it both awkward and somehow inappropriate for me to refer to him differently, just as it is for his many friends. I hope the informality is acceptable.

This book is about how the U.S. Constitution, through its interpretation by the U.S. Supreme Court, deals with the protection of vulnerable people in American society. Key to that discussion is what the role of the Court is in that exercise. In answering the question, Bo departs from what he admits is the conventional view of what judges are expected to do: to decide conclusively disputes between conflicting parties. As seen in his previous scholarship and developed in the book, Bo prefers to focus on the judge not as the sole determiner of equality or protection but as a leader who, through careful observation and guidance, promotes an interactive process among the parties in order to settle the matter in an empathic, mutually respectful way. To Bo, what counts is not the binding decision of a judge but the process of the parties trying to work things out for themselves facilitated by the court. To support this view, along with an exegesis of the relevant jurisprudence, he conducts an interdisciplinary tour through social history, psychoanalysis, morality, and democratic theory, all of which emanate from his scholarship over some five decades. What is especially noteworthy in his scholarship and this book is the weaving into his commentary of those different disciplines to fashion a coherent and illuminating discussion. He then applies the lessons learned from that discussion to some important contemporary issues in America.

Another unusual feature of the book is the infusion of personal experiences that Bo encountered during his extraordinary life and impressive career. He was sensitive to their inclusion because he did not want the book to be autobiographical or otherwise detract readers from his main messages. The fact is that he witnessed or actively engaged in many issues that arose in a period of relentless social and judicial change in America. His life experiences illustrate, if not underscore, the importance and impact of these changes. His skillful handling of the personal episodes not only makes the book's themes realistic but also brings out the humanity of its author.

My involvement in this book stems from my recent teaching collaboration with Bo, and my friendship with him over the last twenty years. When I was a sitting justice of the Supreme Court of Canada we had many discussions on topics of interest as the Court was hearing cases on those subjects; they were of interest to Bo because they related to his scholarly and research work. After my retirement from the Court, those discussions led to our co-teaching an intensive course at the Yale Law School on selected topics in comparative American and Canadian constitutional law. It was somewhat surprising that Bo wanted to do this, since he had stopped teaching constitutional law some years earlier, because of what he regarded as the disappointing jurisprudence of the U.S. Supreme Court. He told me that the promise of the Court in *Brown v. Board of Education*[2] had been so diminished that he found it difficult to teach the subject. But in our collaboration he was enthusiastic and inspiring both to the students and to me. I saw firsthand his profound commitment to teaching and to sharing his views with his students in order to prompt their reactions and engage them in discussion. All of my contact and discussion with Bo led to my reading a number of his manuscripts, including the last one that is now this book. He sent me an earlier draft of the book, and we had a lengthy discussion before he wrote the present version. About ten days after our conversation, he died.

I was then invited to be the editor of the book, which I accepted as a personal and professional honor.

The book is divided into two parts: part I is a historical and theoretical discussion of constitutional law and related disciplines regarding the protection of vulnerable people; and part II deals with practical applications of some constitutional issues in the protection of vulnerable people in contemporary America. In the hopes of providing something close to what Bo would have written for the reader, I now turn to a brief overview of the book.

Bo's profound concern for justice came from his study of and career in the law, which did not get off to a good start. As he describes in chapter 1, he began his law studies in England and was greatly disappointed with what he regarded as an overconcentration on rules that made the subjects artificial. This disappointment vanished when he entered the Yale Law School, which emphasized a much broader and deeper approach to law beyond a set of rules and doctrine. For this transformational change in his attitude toward law and legal education, Bo especially credits two of his eminent instructors, soon to become mentors, who brought to the subject a psychoanalytically informed understanding of people and human conflict. He embraced and impressively built on this approach by enlisting the perspectives of other scholarly disciplines, becoming a major figure in legal scholarship.

Chapter 1 also discusses the concept of law and the legal and social role of the courts—especially the U.S. Supreme Court—as a moral and social agent for change, particularly in protecting the minority or the disadvantaged in society as opposed to favoring the strong or majority over the weak or minority. This raises questions about who is the majority or minority or the stronger or the weaker, and who decides the answers to these questions, all of which he lucidly explores in the book.

As an account of social history, chapters 2 and 3 deal with the judicial and moral authority of the Supreme Court and the Court's promotion of the interests of vulnerable people and of emancipation for subjugated groups. Bo discusses the resulting controversies and conflicts, including the Revolutionary War, the profound disruption of the Civil War, and its aftermath up through the present, from which he highlights modern examples of emancipation. He also discusses the changing role of the Court from curbing the emancipatory platform to expanding emancipatory efforts, and signaling more to come. The springboard for the modern treatment of the subject is the famous "Footnote Four" of the decision in *United States v. Carolene Products Company*.[3] In that case, the Court held that it would not defer to legislation that was hostile to "discrete and insular minorities" and that it would conduct a "searching judicial inquiry" to protect them. Bo returns to Footnote Four many times in subsequent chapters.

In chapter 4, Bo introduces the psychological aspects of subjugative relations in society by examining the psychological obstacles and benefits arising from those relations. This reflects a major contribution of Bo's broad scholarly reach to understand the forces at work in human interaction that he believed the legal system should take into account. He discusses the psychological benefits to the subjugator that result from the subordination of others and that engender profound resistance to the emancipation. This discussion introduces a consideration of the views of an array of great thinkers—Hobbes, Freud, Libet, Baars, Taylor, Armstrong, Goffman, and others—to elaborate on his central topic of the protection of minorities and the weak and the role of the court in that mission.

Chapter 5 deals with the question of whether social institutions can be designed to promote a just resolution of the conflict between oppressor and oppressed, and whether there is a special role for the judiciary in that regard. Bo here notes the suffering that oppressors inflict on themselves and explores how that can be turned into emancipation for the vulnerable. He mines an exceptionally varied mix of commentators (including a plantation mistress, de Tocqueville, Loewald, Socrates, and Callicles) for insights on the role of the judiciary, and, surprisingly at first blush, he provides an interesting and enlightening comparison between judges and psychotherapists.

Ending part I of the book, chapter 6 discusses the Supreme Court's approach to school desegregation. On this matter, Bo argues that the

Court changed from a hierarchical institution to a more egalitarian or conversational democratic model that recognized the work of others outside the court system (such as psychologists whose views outlined the unequal feeling of segregated black school children) and largely left enforcement of desegregation to local federal district court judges. He asserts that overall the Court adopted an impressive strategic approach to school desegregation. After acknowledging the democratic deficit for blacks in their exclusion from legislative representation, he proposes that the local federal district courts served as surrogate democratic chambers for whites and blacks to work out their differences peaceably.

Part II, which deals with practical contemporary examples of constitutional protection of the vulnerable, begins in chapter 7 with the Supreme Court's jurisprudence on the death penalty. Bo makes clear his view that the death penalty must be abolished and submits that even in this context, where mutual respect can be harder to achieve, judicial interventions should foster deliberations among conflicting parties. In this area, he reiterates that the judiciary should not be a hierarchal arbiter of winners and losers that leaves no space for further deliberations. Chapter 7 also draws on his earlier discussion about the similarities between the psychotherapist and the judge in their common obligation to separate personal from public values in their roles. The chapter proceeds to a discussion of the imprisonment of convicted criminals and their treatment as "civilly dead," as shown in particular by the extreme sanction of solitary confinement, and concludes with suggestions to enhance the likelihood of an empathic, mutually respected approach to this vulnerable group.

Chapter 8 deals with gays and lesbians as another group that Bo argues was subjected to serious degradation akin to the terrible mistreatment of blacks. His discussion of the jurisprudence on same-sex relationships is succinct and insightful. Especially enlightening is his description of the tension between the judiciary and legislatures in the evolution of the relationship up to the recognition of a fundamental right to marital status for same-sex couples. In this chapter, Bo characterizes the changes that took place in California, through events that involved the legislature, courts, and the public, as reflecting an egalitarian mode of deliberative authority, the main component of his constitutional theory.

The difficult topic of abortion is the subject of chapter 9. After rejecting as inappropriate the usual justifications for abortion rights, such as privacy and the harm principle, Bo presents the equality guarantee and dignity as providing a better rationale and goes on to offer an analysis of his proposed theoretical foundation to deal with the topic: shared egalitarian authority. He postulates that by conclusively resolving the abortion dispute initially, the Supreme Court missed the chance to invite the disputing parties to face each other to try to ascertain for themselves whether they could reach an accommodation, thereby avoiding a winner-versus-loser result.[4] He goes on to discuss some of the fallout from the Court's attempt to impose a final resolution on a deeply divided public, including the battle between opposing factions to ensure that a majority of judges would be appointed to the Court who would rule their way.

It is in chapter 10 that Bo discusses race relations as the paradigmatic judicial effort to protect vulnerable groups under the commitment made in Footnote Four. In his view, after the Supreme Court correctly held in *Brown I*[5] that racial segregation in schools was unconstitutional, and in *Brown II*[6] wisely paused to enlist the assistance of district courts, the federal Congress, the executive, and others, the Court then failed to continue this approach after the passing of the Civil Rights Act of 1964, the Voting Rights Act of 1965, and the Fair Housing law in 1968 by requiring past intentionally imposed race discrimination in public schools to obtain judicial relief. This view prompts Bo to offer suggestions on what the Court could have done, consistent with his approach of less intervention by the Court imposing its views of equality on the parties and more promotion of deliberation among the parties to achieve democratic equality.

The arena for Bo's thesis in chapter 11 changes from the courtroom to the legislature to point out that judges are not the only actors through whom democratic values founded on empathic mutual respect and accountability can be promoted. Here Bo recounts his experience as a legislative assistant to Senator Joseph D. Tydings from Maryland. At the center of the intriguing story is the Civil Rights Act of 1968, the passage of which was threatened by a Southern filibuster that could be ended by a favorable vote for cloture. It turned out that one senator from Alaska was key to the favorable vote; his vote was cast in a most dramatic way, as he was ultimately persuaded by his realization of the moral significance of what was at issue. Bo notes that the senator was not commanded by party leaders to vote but, left alone to reflect on the matter, he was persuaded by his conscience to do the right thing. Bo relates the story as implicit support for his thesis that limited intervention by courts can enable antagonistic parties to be left to reflect and let their conscience arrive at the morally correct result.

At this point, I wish to refer briefly to the anonymous external reviewers to whom Yale University Press sent the manuscript for their assessment. First of all, I wish to thank these readers for their cogent comments and positive recommendation for publication. One reviewer pointed out how odd it was to review a posthumous manuscript, since making suggestions for improvement, under the circumstances, seemed irrelevant. Obviously, Bo would have responded respectfully to the reviewers, and equally obviously, it is inappropriate for me to presume my comments reflect what he would have thought or written. I can say, however, that some of the points raised by the reviewers reflect differences of opinion among constitutional law scholars that Bo expressly recognized and mentioned, both in the book and to his students. The reviewers' comments, nonetheless, do praise the originality and ingenuity of Bo's interdisciplinary approach, particularly its reliance on psychoanalysis.

One reviewer questioned whether Bo has successfully refuted the conventional view that law's role and legitimacy rests on the ability of judges to provide clear, predictable, and certain closure to disputes, versus Bo's concept of a more therapeutic legal system in which judges recognize the psychosocial dynamics of the antagonistic parties and try to encourage reconciliation between them. I agree with the reviewer when he or she says that Bo's constitutional ideal is treating everyone with equal respect, that is, listening to all concerned to appreciate their perspectives. All of this in turn means that for Bo it is the design of a process for a respectful dialogue that is important, not the judicial search for a definitive answer to the conflict. I suspect that many observers will point to both theoretical and practical difficulties with that approach.

In this respect, one of Bo's closest friends and distinguished colleagues, Owen Fiss, gave an eloquent tribute to Bo at his memorial service at the Yale Law School,[7] in which he pointed to many similarities between himself and his friend. But he also mentioned some differences, including an important substantive one: their views on the role of the judiciary. After referring to Bo's view, as expressed in this book, that the judge must never dictate the outcome of a dispute, since the conflicting parties must work it out for themselves, he expressed quite a different opinion: "I, on the other hand, have always saddled the judiciary with a much more grandiose, perhaps impossible, task: not just to facilitate and enhance a conversation, but rather to discover what justice requires, and then, even if the world must be turned upside down, to make certain the dictates of justice become a living truth."[8]

As a former judge, I find both Bo's and Owen's views attractive and persuasive and I believe both views are instructive. The application of one view over the other will often be dictated by the particular context of a case and the issues before the court. One can argue, for example, that Bo's view recognizes that a final binding decision often ends the legal case but not the human conflict between the parties, and that Bo's proposal for an egalitarian interactive model between the parties has a better chance of resolving the human controversy. I have sat on cases where the court in effect gave guidelines for the parties to negotiate a settlement with no binding decision—a purely Bo viewpoint, support for which can be found in a recent decision of the Supreme Court.[9] I have also, however, participated in many cases where Owen's approach of describing what justice requires in terms of a specific outcome, bolstered by reasoning and respect for the parties, can likewise end the legal dispute as well as the controversy

between the parties. Which approach to employ is another challenge that the judiciary must confront along with the traditional tasks of judges in resolving disputes. This book will be of assistance to lawyers, judges, and law students who are grappling with such issues.

Bo's contribution in writing the book is an enlightening and original addition to our understanding of the protection of minorities in society and of the role of courts in that undertaking. For that, those interested in the law and legal institutions should be deeply grateful.

JUSTICE AND EMPATHY

PART 1

Protecting Vulnerable Groups in Principle

Beings of an inferior order [are] altogether unfit to associate with [superiors] and so far inferior that they had no rights which [others are] bound to respect.

—Chief Justice Roger Taney, *Dred Scott v. Sandford* (1857)

In giving freedom to the slave, we assure freedom to the free.

—President Abraham Lincoln, Message to Congress (1862)

one A LIVING TRUTH

On June 26, 2015, the U.S. Supreme Court ruled that same-sex couples had a constitutional right to state recognition of their marriage. This was an amazing result. Until 2003, states were permitted to impose criminal punishment on same-sex adults who engaged in consensual sexual relations in the privacy of their own homes. The Court had specifically refused to forbid this state punishment in 1986. In 2003, the Court overruled this prior decision, and in a remarkably short time of just twelve years, a constitutional entitlement had leapt from barring state intrusion on the private sexual relations of same-sex couples to requiring state celebration of their marriage.

All of these decisions were strongly contested among the justices themselves. Two of the decisions, the 1986 criminal condemnation and the 2015 marriage celebration cases, were rendered by five votes to four; the 2003 decriminalization case was decided by six to three. Some of the dissenters and their fellow-traveling critics point to the speed of the decisions and the intensity of their popular opposition as themselves demonstrating the illegitimacy of the most recent constitutional rulings. I disagree with those critics.

I do believe, however, that these decisions are not easily justified based on conventional accounts of constitutional lawmaking. If constitutional rulings are legitimate only if they correspond to the original intent of the authors, it is clear that no one envisioned same-sex marriage in 1791 when the Fifth Amendment was ratified or in 1868 when the Fourteenth Amendment was approved.

Originalism is, however, only one school of thought for justifying constitutional interpretations. A competing school, so-called interpretivism, justifies a more expansive basis on the ground that the constitutional grounds of "due process" in the Fifth Amendment or "equal protection of the laws" in the Fourteenth are so generalized that they require (and, indeed, by their very generality were intended by their authors to justify) considerable interpretative latitude by successive generations of judges. But how much latitude is too much? When does the apparent invitation to interpretive free association become license for judges to apply their personal, idiosyncratic values to overrule decisions by popularly elected officials? The justices of the Supreme Court are, after all, life-tenured and beyond any extrinsic controls, unlike elected officials, who must seek periodic approval from their constituents.

And so the argument goes round and round. Restricting constitutional interpretation to the specific meanings of the original language is too narrow and given the majestic generalities of that language even conflicts with the original authors' intentions; but freeing judges from objectively determinative standards excessively opens them to confusing personal preferences with enduring constitutional values.

The apparently irresolvable circularity of this dispute was not my first dissatisfaction with the career I had chosen. A sense of alienation and even boredom emerged from my very first exposure to legal thinking. I began my studies in jurisprudence at the University of Oxford on a Fulbright scholarship, after obtaining my college degree in 1960. Two years later, on a ship back to the United States with my Oxford jurisprudence degree in hand, I could not understand why I had chosen to become a lawyer. The subject seemed artificial to me, finger exercises in which real people were converted into lifeless puppets who were "rational" and "reasonable"—or were required to act and think rationally and reasonably by exerting will power, though everyone I knew (especially including myself) was struggling with confusion, irrationality, unreasonableness.

Then I enrolled at Yale Law School in September 1962 and found a different conception of law's enterprise from a surprising source—not from constitutional law doctrines or abstract formulations of "rights" or "equality" or "liberty" but from the mimeographed class materials that had been assigned for my initial class in family law. I found a beginning path toward a richer, more deeply rooted and humane reading of law in these materials—a path that I have followed for more than fifty years in my career as lawyer and law teacher. My goal in this book is to describe this path—to set out the social, psychological, and morally principled premises that I have come to understand as the predicates for a conception of law that aims toward the cultivation of empathy between people in social conflict with one another.

For my first Yale class in family law, the assigned reading seemed conventional enough—the text of the New York state marriage law and a complaint for financial support that had been filed by a wife now living separate from her husband. The assignment seemed to pose the question that I had already learned in studying English law: how to fit this conflicting couple into the statutory formulas so as to dictate the winner and the loser in their conflict.

Familiar as the text was in these class materials, however, the first footnote in the materials was wildly unconventional. The New York law began by defining marriage as restricted to "one man and one woman." The class materials inserted a footnote to this definition: "[S]tudents of the family and the law must evaluate the assumed preference in this statement for heterosexual relationships. It is, of course, conceivable that decisionmakers may wish to authorize, though not necessarily prefer, a process and criteria for establishing 'marital status' for homosexual partners."[1] Wow. Of course this was conceivable, but it hadn't been conceivable to me until then. (And it didn't become a constitutional right until fifty-three years later.)

An even wider world of possibilities opened in the first class meeting. Two law professors sat at a desk in the front of the classroom, accompanied by some thirty upperclass law students. (I was eligible to enroll because I had second-year status based on my Oxford law degree.) One of the teachers was Joseph Goldstein, a lawyer, political scientist, and lay psychoanalyst; the other was Jay Katz, a psychiatrist and psychoanalyst. Goldstein opened the discussion with a single question: "You've read the statute, the wife's complaint, and the husband's response. What's going on here?"

What's going on in this classroom? How was this a question to begin the discussion about family law? In my Oxford seminars, we would have focused immediately on the legal formulas as they applied to the facts in the case. I had no idea what Goldstein was after in this open-ended question, "What's going on here?"

The other students had no difficulty in responding. Hands shot up throughout the classroom, and different answers were offered. These students had been at Yale for a year and apparently recognized the game in ways that I, a newcomer, did not. For forty-five minutes or so, different students put forward different versions of what we might draw from the legal documents we had read. Goldstein and Katz acknowledged each of the student contributions and engaged in conversation about them. But after each of these interchanges, Goldstein at some times and Katz at others asked, "What else is going on?"

Finally the students seemed to exhaust their imagined possibilities, and the room was silent for a half-minute or so. This also was unique in my prior experience; lawyers are congenital talkers and seem threatened by silence (and not only in England). But Goldstein and Katz were psychoanalysts, and silence was itself an exploratory tool for them. This understanding came much later to me, along with a recognition that psychoanalytically based techniques of exploration could usefully be adapted to legal processes.

Then one of the teachers broke the silence. I have a vivid memory about what was then said, though I forget whether it was Goldstein or Katz who stated, "I have an additional view of what's going on in this case. The husband and wife have lived together for many years, but each has become dissatisfied with the life they have lived while together. Both husband and wife are searching for new and more satisfying paths. They are struggling with themselves about the meaning of their lives. They are literally struggling for their lives. And they have translated that struggle with themselves into conflict with one another." Then, as I recall, Joe Goldstein continued, "The goal of this course is to identify the weapons that the legal system provides to each party in waging warfare with one another and with themselves— to identify these weapons and ask whether and how they help or harm these combatants and people involved with them, especially their three children. And insofar as the legal system inflicts harm, how it might be transformed."

These lessons were pursued during the rest of the semester through close exploration of the case we'd begun to read for the first class. In this detailed examination, a rich portrait emerged of the principal actors in this domestic drama. Of course the portrait was selective and undoubtedly shaped by the lawyers for each disputant. I set out the narrative drawn from the transcript not to claim its accuracy but rather to call attention to its ambition. Unlike conventional accounts of legal disputes, my family law teachers at Yale insisted that law could not be understood or properly evaluated without appreciating the particularities of the parties' psychological and social characteristics. Even if these characteristics are inevitably distorted in legal forums, this is no justification for legal analysts to fall back to stereotyped images of "rational choice makers" or of "morally unworthy" people. If distortions are inevitable and uncorrectable, these are grounds for removing the dispute from legal institutions rather than, as the old joke goes, searching for the missing coin where the light seemed better even though it was miles away from where the coin was lost.

Disguising the names of the warring couple as Sadie and Perry Lesser, Goldstein and Katz pursued their complex vision by providing extensive excerpts of the actual trial transcript, beginning with the wife's first allegations of abuse and request for a separation decree in 1955 through custody disputes regarding their three children in 1957 and, after the couple reached a separation agreement, conflicts about its interpretation from 1961 through 1963.

According to parties' pleadings, the Lessers' marriage began to unravel in 1950 when Sadie renounced her Jewish affiliation and converted to Christian Science. Perry claimed that this conversion violated Sadie's agreement when they first married in 1935 to maintain a Jewish home and raise her children as Jews.

Notwithstanding its dry format, the trial transcript conveyed a Tolstoy-like progression from Perry's relentless attack on Sadie's fitness as a wife and mother, beginning in 1956, to her apparent ultimate unraveling seven years later. Moreover—and most important—it was possible to see through the unfolding of the transcript how the law played at the least an enabling role in this progression.

First of all, the law provided repeated opportunities for Perry's assaults. These interventions were most frequently justified as allegedly protecting the "best interests" of the younger son in obtaining medical care for assorted coughs and the use of eyeglasses, in spite of Sadie's allegiance to Christian Science. In the initial proceedings, the trial judge supported Sadie, awarding her custody of the youngest child as well as occupancy of the family's spacious suburban home and generous financial support for herself and the child. In particular, the judge was adamant that commitment to Christian Science was not incompatible with trustworthy custody of young children. This support weakened over time, however. In part responding to concerns raised by appellate courts to which Perry appealed, the trial judge extracted a commitment for regular medical appointments, apparently based on increased suspicion of Sadie's competence or good faith.

An especially intriguing indication of the trial judge's shifting attitude toward Sadie appeared almost off-handedly in the transcript of the persistent dispute. In early 1957, the judge granted a petition from Perry to remove Sadie from the original family home. At a subsequent hearing in October 1957, the following exchange took place between the judge and Perry's lawyer:

> THE COURT: I was under the impression that Mr. Lesser was living in an apartment. Am I wrong about that?
>
> MR. POMERANTZ: He was at one time in an apartment.
>
> THE COURT: And now he is living at the home?
>
> MR. POMERANTZ: That's right, you were quite correct. At one time he was living in an apartment.
>
> THE COURT: And this house is the original home?
>
> MR. POMERANTZ: Is the original home.
>
> THE COURT: It has not been sold?
>
> MR. POMERANTZ: No, it has not.
>
> THE COURT: The application to me was for the sale of the home and reasons you wanted her [Sadie] to vacate it is so you could sell it.
>
> MR. POMERANTZ: I don't quite recall it that way. My recollection, your Honor, is that he wanted to repossess the home and—
>
> THE COURT: No, the papers before me indicated that he wanted to sell the home and that he fixed a price that he was offering for the

home. I think there was conversation, or there were papers, affidavits, motion papers before me that you prepared.

MR. POMERANTZ: I say my recollection of those papers, your Honor, is that he wanted to be free to sell the home. I don't recall myself at this point whether he reserved the right to occupy the home or to sell it. That is my recollection. He wanted to be free to do either thing.[2]

At that point, the judge returned to directly question Sadie about her medical treatment of the younger son. He marked the transition from his exchange with Pomerantz with one word, "Anyhow." This was not, however, an inconsequential detail. In retrospect, Sadie's expulsion from the original home and Perry's occupation of it was a forerunner of her increasing incapacity. She delayed for months in finding a new apartment, living for the moment in one bedroom in a friend's house. Six years later, in 1963, a new judge in the case awarded custody of the younger son (now thirteen years old) to Perry, and made this observation about Sadie:

> The mother . . . has remarried and at the present time her husband, unfortunately, is confined to a mental institution. She occupies a small apartment which is temporary in character and her economic condition is deplorable. Even her state of mind is unsettled.
>
> . . . She clearly is not in a position to raise the boy under existing circumstances.[3]

The judge then added this final order to his opinion: "The father is directed to continue to pay the mother $25.00 a week for the support of the boy and to pay all sums due to date."

This is a sad coda to this relentlessly litigated relationship. It's difficult to see any legal justification for the judge's order removing the child's custody from Sadie while awarding her a weekly payment for his support. Sadder still, Perry immediately filed an appeal of this payment order. As Goldstein and Katz ironically describe it in their heading to this final entry: "Decisions of the Lessers—"Until Death Do Us Part."[4]

I don't know the outcome of this appeal. Goldstein and Katz ended the transcript with the narrative still in midstream, and their use of pseudonyms makes it impossible for me to find the original court filings. They did, however, identify the judges who presided over the Lesser case. The initial presiding judge was Saul Streit; in 1962 a short biography of him appeared in the *New York Times*. The biography revealed that Streit was born in Vienna, where his father was an Orthodox rabbi. He was brought to the United States when he was three and was married when he was fifty-three to a television actress, the former Jean F. McBride. The *Times* biography does not indicate whether this was the first marriage for either of them, nor does it specify the bride's religious practice. It's plausible, I think, to conclude that Ms. McBride was born into a Christian family and that Streit's origin was Jewish. Before setting out this information, Goldstein and Katz posed the following challenge: "[C]onsider the extent to which the following information about Justice Streit . . . is relevant to understanding and evaluating these proceedings."[5]

This challenge was at the core of their pedagogy. The possibility that this personal information about the judge could be relevant to evaluating the legal proceedings reflected their insistence that we not automatically assume that the judge was an impersonal embodiment of the law's objective nature. Their question, that is, implicitly challenged the conventional view of legal actors as exclusively rational calculators and of law's transparent objectivity. Their challenge was as intriguing and inviting to me as their question in the opening class, "What's going on here?"

The Lessers framed their conflict as a dispute based on different religious commitments. How could Judge Streit be entirely divorced from personal biases arising from the religious differences between him and his wife? Even assuming that he was personally influenced, however, it is not clear whether his background as the son of an Orthodox rabbi who married a non-Jew late in life would lead him to favor Sadie, the converted Christian, or Perry, who ostentatiously insisted on loyalty to the faith of his fathers. Perhaps this background rendered Streit ambivalent—favoring Sadie and harshly critical of Perry at the beginning but vulnerable to Perry's claim of superior rectitude in remaining committed to Judaism. Something must explain Streit's willingness to acquiesce in Perry's eviction of Sadie from the family home while misrepresenting, as the judge clearly believed, his intention to sell rather than occupy the premises. Something must explain Streit's increasing withdrawal of empathy toward Sadie, of his failure to see her need for continued protection against Perry's assaults.

This is what Goldstein or Katz must have meant when they suggested that the Lessers were engaged in mortal combat with one another, that the very existence of meaning in their separate lives depended on one vanquishing the other. This struggle led to the virtual destruction of Sadie, a result that was apparently facilitated by Judge Streit's unwitting collaboration with or surrender to Perry. Perhaps these speculations are wrong. But they seem at least plausible to me. And thinking about their possibility was the beginning of a spacious conception of law, an antidote to the thinness of the conception I had been offered in England.[6]

There was, moreover, another difference from my English legal experience that was amplified by this richer conception of law. There was no written constitution in the United Kingdom at that time, and the British judiciary had no basis for overturning parliamentary acts. When I began my legal studies in England in 1960, only six years earlier the U.S. Supreme Court had overturned Southern race segregation in *Brown v. Board of Education*. It was exciting, thrilling even, to be an American lawyer in ways that were entirely beyond any possibility for British lawyers.

But even so, *Brown* offered a complicated lesson for fledgling lawyers like me. Of course the Supreme Court's decision was morally correct; of course race segregation inflicted intolerable injustice on Southern blacks. But only twenty-five years earlier, a Supreme Court majority had invalidated major New Deal legislation, following precedents in effect for at least the previous fifty years (the so-called *Lochner* lineage) that had obstructed economic reforms benefiting workers and consumers; and in *Plessy v. Ferguson* the Court had explicitly approved race segregation in 1896. It was easy to say that the Court had been wrong for seventy-five years in the *Lochner* and *Plessy* precedents, but those cases had (recently) been overruled and we were now in a new era. Easy to say this, but too glib.

Sadie Lesser v. Perry Lesser provided a miniature portrait of a pervasive characteristic of American law. Perry's capacity to enlist the law in his battle with Sadie and his ultimate success in wholly defeating her, abetted by his implicit alliance with Judge Streit, were entirely familiar instances of the favoritism in American law toward the rich and powerful in their subjugation of the poor and vulnerable. *Brown* was a hopeful harbinger—but its success was uncertain in light of Southern white massive resistance, and there was no assurance that future justices would not revive their old, historically predominant inclinations to favor the strong over the weak.

No guarantee could be extracted from the family law materials that the lion and lamb would be reconciled, that the law would always protect the vulnerable. Indeed, the *Lesser* case seemed to illustrate exactly the opposite lesson—that the lion has extensive capacity and powerful motive to devour the lamb. But I saw how critical evaluation can arise from intensive attention to the texture of the relationships between the conflicting parties, those directly affected by this conflict, and the judge precariously poised between disinterested distance and impassioned participation in the conflict.

The *Lesser* case was a microcosm of a much grander endeavor. It crystallized for me two different conceptions of the law's possibility—as an instrument of oppression or as a means for protecting and emancipating vulnerable people. Judge Streit missed this opportunity; but in 1962, this possibility was in the air, in the larger framework of constitutional doctrine. The Supreme Court's efforts to end racial segregation in *Brown v. Board of Education* and to validate same-sex marriages in *Obergefell v. Hodges* can be understood as a corrective to Judge Streit's failure to protect the weak against the strong in the *Lesser* case. As this connection became clear to me, I began to understand why I wanted to be a lawyer.

From the beginning of the American Republic, courts have claimed a special role for themselves in protecting minority rights against majority oppression; but there has been considerable disagreement in identifying the proper beneficiaries of this judicial solicitude. For most of its history, the Supreme Court insisted that its task was to protect "liberty" and that the core meaning of this right was to forbid any governmental restriction on "private" conduct. This judicial commitment could be described as a protection of minority rights against majoritarian domination; wealthy capitalists were a numerical minority in legislative institutions and thus apparently vulnerable to abuse. Even the Court's refusal from the turn of the nineteenth century to the midpoint of the twentieth to protect African Americans from the oppressions of the Jim Crow regime could be characterized as protection extended to the numerical minority of white Southerners defeated by the white North.

It is, however, misleading to accept at face value the claim that in these cases the Court was protecting the weak against oppression from the powerful. The underlying goal of this judicial enshrinement of liberty was quite the opposite: to ratify and reinforce the existing hierarchy of social and economic order.

In 1938, however, the Supreme Court announced a different agenda, a radical break from its prior history of reflexively favoring the rich and powerful. The case itself—*United States v. Carolene Products Company*[7]—was a routine reaffirmation of the Court's recent retreat from overturning New Deal regulations of economic activity.[8] The Court did more, however, than pledge noninterference in economic regulation; it also prescribed a future affirmative obligation for itself. In Footnote Four of the *Carolene Products* opinion—the most notable footnote in its history—the Court proclaimed that it would not defer to legislatures when they enacted laws hostile to "discrete and insular minorities" who were powerless to protect themselves because of majority "prejudice" against them. The Court promised "searching judicial inquiry" to safeguard such minorities.

There were two implicit premises to this footnote. The first was doctrinal—a conceptual shift from safeguarding "liberty" to protecting "equality." The second premise was less abstract—an instrumental shift from affirming the existing hierarchy of social order to unsettling that hierarchy. In 1938 there was an apparent strategic concern behind this shift. The Great Depression was itself a radical disturbance in the existing social order. The New Deal could itself be understood as a rescue maneuver in response to this dislocation—an attempt that the Court either had to accept or risk more ominous consequences. At the same time, disaffected groups whom the Court (and the rest of American society) had previously ignored themselves appeared to be more ominous threats to social stability, which required recognition and appeasement rather than suppression.

Accordingly, it is not surprising that 1938 also marked the first occasion when the Court critically examined the Jim Crow regime in Southern states. The specific decision was relatively narrow; the Court held only that states were constitutionally obliged to provide "separate but equal" law school facilities within their own territorial boundaries rather than dispatching black law students to neighboring states. This case was, however, an initial harbinger of the Court's systemic assault on Jim Crow sixteen years later in *Brown v. Board of Education*. At the same time that the Court announced Footnote Four, it signaled that the modal "discrete and insular minority" requiring special judicial solicitude was African Americans subjected to racial segregation.

Beyond promising special judicial inquiry in Footnote Four, the Court said nothing specific about the remedies it would prescribe to protect vulnerable people. Perhaps the Court was silent because it regarded the judicial remedy as self-evident: strike down the offending governmental action. But simply erasing the wrongful discrimination does not reliably protect the future welfare of the vulnerable group. The Court might address this problem by holding itself out as ready to intervene again and yet again so long as the abused group needs its protection. But is this an endless guarantee?

The Supreme Court is currently struggling with this question, and it is tempting to see the conflicting answers offered by the justices as reflecting a fundamental disagreement about whether the Court should return to its historically dominant role of protecting liberty and the existing social order or should remain committed to the original goal of Footnote Four by disrupting the existing hierarchical order in order to advance equality. There is some truth to this characterization of the polar disagreement among the justices. But those who support continued emphasis on equality concerns, as I do, must also acknowledge that judicially bestowed protection for this value can ironically obstruct the ultimate goal of achieving an egalitarian relationship between the conflicting parties themselves.

This detrimental result was illustrated by Thurgood Marshall's observation when, as chief counsel for the NAACP Legal Defense Fund, he was preparing for reargument of *Brown* before the Supreme Court. The Court had put several questions to the parties regarding the meaning of the Fourteenth Amendment, including the central issue, "Is it within the judicial power, in construing the Amendment, to abolish segregation in public schools?"[9] After several weeks of exhaustive discussion, Marshall proposed to his colleagues that he offer this answer: "White bosses, you can do anything you want 'cause you got de power."[10]

A serious proposition lies beneath this teasing remark. We can reformulate Marshall's observation as follows. In extending Footnote Four protection to any vulnerable minority, the Court's remedial goal is not simply to invalidate the specific state imposition of inequality but to overturn the entire socially subjugative relationship between the prejudiced majority and the vulnerable minority. The ultimate protective goal is realized only when the subjugative relationship has been replaced by a democratic relationship based on mutual respect. Judicial imposition of defeat on the former subjugators and victory for the former subordinates may not be an effective repudiation but be a reversed mirror image of the prior coercive social relationship.

Footnote Four has since 1938 become more than an instrument for promoting black emancipation. The Court has applied its spirit by protecting women, physically and mentally disabled people, gays and lesbians. Nonetheless Footnote Four has spawned two puzzles. The first is to identify those groups to which the footnote applies. Much has been written about defining a "discrete and insular minority," and the Court has woven a complicated tapestry in answering this question. Full-throated coverage has been awarded to blacks, designating this racial group as a "suspect class";[11] women in turn have been designated "semi-suspect,"[12] while disabled people have been given no special group status but nonetheless have found special protection under a formerly toothless requirement of "rationality."[13] Whether gays and lesbians deserve any special Footnote Four status has apparently been affirmatively resolved by the same-sex marriage case.

Difficult as it may be to solve the puzzle about who is eligible for special protection under Footnote Four, it is even more difficult (and much less studied) to determine exactly what kind of judicial protection follows from that eligibility. The footnote itself promises "more searching judicial inquiry," which is hardly self-explanatory. The footnote would appear to envision judicial invalidation of losses imposed on groups victimized by prejudice and thereby disabled from protecting themselves in majoritarian institutions. But this does not necessarily mean that the judiciary should simply reverse the results of disputes that had been inflicted on a vulnerable group, transforming losers into winners. Abstractly speaking, the constitutional guarantee of equal treatment demands equal respect for everyone. Subordinated groups have been deprived of this guarantee, but the remedy for this deprivation cannot simply be coercive subjugation of the oppressors. Some coercive intervention against the former oppressors might be appropriate, but only so long as that coercion is clearly aimed at establishing a democratic relationship of equality between the conflicting parties.

A democratic cure to the subjugation is achieved when the vulnerable minority is no longer a permanent loser in electoral politics, especially on matters that are intensely important to that group. The deeply puzzling question is prescriptive: How is this ideal goal of a totally reformed relationship to be accomplished? How can this reformed relationship be accomplished through coercive means?

These questions are especially vexing because the prejudiced majority and vulnerable minority come to judicial attention already locked in pervasive hostile conflict. A court can command the prejudiced majority to cease its wrongful subordination of the vulnerable minority. But can it lead the warring parties to a truly democratic outcome—that is, to reformulate their relationship from hostile subjugation to new interactions based on equal respect?

John Hart Ely in his influential book *Democracy and Distrust* proposed restricting judicial interventions to "representation-reinforcing" remedies that assured access to democratic institutions from which subjugated groups had been excluded. When the subjugated groups are numerical minorities, however, and are subjected to such aversive prejudice that they cannot find allies among other groups, open access to litigative institutions is insufficiently protective.

Difficult as this may be in practice, courts must reach for more transformative remedies. By strategic, sensitively devised interventions, courts can structure the litigative process in ways that can emancipate the parties from conflicted confrontation. Courts can guide hostile parties into egalitarian democratic interaction based on mutual respect for one another. This book attempts to chart that path.

A democratic relationship is not conflict free; but conflict must be waged against an acknowledged background of mutually respectful egalitarian engagement rather than coercively enforced dominance and submission. If this precondition can be distilled to one word, democracy depends on an underlying relationship of empathy between conflicting parties—that is, a capacity and willingness to acknowledge a fundamental common identity with one's adversary. If law is nothing more than structured conflict, nothing more than stylized violence, then it is inherently irreconcilable with democratic values. But if the subjugative impulses that the conflicting parties bring to their litigative encounter—including conflictual litigation between individuals and the state—can be transformed by self-consciously adopted processes in litigation, then the law can promote empathy rather than confirming or intensifying antagonism between the parties in conflict. This is the possibility that I have pursued, at least since my reflections on the family dispute between Sadie and Perry Lesser.

Footnote Four of *Carolene Products* exemplified the Supreme Court's embrace of this pursuit and at the same time its uncertainty about the possible means for its achievement. This uncertainty was graphically revealed in an immediate sequel to *Brown*. In 1957, the school board of Little Rock, Arkansas, decided to accept the federal district court's directive to admit nine black students to the previously all-white high school as a gesture of compliance with *Brown*. At the beginning of September 1957, the Arkansas governor, Orval Faubus, dispatched state national guardsmen with instructions to bar the entry of these nine students. Later that month, President Dwight Eisenhower took federal command of the Arkansas guard and also sent federal troops to countermand Faubus's order and to escort the nine students into the school. A chaotic school year followed, marked by white mobs that gathered daily to harass the entering students. The school board asked the federal district judge to suspend his desegregation order because of the disorder; he agreed but was reversed by the federal court of appeals, and the Supreme Court in turn affirmed the appeals court ruling.

The Supreme Court's opinion in *Cooper v. Aaron* pointed in two contradictory directions. First, the Court insisted on enforcing a relationship of dominance and submission—its dominance and the governor's submission—on the ground that the Court is the supreme interpreter of the Constitution and must be obeyed. Second, the Court ignored any characterization of its relationship to the president; but the unspoken background of the case was the independence of the president's authority as commander in chief to decide whether he will support the Court's order. One might say that here too there was a relationship of dominance and submission—President Eisenhower's dominance and the Court's submissive dependence on him. Third, the Court directly addressed the question of the justices' relationship to one another—in particular whether the three new justices who had joined the Court since its decision in *Brown* were obliged to follow the previous command issued by the *Brown* Court or whether their relationship to their predecessors and to their new colleagues was entirely without coercion, based only on the possibility of equal mutual respect.

In the final paragraph of the opinion in *Cooper v. Aaron*, the Court announced that three justices who had participated in the unanimous decision in *Brown* had been replaced and that the new justices joined with their predecessors in unanimously reaffirming *Brown*. None of the parties had asked for this reaffirmation; according to internal Court records, one of the new justices, John Marshall Harlan, had suggested this course. In one sense, the reaffirmation was a statement of internal strength—that the Court was not only initially united in its unanimous decision in 1954 but also remained united. But in another sense, this was an admission of potential weakness—an admission that new justices were entitled to withhold their assent and that *Brown* might be undone by mortality, by forces beyond anyone's control.

At its core, this reaffirmation presented a model for the protection of the weak against the strong, a map for the process by which the democratic promise of Footnote Four might be fulfilled. That means was the willingness of the new justices to withhold their disruptive power and to seek voluntary concordance with their colleagues. This pursuit of unanimity is freely chosen, but it is at the same time an act of submission to the moral imperative of democratic life—that equality does not arise magically or from the impersonal workings of the economist's "invisible hand" that converts selfish pursuit into communal wealth.

Democratic equality requires self-conscious effort to reach agreement with adversaries. Courts are powerless to enforce this effort, notwithstanding their apparent supremacy in interpreting the words of the Constitution. Courts are able to teach this fundamental democratic principle in numerous ways, including the example of their own deferential conduct toward disputing parties, whether other judges, litigants, or the general public witnessing their actions.

In *Cooper v. Aaron*, the Court appeared to understand its pedagogic role in this transformative process in its final paragraph, its capstone:

> The basic decision in *Brown* was unanimously reached by this Court only after the case had been briefed and twice argued and the issues had been given the most serious consideration. Since the first *Brown* decision three new Justices have come to the Court. They are at one with the Justices still on the Court who participated in that basic decision as to its correctness, and that decision is now unanimously reaffirmed. The principles announced in that decision and the obedience

of the States to them, according to the command of the Constitution, are indispensable for the protection of the freedoms guaranteed by our fundamental charter for all of us. Our constitutional ideal of equal justice under law is thus made a living truth.

In this final paragraph, the Court bows respectfully to the conflicting parties who argued twice before the Court and were given "the most serious consideration," to the three new Justices who voluntarily joined with the others, and to the states, which offer "obedience . . . to the commands of the Constitution." Is this sequential ordering of this paragraph more than simply lexical? Is it a logical deduction that the constitutional commands are satisfied only by open argument given "serious consideration" by all participants, followed by the self-conscious pursuit of unanimous agreement not only on the Court but also in the states? Is it "thus," is this the causal mechanism by which "our constitutional ideal of equal justice under law is made a living truth"?

I would say so.

Demonstrating this proposition is the goal of this book.

two JUDICIAL POWER TO COMMAND

The Supreme Court may have formal hierarchic authority to interpret the Constitution, but its actual power to enforce its will is limited. There is, however, one clear power in its actual possession. That is the power to command attention, to demand some response even if that response is "massive [or passive] resistance." This is a considerable power, and it has distinct moral dimensions. The Court speaks in the lexicon of morality: "You ought to do something or refrain from something because our communal morality, embodied in the Constitution, requires this." The addressees of this command may choose to defy it, but they can't ignore it; they must respond, even if only in their own minds, in moral terms: "You say I am morally bound to do or to refrain, but I am not bound by your moral claim, I reject it." This judicial power deserves to be acknowledged as a separate weapon in the Court's effective armamentarium. It should be purposefully deployed.

In my personal experience, I have found myself subjected to this power, forced to respond to the Court's command that I must morally justify myself.[1] When *Brown v. Board of Education* was decided, in May 1954, I was just about to enter tenth grade at Montgomery Blair Senior High School in Silver Spring, Maryland. This was a huge establishment with more than two thousand students—none of whom was black. I had noticed this demographic fact but had ascribed it to the absence of any black families in my all-white suburban collective. As I then saw it, this absence occurred because, like the small numbers of Jewish families that clustered together in parts of Silver Spring, blacks preferred to live among themselves in the neighboring District of Columbia itself.

I was wrong. There were black schoolchildren living in close proximity, but they had not been attending Montgomery Blair Senior High School. In September 1955, when I returned to begin eleventh grade, there were some twenty blacks who appeared, unexpectedly for me, among the student body. Where had they come from? After a moment's reflection, I knew.

About a mile past my junior high school was an enclave known as Montgomery Hollow. According to local legend, this small patch of land had been deeded by Abraham Lincoln himself to a group of freed slaves. In Lincoln's time, the Hollow had been on the far outskirts of residential properties in Washington, but by the early 1950s it had been surrounded and submerged by the explosive growth of all-white suburban sprawl. I had known about the existence of the Hollow but had never taken the dirt road that led from behind my junior high school to see it for myself. Nor had I thought about the reason for the absence of any age-peer Hollow residents from my school.

Now equipped with my newly minted driver's license and my parents' car, and provoked by the sudden unexpected appearance of the small group of black students in my high school, I drove down this dirt road and in less than a mile found ten or fifteen contiguous buildings—a collection of small shacks really. All the people I saw outside these buildings were black. The buildings themselves were wooden and appeared insubstantial, unlike the sturdy suburban brick homes immediately outside the Hollow. There were aged refrigerators visible on the front porches of several of these homes, small sheds behind many of them that appeared to be outhouses, suggesting that there was no plumbing inside the homes. The source of water for the entire community appeared to be several outside hand pumps atop wells.

I had never seen anything like this collection of dwellings; it most resembled photographs I had seen of shantytowns in the Deep South. Here was this black community located a mile behind my junior high school (closer than my own home, from which I had walked to school every day). And yet I had never seen any black students in my junior or senior high school until 1955, the year after the Supreme Court's ruling in *Brown v. Board of Education*. I had been attending a racially segregated school district—a fact that I had not seen or acknowledged though the evidence was blatantly available.

The legal explanation for this situation was quite simple and also readily visible for anyone who had looked. Unlike state legislatures in the Deep South, the Maryland legislature did not require racially segregated schools but instead gave each local school board discretion to impose racial restrictions. Montgomery County—my home county, a seeming outpost of Northern liberalism—had decided on separate facilities for whites and blacks. I had assumed that my home county was a liberal bastion even though it was located just below the Mason-Dixon Line separating North from South. But I was wrong.

The Montgomery County School Board did decide to comply immediately with the *Brown* ruling, though the former Confederate states embarked on a long campaign of opposition. I knew that my public school was all white, but I had not previously realized that this was because of an official policy of race segregation. But now in 1955, the sudden appearance of a small cadre of black students in my high school forced this knowledge on me. That was the first educational lesson for me that came from the Supreme Court's decision in *Brown v. Board of Education.*

The second lesson came a year later when I was in twelfth grade and a member of the high school Student Council. I had been elected chief justice of the student court, with jurisdiction to adjudicate minor matters of disciplinary infractions; this was the only judicial office I've ever held, and with it came membership on the Student Council, which was responsible for overseeing various student activities. One of these activities was the senior class beach party, an outing near the end of the school year in June that for some considerable time had been a traditional graduation celebration. The nearest beaches were on the Eastern Shore of Maryland, and the location for our high school event had always been Beverley Beach.

I knew Beverley Beach. Three years earlier, I had worked as a waiter at a summer camp, and on one of my days off several senior counselors and I had driven past the beach and were startled to see a sign at its entrance announcing, in descending order, no dogs, Gentiles only (in other words, no Jews), and among Gentiles only those with northern European ancestry (in other words, no blacks and possibly no Italian Catholics). This was, remember, 1953.

If the senior party were held at its customary site, members of the small Jewish cohort at my high school could attend only if they were willing to pass as Gentiles. Whatever the moral status of this dissembling decision, it was not available to black students. There were no blacks on the Student Council, and I was the only Jew, but when we began planning for the party, I said nothing about the exclusion of Jews from Beverley Beach. Along with several other members of this all-white group, however, I did raise the issue of black students being unwelcome there.

We then considered several alternatives. Was there another beach to which we could turn? The answer was no; all of the nearby beaches were on the Eastern Shore and either refused admission to blacks or maintained racially separate swimming areas. One council member then suggested that we send a delegation to the handful of black students in the senior class, perhaps ten out of some seven hundred seniors, and ask them to forgo attendance at the beach party rather than cancel it and deprive everyone of this traditional celebration. The other council members were virtually unanimous in rejecting this suggestion on the grounds that it put an unacceptable burden on the black students by forcing them to conclude that their very presence in the school was causing harm to other students.

But what if we canceled the party because of the Beach Club's restrictive policy? Wouldn't both black and white students know this? Wouldn't the whites resent the presence of the blacks? After much discussion, the Student Council resolved to cancel the beach party and explain (falsely) to the entire student body that the beach had prohibitively raised its admission fees. We resolved to keep the real reason strictly to ourselves. With one exception: we voted to instruct the faculty member, Mr. Fox, who supervised the Student Council and attended all meetings, that when he contacted the members of the Beverley Beach Club to inform them that we had canceled the traditional outing, he should tell them the real reason—that we knew and disapproved of their policy toward black people.

I said nothing, however, about my own personal reason for opposing the club's racial policy—because it excluded Jews as well as black people. I spoke in opposition to the club's exclusion of blacks but said nothing about Jews. Most likely, I would have boycotted the party at Beverley Beach rather than pass as Gentile but, aside from informing a handful of Jewish classmates at the school, would not have mentioned the anti-Semitic policy as the reason for my absence.

Was I hiding my Jewish identity behind my opposition to the anti-black policy of the beach club? Was I taking advantage of an unspoken connection between blacks and Jews, an imagined alliance that would have had very little salience for blacks but was for Jews a way to fight for ourselves without acknowledging our true stakes in this fight?

There has been much dispute in the sixty years following this decision about the social power behind the Supreme Court's rulings: dispute about the Court's reluctance to insist on immediate compliance in *Brown II;* dispute about the Court's practical capacity to enforce its will on its own; dispute about the existence of a presidential or congressional obligation to support the Court. Some have concluded that the Court should have insisted on immediate compliance, notwithstanding its apparent incapacities;[2] others have concluded that the Court offers only a "hollow hope" of reform on any front because of these incapacities.[3]

My own experience suggests that the Court wields an authority deeper than its practical capacity to enforce its will. That authority is the ability to force into conscious awareness aspects of our relationship to scorned groups that are easily shut away from acknowledgment, often because of unease and even guilt. I was attending a racially segregated school and was advocating racial equality on behalf of blacks while silently and therefore uncomfortably acting to protect my own Jewish identity. These two lessons were forced on me by the Court's decision in *Brown.*

A court order commanding me or my school board to accept black students would have changed the terms of *Brown*'s moral challenge. The issue would be instead be joined with, and even superseded by, the question whether I would acknowledge the court's authority over me. This is a moral choice in itself, but it radically differs from my acceptance of personal responsibility for the commission or continuation of past inflictions.

As a result of the Supreme Court's decision in *Brown*, this challenge was conveyed to the entire nation by the widely circulated photographs of the Southern white woman, the purported epitome of feminine gentility, screaming at one black student who dared to enter the formerly all-white high school in Little Rock.

The hatred and violence that lay just beneath the seemingly peaceable surface of race relations had been unmasked by *Brown I*. Would the white South accept personal and communal responsibility for transforming this oppressive relationship? Would the white North acknowledge responsibility for its passive acquiescence and now accept a moral responsibility for corrective action? These were the central questions posed by *Brown*. There was no way that the white South or North could evade answering them, whether its response was yea or nay.

The Court thus is the instrument of moral accountability. Even when it demands compliance, it can effectively do no more than force us to accept responsibility for our moral choices. This is a considerable power.

three ALL THAT IS SOLID

Can the Court do more than this in carrying out its basic mission of protecting vulnerable people? Is there a way that the Court can promote, even if it cannot directly enforce, the basic tenets of democratic principle, of relations based on respect for equal status, of empathic fellow feeling for others?

There have been times in American social history when this democratic commitment was dominant, eras characterized by self-conscious efforts at emancipation from subjugation. These eras have been brief compared to the times when the predominant characteristics of social relations were hierarchically subordinating. Courts have supported the emancipatory impulse only in its most recent appearance after 1938; this is the import of the Court's commitment to Footnote Four. This most recent era has been more prolonged than the earlier intervals of emancipation—perhaps because of the supportive role played by the Court, rather than its efforts in past eras to stifle egalitarian efforts. Even so, the Court—and the country at large—are deeply divided between those who favor and those who oppose the continuation and expansion of the egalitarian emancipatory commitment.

What might we learn by examining this social history?

There has been a recurrent pattern in American social history of alternating eras predominately characterized either by rigid hierarchical boundaries between superiors and inferiors or by more fluid, egalitarian modes of social authority. The hierarchic eras have focused on fears of social disorder and the consequent need to subjugate disruptive (or potentially disruptive) forces. The more fluid eras, by contrast, have been less fear-filled and more attentive to empathic, egalitarian fellow feeling.

There was never a time in these alternating social eras when disorder was entirely suppressed or when the lion and lamb peaceably lay down together. The alternation was more a matter of social emphasis; but the social emphasis did change. When we acknowledge the existence of this alternation, we might also identify social causes that precipitate the dominance of one era rather than the other. We can then ask whether these precipitating causes are amenable to self-conscious deployment in order to favor one era over the others—and in particular what social forces are especially available to judicial interventions.

Broadly speaking, there have been three moments in our history when emancipatory efforts were highly visible and widely supported: during the generation following the Revolutionary War through the 1820s; from the middle of the Civil War (when abolition of slavery became a central goal, at least as much as preserving the Union) through postwar Reconstruction until 1876; and from the era stretching from World War II until today (most prominently espoused in the 1960s and 1970s and, though now subject to intense polarized dispute, still in contention for social attention).

For most of American history our actual organizing principle has been the imposition of social order based on the subjugation of some by favored others. This proposition is brutally confirmed by the institution of slavery and its replacement after formal abolition by segregation laws, exclusion of blacks from voting, and the regime of fear imposed on them by lynchings and other depredations. In 1857, the U.S. Supreme Court explicitly held that the equality of all men proclaimed by the Declaration of Independence actually applied only to white men, thus excluding all blacks, whether they were formally slaves or free men. In its *Dred Scott* decision, the Court ruled that if equal status applied to black as well as white men, the authors of the Declaration would be guilty of inconsistency, since many of them were slaveholders. However, the Court opined, all of the authors were men of such high distinction that it was impossible that they might hold self-contradictory views.[1] The Court thus apparently viewed the logical error of inconsistency as a more grievous sin than the enslavement of some human beings.

There have, however, been some times in the sweep of the American experience when the promise of equal justice and liberty has been avowedly more universal, when we have acknowledged the betrayal of this promise for some and have resolved to correct this contradiction. Thus the *Dred Scott* decision withholding national citizenship from all blacks was overruled by section 1 of the Fourteenth Amendment, enacted just after the Civil War.

The status of blacks is not the only instance of alternating eras of suppression and liberation in American social history. In retrospect, we can see a recurrent pattern regarding when and why the dominant social ordering either justified or disavowed extreme status differences between groups of people—between blacks and whites, women and men, Native Americans and whites, laborers and capitalists, homosexuals and heterosexuals, Jews or Catholics and Protestants, people with mental or physical disabilities and the "able-bodied."

The conventional account of the occurrence of a shift in social emphasis from subjugation to emancipation gives great causal weight to the protests of the subjugated groups—in modern times, the rise of the black civil rights movement in the mid-1950s and 1960s, the rebirth of the women's liberation movement in the late 1960s (succeeding the women's suffrage movement of the early twentieth century), the gay protests beginning with the Stonewall uprising in 1969, the disability rights movement beginning in the 1970s. These open protests by subjugated groups were certainly important contributions to their changed status. But deeper causal puzzles still remain.

Many members of all of these subjugated groups experienced oppression long before they engaged in open protest. What led them to throw aside the fears of retaliation and the self-devaluations that had kept them silent for so long? The contagion of their successive efforts is a partial explanation, as open demands for emancipation moved by example from one group to another. But even so, what sparked the initiation of these efforts? And why were the open protests not successfully (and brutally) suppressed by the dominant oppressors, as had occurred many times earlier? What might have occurred within the groups of oppressors that led many of them to hold back from suppressing these protests, first to tolerate and then to attend to them?

To be sure, the path from oppressors' resistance to their responsiveness to open protests was not smoothly or quickly traversed. But some force undermined the ruthlessness of the oppressor groups, leading perhaps to failures of nerve that had not previously inhibited the oppressors or to new awareness of empathy by oppressors that had not previously restrained their retaliations against the rebellious subjects. Whatever the source of these restraints operating on the oppressors, I believe that the oppressed groups sensed the new restraints, if only dimly, and this sense encouraged in them—literally, gave them courage for—open protest about grievances that had previously afflicted them only in silence.

If open protests by oppressed minorities played only a limited role, what more potent force might explain this shift from subjugation to emancipation? Some suggest that moral ideals favoring emancipation have an internal expansive logic.[2] The problem with this hopeful idea, however, is that emancipation at least as a matter of American historical experience has regularly been followed by reimposition of more rigid and brutal impositions of social order. This has at some times been directed at the same previously victimized groups and at other times at different groups, but the subjugative impulse remains strong.

We can see this cycle in action by examining the fate of the first emancipatory moment in American history. This occurred in the aftermath of the colonists' overthrow of British rule. The American revolutionaries repeatedly claimed that Great Britain was treating them like "slaves."[3] This complaint appeared hypocritical on its face, since many of the most ardent advocates against their British enslavement were themselves slaveholders. As Samuel Johnson acidly observed, "[H]ow is it that we hear the loudest yelps for liberty among the drivers of negroes?"[4]

The revolutionary colonists might have justified themselves, as *Dred Scott* held, by claiming that black slaves were a different order of humanity from whites and were inherently dangerous to social order in ways that whites generally were not. This was indeed the justification that many Southern slaveholders offered in the nineteenth century and had been, as the American historian Edmund Morgan has tren-

ALL THAT IS SOLID

chantly analyzed, the foundation for the white colonists' commitment
to the ideal of liberty, but restricted to themselves.[5] In colonial America generally, the most visible and forcible subordinating degradations
had been directed against black slaves (located mostly in the South but
an important part of the commerce in the Northern colonies) and Native Americans (against whom the white colonists in all sections of the
country engaged in brutal, land-grabbing aggression).[6]

The Revolutionary War unsettled these subjugative relationships.
This war was accompanied by considerably softened white attitudes
in the Northern and Upper Southern states toward black slaves and
Native Americans. A new empathy appeared as the revolutionary
colonists themselves were explicitly and openly troubled about the
inconsistency of their claim for liberty as compared with their own
treatment of black slaves and Native Americans.[7]

Thus most Northern legislatures abolished slavery during the
generation after independence,[8] and legislatures in the Upper South
made it easier for slaves to buy their freedom or otherwise be emancipated by their masters.[9] Moreover, the U.S. Congress outlawed the
international slave trade in 1807, even though article 1, section 9, of
the Constitution had withheld this authority until 1808. Regarding
Native Americans, a new policy was embraced that accentuated treaty
making rather than warfare; these treaties, moreover, were ostensibly
beneficent toward the Native Americans.[10] This era dominated by the
postindependence generation was, broadly speaking, an emancipatory
moment.

To be sure, egalitarianism was not uniformly embraced in this moment. The impetus for the replacement of the Articles of Confederation with the Constitution was in effect a reactionary reassertion of
hierarchic social authority by the old colonial ruling elite who saw
their status threatened by the democratic grasping of the masses (that
is, the white male artisans and small-scale agriculturists).[11] The new
constitution was hardly an emancipatory document, especially in its
entrenchment of slavery in the South.

But even here, some new empathic connection is revealed by the
fact that, for all the Constitution's deference to Southern plantation

slaveholders, the word "slave" never appears in the text. James Madison, one of the richest men in Virginia and one of the largest slaveholders, was explicit in his insistence that the word would stain the document and that its absence would implicitly convey the hope that the institution of slavery might someday be abolished.[12]

This new social attitude was based on some new measure of empathic identification among the white elites toward blacks and Native Americans; but it lasted only during the life span of the Revolutionary War veterans. By 1832 the post-Revolution emancipatory impulse had run its course in the Upper South and the North, and a new and even more rigid social hierarchy was imposed. The last gasp of the emancipatory impulse was the extended debate of the Virginia legislature in 1831–32 regarding the possible abolition of slavery, a measure that was defeated by the narrow margin of sixty-five to fifty-eight.[13] For some time before then, however, conditions for freed blacks had become more harshly repressive in the Southern states. For example, by 1820 many Southern states forced free blacks to leave their territory, and these states concurrently made it almost impossible for slaves to buy their freedom even if their owners agreed.[14]

Regarding Native Americans, the previous national goal of conciliation was essentially abandoned in favor of an openly avowed policy of literal extermination, of genocide. The marker for this shift was the election of Andrew Jackson as president in 1828.[15] All the preceding presidents had been charter members of the American founding elite (and all but two, Adams father and son, had been Virginia plantation owners of vast wealth). Jackson represented the "new man" (as the common account had it, tracking mud into the White House and stomping on old manners).

The Age of Jackson may have been an egalitarian embrace of middling white men, but it was also a return to and intensification of the subjugation of blacks and of Native Americans. The Jacksonian categorical restriction of egalitarianism to whites while more rigidly excluding blacks and Native Americans as a different and inherently subordinate rank mirrored the social order that Edmund Morgan described in pre-Revolutionary Virginia: "Racism ... absorbed in

Virginia the fear and contempt that [elite] men in England, whether Whig or Tory, monarchist or republican, felt for the inarticulate lower classes. Racism made it possible for white Virginians to develop a devotion to the equality that English republicans had declared to be the soul of liberty."[16] Even regarding white males, the Jacksonian commitment to egalitarianism was more popular rhetoric than actual endorsement. Though universal white male suffrage was adopted in all states by the end of the Jacksonian era, this era also marked the intro- duction of party politics which in practical terms subjected members to party discipline rather than permitting them to think and speak for themselves.[17] (As Tocqueville observed, political parties became the medium through which "the absolute sovereignty of the majority" could exercise its dominion. Majority power was "not only preponder- ant but irresistible.")[18] The party structure didn't subordinate middle- class white males with the same ferocity as was inflicted on blacks and Native Americans. But generally speaking, the Age of Jackson embraced a subjugative mode of social authority, notwithstanding its rhetorical commitment to the equality of all (white) men.

This rigid Jacksonian reimposition of social order was in turn un- raveled by the Civil War. From this cataclysm, a moment followed—a very brief moment—predominantly favoring emancipation accompa- nied by some degree of empathic fellow feeling with the oppressed blacks. The Revolutionary War had disrupted prior social orderings but nonetheless had a stabilizing connection with the prior order be- cause the postindependence domestic elite moved from the previous shadow of British colonial rule into full daylight in the exercise of its social authority. By contrast, the Civil War effected a radical, al- most total breach of prior assumptions about the structure of social authority.

The war fundamentally changed the character of the American Union. President Lincoln had initially insisted that the goal of the war was to preserve the Union. He failed to achieve that goal; the Union that emerged after the war and as a result of the war radically differed from the Union that Lincoln wanted to save. Before the Civil War, the Union had been a voluntary association among states;

as a result of the war, the Union was transformed into a forced alliance between dominant and subjugated states, North and South.

The Civil War, moreover, shattered much more than the previous conception of American political relationships; it destroyed human lives in a magnitude that exceeded all past recorded experience of warfare, not just in the United States but perhaps in the entire history of the Western world. The total number of Civil War deaths is now reliably estimated at seven hundred and fifty thousand. In the Second World War, there were four hundred and five thousand American deaths. If the total U. S. population had been the same in 1865 and 1945, the proportionate loss in World War II would have amounted to 7.5 million deaths rather than the actual loss of four hundred and five thousand. Indeed, there were more American combatant deaths in the Civil War than the combined total of deaths in all other wars this country has fought, from its beginnings in 1776 until today.[19]

The Civil War thus plunged everyone into an atypically shared state of grief. Historians of the period concur in ascribing "the central roles occupied by loss and trauma in postbellum America."[20] This dislocating sense of loss and trauma vividly persisted for almost a century—especially in the conquered South, where approximately one-quarter of the white males aged twenty to twenty-four had died in the war.[21]

The profound disruption of the Civil War was not only the impetus for emancipatory empathy with the oppressed blacks but also paradoxically set the stage for a subsequent more totalizing and brutal imposition of social order than had existed in the prewar Jacksonian era. Before the war, the possibility of rebellion had been the dominant fear among whites regarding black slaves in the South. After the war, sexual aggression by black men against white women ("the black beast rapist") became the whites' predominant expressed fear.[22] White lynching mobs were propelled into an especially murderous rage against blacks accused of raping (or simply having sexual intercourse with) white women.[23]

This new fear of black male sexuality found comparable expression in the changed social signification of sexual deviance generally and homosexuality in particular after the Civil War and Reconstruction. Condemnation of same-sex sexual relations has a long history in Western culture, stretching back to biblical times. But in the United States, this condemnation was transformed in the late nineteenth century. Forbidden sexual acts that anyone might indulge were no longer simply condemned as such. The condemnation took on a new format. The status of being homosexual was proclaimed to designate a firm category of people distinct from heterosexual people. This was not simply a repudiation of the acts of same-sex intercourse; the entire social category of The Homosexual was at once invented and condemned.[24]

This reconceptualization occurred at virtually the same moment when American culture explicitly took on the task of controlling sexual conduct in new ways, similarly based on new social categorizations. Thus, also in the late nineteenth century, laws were enacted that for the first time required a man and a woman who wished to be married to obtain a prior license from the state.[25] Before this time, state recognition of marriage took place only on a post hoc basis when there was some controversy about whether a couple should be considered married—that is, when one alleged spouse had died intestate or when a merchant after advancing credit to one alleged spouse sought to recover the debt from the other alleged spouse. If the couple's relationship had been formalized as "marriage" by some church ceremony, this was sufficient for the state's purpose; but even without this ceremonial celebration, states were prepared to retrospectively recognize these prior relationships as so-called common-law marriages. In the early twentieth century, most states abolished the status of common-law marriage on the ground that this status in effect allowed couples to marry themselves rather than requesting prior permission from (and, in effect, subordinating themselves to) the state.

The new marriage permission laws, moreover, did not accept every applicant. Marital status was now categorically withheld from people who were considered "mental defectives"—not simply or even primarily because such people lacked capacity to enter any contractual arrangements but because they allegedly would reproduce children who themselves would be mentally defective.[26] This state policy against reproduction by so-called mental defectives was not restricted to withholding permission to marry. Coerced sterilization of people found to be mentally defective became legally recognized and widely practiced in most states during the late nineteenth and early twentieth centuries.[27]

At this same time, states enacted new restrictions on a wide range of sexual behaviors. Sale of contraceptives (and in some states even use of contraceptives) was prohibited by state and federal laws.[28] Before the Civil War, abortions had been available without legal restriction during the first trimester (or before "quickening," the perceptible movement of the fetus in the womb). By the end of the nineteenth century and the beginning of the twentieth, every state had adopted new abortion restrictions, limiting availability only to pregnancies that threatened the "life" (or sometimes simply the "health") of the woman.[29] These new laws assigned the regulatory task exclusively to licensed physicians, as was also the case with implementation of the new sterilization laws. (It was only in the late nineteenth century that the state undertook the licensing of physicians as a prior requirement to engage in the practice of medicine.)

Perhaps the most vivid expression of the post–Civil War hysteria about "out-of-control" sexuality was the open warfare waged by the federal government against polygamy in the Utah Territory. In his 1871 State of the Union address, President Ulysses S. Grant referred to the Mormon practice as "a remnant of barbarism, repugnant to civilization, to decency, and to the laws of the United States."[30] During the latter half of the nineteenth century, the federal government escalated its attempt to suppress polygamy by seizing the assets of the Mormon Church of Jesus Christ of Latter-day Saints and even dispatching federal troops.[31] From this quick sketch, we can see that invention of the new category "homosexual person" was accompanied by a wide range of previously nonexistent public regulation of sexual conduct during the late nineteenth century.[32]

One other instance of new categorical conceptualizations in late nineteenth-century America casts special light on understanding the demonization of homosexuality as such. That is the emergence of race segregation in the former slaveholding states of the Confederacy.[33]

The Jim Crow regime threw a pervasive regulatory net over all aspects of social relations between blacks and whites in the South. The establishment of rigid social separation of the races was, in one sense, meant to reassert the subordination of blacks to whites that had been at the core of the institution of slavery. But the new format of that subordination had an underlying connection with the new status of homosexuals after the Civil War. Racial segregation did not invent but did solidify the conceptual categorization of black people—that is, *all* black people as such—as intrinsically inferior to whites. Before the war, all slaves were black, but not all black people were slaves. Some black people were free, that is; although free status was increasingly restricted in the South and blackness viewed as categorically different from whiteness from the beginning of the nineteenth century until the eve of the Civil War, this categorical distinction was reified and made explicit in public policy during the generation after the war by the emergence of racial segregation. For the Jim Crow regime, all blacks were the same—categorically distinct from and inferior to all whites as such. This is the new conceptualization that had taken hold at the same time as the distinguishing of all homosexuals from all heterosexuals.

Thus a vast range of novel categorical restrictions in sexual conduct and race relations was imposed by the generation that came to maturity after the Civil War. This generation was deeply unsettled by the war, perhaps even more so than the prior generation that had directly presided over it but had entered into that traumatic conflagration as adults with the prior experience of having lived in a world that seemed reassuringly ordered. To be sure, that world exploded for everyone; but unlike their forefathers, the young foot soldiers in the war could not pass on to their children and their children's children the sense of having lived in an ordered world with an organic connection to the social life that preceded them.

Thus it is not surprising that some time should elapse between the disruptive event of the Civil War and the imposition of rigid compensatory hierarchical subordinations. The greater confidence of the older generation in the existence of an underlying stratum of social order provided a psychological space in which emancipation—that is, the very idea of doing without the old social hierarchies—could take hold. For large numbers among the subsequent generations, however, the Civil War in retrospect rendered the world unintelligible. The old social categorizations had apparently failed to provide reassurance about the coherence of the world.[34]

After the Civil War, Americans—both Northerners and Southerners, white and black—could not simply resume social life as if the old antebellum presuppositions about the forces of order still were intact. Thus they devised new forms of social order, which were given expression in novel and newly rigid terms not only of domination of whites over blacks and heterosexuals over homosexuals but also of the rule by men over women (enforced in newly created "separate spheres" between public and private lives) and the control by so-called mentally normal people over mentally disabled people (enforced by geographically remote institutional confinement). The rigidly hierarchical terms of all these social relations were in the service of appeasing the sense of disorder, of social chaos, that had emerged from the torrent of the Civil War.

These new terms had their desired effect for almost one hundred years. This effect can be measured not simply by the self-serving proclamations of dominance among the top dogs—the white, male heterosexuals—but also by the widespread silent submission of the bottom dogs, the women, blacks, gays, and mentally disabled people who acquiesced in their own subordination and devaluation (albeit in the face of the pervasive threats of violent reprisals).

What, then, happened to these seemingly rock-hard degradations of vulnerable groups so that today we have seen the election of a black president, the emergence of a woman as the leading contender from his political party to succeed him, and the availability of same-sex marriage in the entire nation? These data points do not demonstrate that the old subordinations of blacks, women, and gays have entirely disappeared. But the categorizations no longer have the widespread force of seemingly unchangeable elements in the "natural order of things." The categorizations are now publicly contestable and fiercely contested.

There are many possible explanations for these dramatic changes. It can be plausibly argued, for example, that the Second World War brought women out of the home and into the workplace for the first time in substantial numbers and that this changed their own and others' sense of their recategorization as no different from, as equal to, men in economic endeavors. It can be plausibly argued that the war brought large numbers of Southern blacks to Northern cities with greater fluidity in racial practices and that service in the armed forces by blacks gave them a new sense of possibilities and self-evaluation.

The list of possible causal factors is immense. I want to return, however, to one common explanation for social change—that is, the new expressions of open resistance by the previously degraded groups—not in order to dismiss this explanation but to suggest its incompleteness.

What explains the newly vocal protest of the formerly oppressed but silent groups? Why did large numbers of African Americans rise up in the 1960s to challenge the segregationist regimes after almost a century of public silence? Why did large numbers of women suddenly characterize themselves as oppressed and embrace a feminist agenda in the 1970s? Why did gays rise up beginning with Stonewall in 1969 and since then gathering in numbers, force, and openness? Why did mentally disabled people protest their remote institutionalization and seek more publicly visible community placement instead?

These groups always knew that they were suffering from oppression. But I believe these groups were led to open protest because they suddenly sensed a sympathetic audience among the oppressors who had previously been blind to their suffering. They suddenly sensed that considerable numbers of their former oppressors were now prepared to extend a new sense of fellow feeling toward them, of empathic identification with them.

This new openness among many (though certainly not all) of the former oppressors did not occur because of the open protests. It is more accurate, I believe, to say that the protests from the previously subjugated groups initially occurred because these groups sensed (however indistinctly, however unconsciously) that large numbers of their oppressors themselves already felt vulnerable and oppressed by the emotional and cognitive disruptions that they were experiencing. The newly open protests in effect built on and reinforced the sudden emergence of fellow feeling among large numbers of the oppressors.

The protests brought these empathic identifications into high visibility and conscious awareness. But these identifications arose from a deeper source. While multiple factors gave impetus to the destabilization of degrading categorizations, the initial spark for this social process came from a series of external shocks comparable to the impact of the Civil War in the nineteenth century and the Revolutionary War in the eighteenth.

To produce the third emancipatory moment in American history, there was no single event that had the impact of the Revolutionary War or the Civil War. There was, however, a prolonged succession of events between the late nineteenth century and the mid-twentieth century that led ultimately to radically unsettle the previous social ordering. Among these disruptive events were open warfare between capitalists and labor in response to the transformation of the American industrial workplace, a series of economic setbacks culminating in the Great Depression of the 1930s, the shocking example of Nazi Germany and its fearful resemblance to American social practices, the two World Wars, the subsequent Cold War, the threat of nuclear holocaust, and the Vietnam War. The accumulation of these events led to a pervasive undermining of the old order by the decade of the 1960s. With all this taken together, by this time substantial numbers of Americans experienced a full-blown loss of confidence in the beneficence and coherence of the existing social order.

One social experience in the 1960s had special impact in contributing to this sense of loss. Just as widespread, deeply unsettling grief was engendered by the Civil War, the assassination of President John F. Kennedy precipitated a state of grief that was amplified by the subsequent killings of Martin Luther King Jr. and the president's brother.

Robert Kennedy's killing while campaigning for the presidency in particular converted the imagined resurrection of the brother's presidency into a reenactment of his death. This mounting grief may not have been as personal as the losses experienced by the Civil War survivors, though Lincoln's assassination points to the existence of links between the personal and societal experiences of loss. The trauma of the Civil War may have been more intense than the social response to the assassinations of our leaders in the 1960s. But grief over the irreparable loss of these national leaders in the 1960s was a chronic undercurrent that markedly contributed to a loss of confidence in the prior belief that we could rely on customary caretakers to protect us from harm.[35]

The social turmoil surrounding the Vietnam War, the explosions of racially motivated riots in black urban ghettos, and the widespread violent assaults on blacks by segregationist white Southerners were also chaotic social disruptions. These eruptions brought into high visibility and intensified the loss of faith in the beneficence and effectiveness of traditional caretakers.

This loss of faith is related to the reevaluation of the status of gays and lesbians after the turmoil of the late 1960s. We can see this link by examining the terms of debate about the most polarizing public dispute that emerged in the 1970s—the conflict between pro-choice and pro-life advocates regarding state restrictions on the availability of abortion. Beneath their clamorous antagonism, there was one proposition—one critique of American culture in the 1970s—that was shared ground between the two warring camps. The pro-choice and pro-life forces actually agreed on the same fundamental premise that traditional caretakers could no longer be trusted to faithfully discharge their socially protective roles.

From the post–Civil War subjugative era until the late 1960s, there was widespread social agreement that physicians should decide if and when abortions would be available to pregnant women. Starting in the mid-1950s, reform efforts arose to liberalize the standards that physicians should apply in making their decisions. But these efforts were led by physicians and were still confined by the premise first articulated immediately after the Civil War—the premise that doctors should be in control of the abortion decision.

It was not until the late 1960s that a new conviction rose into public visibility—the view that doctors could not be trusted as the decision makers and that women were entitled to decide for themselves. The pro-choice critique rested on a broader rejection of trust in men generally to act in women's interests and a reevaluation of the relative social status of men and women, transforming the understanding of status differences in separate spheres (women dominant in the private home, men dominant in the public world) into acts of oppression directed by men against women.

At the same time that this reevaluation of the beneficence of social ordering of men and women was taking place among pro-choice forces, the pro-life forces emerged into high public visibility driven by the same basic premise. For the pro-life forces, the traditional caretakers who had betrayed their trust were not so much physicians (though physician providers were regarded by pro-life advocates as violating the professional obligation to do no harm). Vehement accusations of betrayal were aimed at the Supreme Court justices who reversed the old rules and gave complete authority to women as such. Underlying this pro-life rejection of the beneficence of abortion providers and judges was an even more fundamental loss of confidence. The old faith that mothers instinctively protect their children from harm was replaced by a new image among pro-life forces, that is, mothers as socially approved killers of their babies.

This loss of faith in traditional caretakers was starkly revealed by but was not restricted to the abortion debate. This loss can also be seen as a driving force in another dramatic and surprising cultural development—that is, the virtual disappearance since the 1950s of the elite status in American culture of WASPs, white Anglo-Saxon Protestant men. This is an amazing social transformation. Just fifty years ago, when I graduated from Yale Law School, it was a seemingly settled fact that WASP males owned American society. During the past half century, however, the WASP male dominance has virtually disappeared.

This is exemplified by the current composition of the Supreme Court. During its entire history until 1993, only six Catholics and five Jews had served on the Court; all of the other ninety-five justices were Protestants. Moreover, there was usually no more than one Catholic from 1835 onward and one Jew beginning in 1915; in any event, there were never more than two Catholic or Jewish justices on the Court at the same time. Thus even when Protestants were not the sole members of the Court, they always were numerically predominant. Since 1993, however, every justice appointed has been either Catholic or Jewish. Today there are no Protestants—*zero* Protestants—on the Court. The entire Court is now composed of six Catholics and three Jews.

There has been virtually no mention of this phenomenon in the popular press. The presence of three women has been widely commented upon; but there is relatively scarce notice that two of these women are Jewish and one is Catholic. Almost no one publicly observed that both of President Clinton's appointees were Jewish. The fact is commonly mentioned that all of the current justices studied at either Yale or Harvard Law School, accompanied by the typical complaint that these limited educational affiliations mark them as an out-of-touch elite unrepresentative of American society and even among the American legal profession. But virtually nothing is said about the current absence of Protestants, even though they make up approximately half of the American population.[36] This pervasive public silence about the religious affiliation of the justices did not occur because of its sensitivity or controversial character; this inattention arose, it seems, because their religious affiliation suddenly appeared irrelevant and uninteresting.

To summarize, we can see a repeated cycle in American social history: from the stable hierarchical social order in colonial times; to the disruption of that order in the violent break with Great Britain; to the egalitarian emancipations that followed the Revolutionary War and intensified after Thomas Jefferson's election in 1800; to the imposition of more rigid hierarchies leading up to Andrew Jackson's election in 1828; to the eruption of the Civil War followed by the brief emancipatory moment of the Reconstruction era and enactment of the three postwar liberating constitutional amendments; to the imposition of even more rigid hierarchies between 1876 and 1930; to the accumulation of disruptive events after the Great Depression into the 1960s that undermined the post-Reconstruction hierarchies (of whites over blacks, capitalists over labor, men over women, straights over gays, mentally "normal" over mentally ill or retarded); to the egalitarian emancipations that gradually unfolded after 1938 and virtually exploded during the decade of the 1960s.

The striking aspect of this progression is the regular recurrence of emancipatory interludes between the impositions of oppressive social ordering—episodes of "liberty and justice for all" rather than only for some. During the oppressive times, the favored status of some is apparently purchased directly at the expense of the oppressed as if the oppressors can only see themselves as favored by comparison with the degraded groups. This stable social order is regularly disrupted, but the disruption does not fundamentally arise from the revolt of the oppressed; there were occasional outbursts by small groups of the oppressed, but these mini-revolts were quickly and even ruthlessly suppressed by the dominant groups. The stable social orders were instead initially and fundamentally overturned by events exogenous to the degradation or self-evaluation of the oppressed. This is the sense of Karl Marx's prediction of an imminent revolution in which "all that is solid melts into air."[37] The old social categorizations now lose their referents and the old hierarchies seem arbitrary, irrational, unjust. A sense of liberation takes their place.

When substantial disorder erupted and undermined the confidence of the oppressors in their favored status, the oppressed groups took advantage of this weakened condition, this loss of self-confidence among the oppressors. The newly overt protests of the oppressed gave added impetus to the forces already at work to undermine the prior social hierarchy. But the primary moving force in the unraveling of the hierarchy was an unaccustomed sense among the oppressors that the oppressed were not as radically different from them as their rigidly differentiated prior status degradations had proclaimed.

The novel weakness, the loosened grasp of their hierarchic social dominance, led large numbers of the oppressors to feel an unaccustomed kinship, a fellow feeling, for the oppressed.

This empathy was not long lasting in the first emancipatory era led by the Founding Fathers' generation, and sympathetic identification was even more brief during the emancipatory era that followed after the Civil War. But empathy for the oppressed among the oppressors and the emancipatory implications of that empathy were real, if only for a time.

The post-1960s challenge to oppressive-status hierarchies has proven to be more resilient than the prior eras of emancipatory indictments. To be sure, there have been strenuous demands for the reimposition of subjugative controls in the wake of the 1960s disruptions. But these reactionary moves have not come to dominate our social lives with the same completeness and rigidity that were evident in the Jacksonian and the post–Civil War eras. In our time, struggle is openly avowed between those urging reimposition of stable social hierarchies and those demanding preservation and enlargement of the new emancipations as well as their extension to additional oppressed groups (from African Americans, to women, to disabled people, to gays and lesbians). The emancipatory impulse has not retreated as in past eras; it persists, though locked in public competition with the subjugative mode. The continued combat of these two forces is exemplified by the election in 2008 and reelection in 2012 of our first African American president, on one side, and the surging influence of the Tea Party and the rightward shift of the Republican Party, on the other.

Notwithstanding the difference between the resilience of the three emancipatory eras in American history, they share one fundamental characteristic—that is, the unaccustomed strength of empathy between former subjugating and subjugated groups based on the dissolution of the rigid differentiation between members of these groups (between whites and blacks, men and women, straights and gays, mental normals and abnormals). This new empathic sense of fellow feeling arose as a consequence of the dissolution of the prior categorical differences between "superior" and "inferior" groups—a dissolution that emerged from the exogenous force of the social disruptions of warfare, death, and economic disaster.

The sense of stabilizing social order expressed by rigid categorical group differentiations not only mirrored actual social stability; the social stability itself was widely ascribed to the existence and continued maintenance of the categorical differentiations. (Here is an instance of the *post hoc propter hoc* fallacy at work.) By this fallacious though extensively held conviction, the disruption of external order was understood as demonstrating the failure of the existing social hierarchy to achieve its goal of enforcing a stable world order. A new ordering principle was needed, and, for a time at least, this need was met by a widespread feeling of universal social solidarity based on an empathic identification equally shared among everyone. This does not mean that everyone is the same in every dimension—intelligence, height, weight, eye color; it means that we all share a fundamental similarity notwithstanding surface differences among us. This is the conviction that underlies the egalitarian norm.

It is difficult to explain the unusual persistence of the contemporary emancipatory impulse. There are, of course, many differences between past eras and ours, and accounts of historical causation are always driven more by hunches than by verifiable data. There is, however, one difference between past and present emancipatory efforts that seems especially significant to me. That is the different role of the judiciary between then and now regarding these two modes of social authority.

While other governmental institutions promoted emancipation during the generation after the Revolutionary War and then again immediately after the Civil War, the Supreme Court entirely exempted itself from this enterprise for a full century and a half after the founding of the republic. The Court instead consistently favored social subjugation as an instrument of maintaining or reimposing order. Most notably, before the Civil War the Court regularly supported the institution of slavery by invalidating measures by some Northern state legislatures and state courts to limit the recapture of fugitive slaves[38] and Congressional efforts to ban the extension of slavery in the territories.[39] After the Civil War, the Court effectively undermined federal efforts to protect the freed slaves by narrowly construing the emancipatory goals of the new constitutional amendments,[40] by approving race segregation notwithstanding the abolition of slavery in the Thirteenth Amendment and the guarantee of equality in the Fourteenth Amendment,[41] and by ignoring blatant Southern restrictions on black voting rights notwithstanding the promises of the Fifteenth Amendment.[42] At the same time, the Court converted the guarantees of the Fourteenth Amendment into a mandate for preferring the property interests of the new capitalist class against state regulatory efforts to protect consumers and workers.[43]

In the late 1930s, however, the Court adopted a dramatically new allegiance in the struggle between subordinating and emancipatory conceptions of social authority. The first indication of this change appeared when the Court upheld both state and federal legislation regulating economic activity[44]—legislation that almost certainly would have been overturned under the Court's previously prevailing doctrine that had favored the subordinating authority of capitalist enterprises over the claims of labor and consumers.[45] This shift might be explained as a response to the overwhelming electoral victories for New Deal congressional regulatory measures and related enactments in state legislatures—as evidence, as one observer put it, that the Supreme Court "follows th' ilection returns."[46]

In this new self-depiction, however, the Court did more than ratify emancipatory efforts of other institutions. It also promised to initiate efforts on behalf of a variety of subjugated groups well in advance of other federal and state institutions. This promise first appeared in Footnote Four of the *Carolene Products* case,[47] decided in 1938. This new vision moved from footnote to the main text of a Court opinion in two cases decided very soon afterward.

In 1940, the Court upheld the authority of a local school board to compel students to pledge allegiance to the flag at the beginning of each school day, notwithstanding the students' religiously based conviction that the flag salute was forbidden idolatry. Only one justice dissented from this ruling—Chief Justice Harlan Fiske Stone, not coincidentally the author of *Carolene Products* Footnote Four. The Court's opinion in the Jehovah's Witness flag salute case, *Minersville School District v. Gobitis*,[48] was written by Felix Frankfurter (the foreign-born Jewish justice). In that opinion, Frankfurter extolled the flag salute as an instrument for the "promotion of national cohesion"[49] and dismissed the resistant school children as "dissidents" who were asking for "exceptional immunity" for their "individual idiosyncracies."[50]

Just three years later, the Court reversed this ruling. In the interim, one new justice (Robert Jackson) had joined the Court, and three other recently appointed justices who had participated in *Gobitis* (Hugo Black, Frank Murphy, and William O. Douglas) had subsequently announced publicly that they had changed their views and were prepared to overrule that decision.[51] In 1943, Jackson wrote the Court's opinion overturning *Gobitis* by a six-to-three margin. In *West Virginia Board of Education v. Barnette*, Jackson rejected the very conception of coercive subordinating authority that Frankfurter had endorsed in the service of promoting national cohesion. Jackson instead concluded, "As governmental pressure toward unity becomes greater, so strife becomes more bitter as to whose unity it shall be. . . . Those who begin coercive elimination of dissent soon find themselves exterminating dissenters. Compulsory unification of opinion achieves only the unanimity of the graveyard."[52]

Jackson did not cite Footnote Four in coming to this conclusion. He overturned the compulsory flag salute on the ground that this coercion violated the students' First Amendment right of free expression. But the protective embrace that he offered the Jehovah's Witness children can readily be understood to ratify the footnote's promise of judicial solicitude toward "discrete and insular minorities." Indeed, these school children had an especially urgent need for protection from someone in 1943, as the United States was engaged in world war and Jehovah's Witness adherents generally were subjected to majority prejudice because of their pacifist views. In offering this protection, the *Barnette* Court relied on the conception of social authority that I have described as emancipatory—that is, egalitarian rather than hierarchical, fluidly interactive rather than rigidly dictatorial.

The Court exemplified this fluid conception of its own authority in its rapid overruling of its own prior precedent, in the willingness of three justices publicly to renounce their prior votes and thereby invite further interaction with the previously defeated litigants, and in its vivid warning about the ready progression from "coercing dissent" to "exterminating dissenters." But to repeat, the Court could have cited Footnote Four; in any event, its actions were emblematic of it.

The path from *Gobitis* to *Barnette* was in effect only the first instance of the Court's radical shift from reflexive support of established authority to protective scrutiny of state actions imposing disadvantages on vulnerable groups. This shift was initially most visible in the Court's increased scrutiny of Southern racial segregation practices. In 1938, at virtually the same moment that it formulated Footnote Four, a Court majority ruled that Missouri could not constitutionally refuse to establish an in-state law school for black students, though it paid for black legal education in neighboring states.[53] During the subsequent sixteen years, the Court invalidated race segregation in buses that traveled in interstate commerce,[54] prohibited political party primaries in which blacks were forbidden to vote,[55] forbade governmental enforcement of residential racially restrictive covenants,[56] and overturned racially separate graduate school admissions.[57]

In retrospect, the Court appeared engaged in a relentless march toward invalidating all Jim Crow laws—all state maintenance of "separate but equal" accommodations for blacks and whites. As it actually occurred behind the face of the Court's unanimous rulings, however, the justices privately seemed uncertain and divided about whether to strengthen equality demands while preserving the regime of racially separate public facilities. Nonetheless, during the lapse of sixteen years during which it moved finally to invalidating race segregation in *Brown v. Board of Education*, the Court was visibly impelled by the shift in the social ethos generally from endorsing subordinative relationships to prizing egalitarian interactive relationships.

At the same time, it seems likely that the Court's endorsement of that shift and its extension of this social ethos to other subjugated groups in itself contributed to the unusual longevity of the emancipative impulse as compared to the relative brevity of past emancipatory eras. If this is true, can we identify specific characteristics of judicial interventions that might explain the special impact of courts in this enterprise?

Courts have a special moral status in American society, and they, more than other institutions, can drape themselves with the text of the Constitution, our secular holy writ. Accordingly, judicial interpretations of the Constitution carry a substantial moral weight. But I believe that this weight derives less from what judges say than from the settings in which they speak. To explore this proposition, we must dig deep into the individual psychological forces that resist or promote empathic connections, that lead to subjugative or egalitarian social relationships.

four THIS WORD "REASON"

What are the psychological obstacles encountered in attempting to turn away from subjugative relations? What are the psychological benefits of subjugation that must be overcome in order to implement a normative preference for emancipation?

These questions might seem to answer themselves. The autocratic master enjoys immense pleasure, one might say, from his superior social status and consequently is prepared to deploy all of his power to maintain that status. This may be a sufficient answer to explain the stubborn resilience of subordinative relationships. But I believe there is a deeper psychological benefit that comes from subjugating others, a benefit that engenders deep-rooted resistance to emancipation and affects both oppressors and oppressed.

Subjugation of some by others can readily form the basis for a sense of ordered safety and even for cognitive coherence on the part of everyone, whether situated at the top or the bottom of the hierarchy. Subordination of some by others bolsters the fragility of the sense of self-control, of rationality, and of objectivity. This fragility expresses itself in the cognitive differentiation of "self" from "others." Domination of some by others clearly asserts these boundaries ("I am different from—and in control of—them").

There is, however, an inherent psychological tension in this separate differentiation, an unavoidable pull toward dissolved barriers from others. This impulse is often unwanted and unacknowledged, often lodged in unconscious thinking where it can be shielded from conscious awareness. In times of widespread social disruptions, the psychological tension underlying the maintenance of these boundaries can readily lead to their cognitive attenuation. This weakened conceptual distance can promote an unaccustomed sense of connection and fellow feeling, a boundlessness in social relations in comparison to the relatively fixed boundaries that characterized the prior regime of social subjugation.

This relative dissolution of established boundaries between people can be liberating and energizing. But here's the rub: the attenuation of the boundaries can also inspire intense anxiety, even primitive terror. This fear can overwhelm the sense of liberation and unleashed energy and can provoke a resurgent subordination of some by others.

This individual cognitive problem arises from the fact that our brains are constantly bombarded by sensory perceptions that have no intrinsic structure or meaning. We construct meaning, we give order to disordered perceptions;[1] and through our mutual depiction of social relationships with one another, we bestow meaningful order. Distinguishing between self and other is one of ways that we organize coherent conceptual representations of the world. Drawing polar distinctions between conscious and unconscious thinking, rationality and irrationality, objectivity and subjectivity, dream fantasies and wakeful reality are other ways. All of these polar distinctions are fragile,[2] but the fragility of the self/other distinction casts an especially strong shadow over efforts to conceptualize and regulate social relations.

An early intuition of the fragility of cognitive ordering was offered by Thomas Hobbes in *Leviathan*. The treatise is an extended account of political relationships, but Hobbes begins with the individual's capacity for rational thinking. He asks, "[W]hat is meant by this word *reason*, when we reckon it amongst the faculties of the mind"; and he illustrates the puzzle with the observation "[I]t is a hard matter, and by many thought impossible, to distinguish exactly between sense and dreaming. For my part . . . being awake I know I dream not, though when I dream, I think myself awake."[3]

The problematic differentiation between wakefulness and dreaming translates more directly into political theory when we consider the tenuousness of the related distinction between "self" and "other." The cognitive development of this distinction and the reasons for its psychic fragility are well portrayed in the work of Sigmund Freud.

Freud's basic data was limited—a combination of his introspections and accounts from his patients of their waking fantasies and dreams while asleep. He lacked tools to observe the neurological functioning of living brains. We have only recently developed such tools, and even now their observational capacities are limited and imperfect; but these new brain-scanning tools promise to remedy the incapacity of Freud to rigorously distinguish between what he observed in his patients and what was transpiring in his own mind that confused and distorted his perceptions of what was happening in them.

Freud's incapacity is the basis for still-persistent complaints that his observations were not objective and therefore do not qualify as science. There are, however, two answers to these complaints. The first answer comes from experiments with the new brain-scanning tools that have provided the first objective demonstrations, by conventional scientific standards, of the existence of unconscious thinking. The second answer transforms the shortcomings of Freud's capacity for objective observation into a strength of his methodology. Objective measure of thought processes itself can be seen as a distortion. Objective observation depends on distinguishing between "inside" and "outside" worlds of mentation. Freud, however, took seriously what purported objectivity about mental functioning is inclined to ignore—that is, the proposition that subjectivity is an inherent characteristic of mentation.

This is not to say that objectivity is always an illusion. Objectivity depends, however, on a rigorous separation of "self" from "other" that is not acknowledged in all cognition; separation has no place in unconscious thinking. Freud speculated, based on his study of dreams (which are the "royal road to the unconscious," as he said in *The Interpretation of Dreams*), that there are systematic differences between conscious and unconscious thinking and that mental functioning consists of interwoven relationships between these two fundamentally different and incommensurable modes of thought.

At times, Freud seemed to envision a Hobbesian response to the conflicting modes—a forced or self-enforced surrender to rationality. This conception was especially evident in his reports about the conduct of psychotherapy when he would claim superior knowledge and authority in interpreting the unconscious meanings of patients' symptoms and thereby declare them cured. At other times, especially in his late publications, Freud was more modest about both his capacity and his patients' capacities to control unconscious forces.[4]

Freud never articulated the precise relationship between conscious and unconscious thought processes. He never gave a clear account of whether unconscious and conscious thought processes are rigidly differentiated or whether they stand in a hierarchical relationship. But these issues are less important than Freud's basic insight: unconscious thinking exists; it rests on premises different from and logically inconsistent with conscious thinking; and it influences behavior even though it is not directly accessible to awareness.

The limitation of his observational capacities should not be a reason for dismissing the basic insights of Freud any more than the failure of Darwin to understand the mechanism for genetically transmitted inheritance undermined his claim that evolution through reproduction is a basic characteristic of all life forms. The empirical lacunae in Darwin's conception has now been filled by our modern understanding of genetic transmission. Modern observational capacities regarding brain function have not yet advanced as far as our new knowledge of genetics. But regarding the existence of unconscious thinking, we no longer need to rely solely on inference as Freud did. We now have direct empirically verifiable observation of unconscious thinking based on modern brain-monitoring capabilities.

The first empirical demonstration of unconscious thinking was accomplished in the 1970s by Benjamin Libet at the University of California, San Francisco. Libet asked subjects to lift their right index finger whenever they felt an urge to do so. Based on readings from electrodes attached to the subjects' scalps, Libet observed that electrical activity regularly occurred in the brain three hundred milliseconds before a subject was aware of the urge to move his or her finger. "Merely by observing the electrical activity of the brain, Libet could predict what a person would do before the person was actually aware of having decided to do it."[5] Libet thus saw directly what Freud was capable only of inferring—that brain activities indistinguishable from consciously perceived thoughts take place outside conscious awareness.[6] We can now see unconscious thinking in operation.

What are these unconscious thoughts? What meaning do they contain? We know from Libet's experiments and those of others who have followed him that this observable, unconscious brain activity is not random electrical noise. The scalp readings that preceded his subjects' awareness of an impulse to lift their index fingers repeatedly revealed the same patterns as after conscious awareness. The readings have meaning of some sort, though to decipher this meaning we are still dependent on a reconstructive process carried out by the subjects themselves—a process that retrospectively teases these impulses into some form of conscious awareness. This reconstructive process is in its essence identical to the waking recall of dreams.

The relationship between conscious and unconscious thought is not, however, a one-to-one correspondence. Far from it. There is an immense reservoir of unconscious thinking that never becomes conscious, located in what the neuroscientist Eric Kandel describes as a "vast array of unconscious, autonomous, specialized brain networks that contribute to the small amount of conscious information that is the spotlight of attention."[7] The content of this spotlight is "the momentary, active, subjective experience of working memory." Conscious attention in effect "corresponds to our working memory for a single event, a memory lasting only sixteen to thirty seconds."

Behind this consciously experienced memory, however, there is an immense network of memories that is selectively scanned, as it were, backstage. As Libet's experiments showed, this unconscious scanning occurs with incredible speed; the interval Libet identified between the unconscious prelude to and the conscious awareness of the urge to lift one's finger occupied only three hundred milliseconds. But during this tiny interval, it seems as if the urge to lift one's index finger is processed through an interwoven neural chain of associative memories—memories, perhaps, of past uses of the index finger, of body activity, of following instructions, of independent choice making, of this and that and cabbages and kings.

This scanning of past memories must inevitably leave some residual tracings in the final conscious idea. To pursue the theatrical metaphor, only a limited number of memories step forward from backstage to center stage to be incorporated into the spoken play, the consciously acknowledged idea. The vast number of other memories that remain unconscious are not entirely effaced, however, but retreat offstage, where they remain ready to be recalled.

This theatrical metaphor was notably used by the cognitive psychologist Bernard Baars to describe the way unconscious ideas come into conscious awareness from a widespread network that he called the "global workspace" of the brain. He analogized this workspace to a theater with three parts: "(1) a bright spotlight of attention focused on the action of the moment; (2) an unseen cast and crew who are not part of the immediate action; and (3) the audience. . . . Mind is not simply the actors, crew members, or audience, but the network of interactions among them."[8]

The relationship between the conscious idea at center stage and the offstage memory may be harmonious—that is, the unconscious memory may be comfortably enfolded into the conscious thought, though it remains outside conscious attention. Or the relationship may be adversarial—with the offstage memory banished from the center of conscious attention but unreconciled to its exile, shouting angrily from the wings and even disrupting the action onstage. Whether harmonious or conflictual, this portrait of cognitive processing between unconscious and conscious memories is captured by William Faulkner's observation "The past is never dead. It is not even past."[9]

The conventional scientific method of objective observation has inherent limitations. Because it relies on rational premises, the conventional method is biased toward excluding subjectivity and readily distorts the experience of mental functioning that is antithetical to objectivity. Freud's failure to limit his vision to what he was able to observe objectively is paradoxically not a weakness but a strength of his method in accounting for mental functioning. If properly understood, Freud's position leads to a different conception of scientific observation, a corrective to the conventional scientific effort to exclude subjectivity.[10]

Freud himself did not fully grasp the revolutionary implications of his conception of mental functioning. In particular, he was inclined to array aspects of conscious thinking as hierarchically superior to unconscious thinking. This was an especially marked inclination in his practical experience and writing about therapeutic technique. The goal of psychotherapy, Freud frequently opined, was to bring unconscious thoughts and conflicts into conscious awareness and thereby to facilitate rational control over irrationally based beliefs and conduct. This was the basis for his famous aphorism "[W]here id was, there ego should come into being."[11]

Freud's psychoanalytic successors saw this as a limitation, only a partial truth. The corrective was most vividly articulated by Hans Loewald's revised version of Freud's aphorism—not to disagree with it but to supplement it by prescribing also that "where ego is, there id should come into being."[12] This is not a hierarchic contest between ego and id, as Freud had envisioned it, but an alternation, an intertwined equality of authority, between the conflicting forces in individuals' minds.

One of the conflicting forces is the inconsistent, incommensurate conceptions of bounded and boundless selves. Freud portrayed these different self-conceptions in developmental terms: "[T]he infant at the breast does not as yet distinguish his ego [sense of self] from the external world as the source of the sensations flowing in upon him. He gradually learns to do so [so that] the ego detaches itself from the external world. Or, to put it more correctly, originally the ego includes everything, later it separates off an external world from itself. Our present ego-feeling is, therefore, only a shrunken residue of a much more inclusive—indeed, an all-embracing—feeling which corresponded to a more intimate bond between the ego and the world about it."[13]

This developmental account might appear to imply that as individuals grow from infancy they learn that every person has a separate self, and this new idea entirely supersedes or corrects the infantile belief in unbounded selves. But this was not the view Freud took; he claimed, paradoxically enough, that all adults "somehow preserve" the idea, instilled in their infancy, that they are not separate from the surrounding universe of animate and inanimate objects but are instead indissolubly linked to it. In short, adults continue to believe that they have no separate "self" at the same time that they learn to understand themselves as selves separate from others.

In this sense, Freud posited, the minds of all humans (except those of newborn infants) are divided against themselves. Insofar as we struggle to suppress a sense of boundless self and prefer to see ourselves as rationally in control of ourselves, of our rigidly bounded selves, we are at war with ourselves. This internalized warfare between incommensurate forces is the intrapsychic counterpart to Hobbes's "war of all against all" in the external regime of social relations. The absence of any overarching principle of "justice" or "right reason" for resolving this conflict is the reason that Hobbes prescribed universal surrender to an unaccountable Sovereign as the only escape from this conflict.

For many people, this internal struggle equally seems to require surrender to an unaccountable embodiment of self-control, the mental existence of an internal "super self" (rather like the invisible genie who controls the refrigerator light switch). But this homunculus does not exist. The very idea of a master self that controls the disparate aspects of our cognitive activities is subject to an infinite regress. From this belief, the question inescapably arises, "Then who or what controls this controller?" And once we have identified the super-controller, who controls it?[14]

This search for an ultimate self is a fantasy that we can ultimately find an impermeably bounded self. This search is fruitless, a snark hunt in Lewis Carroll's sense. Like it or not, acknowledge it or not, in everyone's mental structure, a fantasied bounded self permanently coexists with a fantasied boundless self.[15] The two contradictory modes of perception exist only in juxtaposition to one another, only in continuous interaction, and not as independent, clearly defined entities.

This proposition that the idea of a bounded, rationally objective self never banishes the boundless irrationally subjective self seems to defy common sense. We empirically observe that boundaries exist between our own body and the bodies of others. This may not be true for fetuses in their mothers' wombs; and common sense suggests that it may take some time even for newborns to revise their unbounded view of the universe. But common sense nonetheless seems to dictate that at some point, every child learns to refute the incorrect, irrational view.

Psychoanalysis teaches, however, that this conclusive refutation, this exclusive commitment to rational thinking based on the bounded separation of self and other, never takes place. Rather than refuting the idea of boundlessness, we instead only bury this idea in unconscious thinking and thereby preserve it. This proposition is a cornerstone of Freudian psychology.

Freud illustrated this proposition by a poetic invocation. He asked the reader to visualize the archaeological history of the city of Rome, noting how new structures were successively built on top of the old so that the former history of the city was effectively preserved though buried. He then continued,

> Now let us, by a flight of imagination, suppose that Rome is not a human habitation but a psychical entity with a similarly long and copious past—an entity, that is to say, in which nothing that has once come into existence will have passed away and all the earlier phases of development continue to exist alongside the latest one. This would mean that in Rome the palaces of the Caesars and the Septizonium of Septimius Severus would still be rising to their old height on the Palatine and that the castle of S. Angelo would still be carrying on its battlements the beautiful statues which graced it until the siege by the Goths, and so on. . . . And the observer would perhaps only have to change the direction of his glance or his position in order to call up the one view or the other.[16]

Freud thus posited the existence of an unconscious mind as a structured entity coexisting beneath or alongside a conscious mind. The distinction between conscious and unconscious does not appear full-blown in early infancy; it is a developmental achievement. One might say that the unconscious comes into being to serve as an ineradicable repository for early ideas (such as the boundless self) that are diametrically opposed to later-acquired ideas (such as the bounded self). These contradictory ideas coexist, though experienced in rapid (typically unconscious) alternation.[17]

The fragility of the self/other distinction and yet its stubborn pursuit in individual psychology has been extensively documented, building on Freud's account. Thus, for example, one revelatory marker of the capacity to conceive a separate self is understanding that knowledge I possess is not necessarily and automatically possessed by others. This understanding rests on the belief that my mind is separate and different from the minds of others and that to obtain knowledge they must either learn it as I have done or I must communicate it to them. This seemingly commonsense proposition about the existence of "other minds" is not grasped by virtually anyone until around three years of age.

In a classic experiment carried out by the developmental psychologist Jean Piaget, this has been demonstrated by hiding a ball in the presence of the child and another person, then removing the other person from the room, relocating the hidden ball and asking the child to predict where the other person would look for the ball when he reenters the room. Children younger than three typically respond that the other person would immediately look in the new hiding place, ignoring the fact that the child alone knew that location. Only after the age of three does the typical child grasp that the absent person would look in the original hiding place.

Another observable marker of the incapacity of newborn infants to see themselves as separate from others is their inability to recognize themselves in a mirror. Until around eighteen months, typical infants fail to respond to their own mirror image with any special recognition or differentiation. Notwithstanding that the infants smiled or grimaced or cried at the precise instant that their mirror image made the same move, typical infants make no connection between themselves and their reflected image.

After eighteen months, typical infants recognize themselves in the mirror by intentionally playful exchanges between themselves and their mirrored image. The infants thus demonstrate a newfound capacity to see themselves as separate from the rest of the world. Whereas previously the mirror image had been for the infants a perceived object no different from all others, now the infants see the mirror image as a unique expression of an "I" or a "me."[18] Though the concept of a distinct "I" is thus revealed in rudimentary form, the infants still have not fully absorbed this idea until much older than eighteen months. Accordingly, the typical verbal infant remains confused about the use of personal pronouns until well into the third year, finding it difficult to understand that he or she is a "me" to himself or herself but an objectively observed "you" to others.

I made a further personal observation recently when I spent some time with my seven-month-old great-nephew, Beckett. As he sat on a blanket covering the floor, he tugged repeatedly at the blanket's edge apparently intending to lift it off the floor and over his head. He couldn't lift the blanket because he was sitting on it—a difficulty evident to me but not to him. He kept pulling. It seemed to me that Beckett had no sense of himself as an object in the world; he was, that is, unable to conceive himself as a separate object weighting down the blanket. So he tugged and tugged to no avail.

Freudian developmental psychology is not the only way to understand the fragility of the self/other distinction on which our sense of self-control ordinarily rests. The philosopher Charles Taylor has offered another perspective on this difficulty. In *Sources of the Self: The Making of the Modern Identity* (1989), Taylor identified what he called "the continuing philosophic discomfort" with the post-Enlightenment conception of the self. He located the source of this discomfort in the confusing shift between "radical objectivity" and "radical subjectivity" within the self's conceptual structure.[19] Self-conscious human beings can both observe themselves from a third-person perspective and experience themselves from a first-person perspective. But Taylor observed that the two perspectives are incommensurate; they start from different premises, and these premises lead to radically different mental representations of the individual and collective worlds.[20]

Taylor characterized the defining difference between the premodern and postmodern Enlightenment views of the self in a vivid way. He said that the self-objectifying modern self "stands in a place already hollowed out for God; he takes a stance to the world which befits an image of the Deity."[21] When God is firmly in his place, the incommensurate distinction between the third-person and first-person perspective in human thought is stabilized. That is, God embodies the third-person perspective; he observes and controls us. We in turn embody the first-person perspective, observed and controlled by him. The conceptual instability occurs when God disappears from the equation and when these two perspectives of radical objectivity and radical subjectivity are thought to exist in a single entity that is the modern self.[22]

If the modern self combines the two perspectives, it is easy to understand the premodern embodiment of the third-person perspective in God as a psychological projection—that is, as a psychological defense mechanism by which individuals project their own attributes onto someone or something in the external world (in this case, a projection of the capacity of individuals for seeing themselves as third persons) because acknowledgment of the attributes as their own would be too uncomfortable. Though the individuals psychologically separate themselves from ownership of or personal responsibility for the attribute, this conceptual maneuver in fact rests on the premise that the individuals and the object of their projection are seamlessly intertwined. The psychological defense mechanism of projection rests on the unacknowledged, unconscious premise that the self is not separate from the external world. The modern self is at once bounded (distinct from the external world) and boundless (seamlessly woven into the world).

We can comprehend both the depth of this contradiction and the persistently urgent impulse to achieve its resolution by exploring a further implication of Taylor's observation that the modern post-Enlightenment concept of "self" occupies a "space hollowed out for God." When God is the first-person creator and we are the third-person objects of his creation, it becomes easy to identify the uncaused cause in a hierarchical structure of the universe. God is the originator who causes everything to happen, but nothing or no one has caused him to come into being. God is the uncaused cause. But if God disappears (or is in hiding and unavailable), who or what takes his place as the uncaused cause? Taylor observed that we moderns have taken God's place. But if that is so, how can we cause us?

Contemporary neurology offers a further perspective on the evanescence and multiplicity of the very idea of a self-controlling self. "The consensus from contemporary neuroscience is that neurological processing is for the most part distributed across various brain regions. There is consequently no real unified neurological center of experience, nor is there any real identity across time that we could label the self. . . . [The self is not] located and hidden in the head."[23]

Paul Armstrong elaborates on this idea by noting that the notion of the self has a temporal foundation that bridges past recollection and future anticipation and therefore "is always slipping away and is never at one with itself." He invokes the metaphor of a symphonic orchestra as "representing the brain's distributed multiplicity of activities, which are not reducible to a single processing site"; and he varies the metaphor by observing that the orchestral conductor "does not preexist the performance . . . but is produced by it, just as there is no central manager—no man in the machine—directing the brain's activity." Armstrong continues, "The conductor may come to stand metonymically for the orchestra . . . but [this] is necessarily a misrepresentation of the distributed, temporally fluid, ever-shifting phenomenological and neurological bases of selfhood."[24]

Yet another path for appreciating the fluidity underlying the idea of a bounded self comes from a sociological perspective on the interactive processes from which individual self-definition arises. Erving Goffman has especially illuminated these processes in his mapping of the elaborate social rituals that bolster the fragile boundaries between self and other. Writing in the 1960s, Goffman minutely observed the rules of etiquette regulating public encounters among strangers.[25] Beneath these simple regulations, he discerned underlying forces of aggression and threats of psychic incoherence.

Two of Goffman's most revelatory examples were the mutually choreographed conduct of strangers who enter an elevator on successive floor stops and the mutual regulation of eye contact between strangers who pass one another on public streets. Regarding the choreographic regularities in elevator conduct, Goffman observed that when a second passenger joins the first, the two almost invariably take up the furthest distanced positions diagonally across from one another; when a third and fourth passenger enter, all of the occupants retreat from one another to occupy the four corners of the elevator, as far as possible from one another; and when a fifth enters, he or she almost invariably stands dead center. This patterned spatial separation breaks down when a sixth enters; there simply is too little space for all of the passengers to take fixed, equidistant stands—but the impulse for demarcated territoriality still persists in the effort among the members of this crowd to avoid touching one another.[26]

Goffman's second example, of eye contact on public streets, was equally striking in his identification of regular rules regarding spatial distance. Goffman observed that as strangers approach on a public street, they initially look at one another from a distance, often somewhat furtively, in order to chart a course that averts collision between one another. But when these approaching strangers reach approximately eight feet apart, they almost invariably cast their eyes downward to demonstrably break eye contact and look away from one another. Goffman called this implicitly regularized street conduct a "dimming of the lights."[27] He speculated that this regularly observed conduct in public streets served the same goal as public elevator etiquette: to reassure people who have never previously met that they have nothing to fear from one another.

The fact is, as Goffman noted, that our everyday encounters among strangers continuously offer the possibility of mayhem of some sort. All of us do have reason to fear one another. Statistically speaking, people are more at risk in their dealings with intimates or acquaintances; perhaps this is, at least in part, because we let our guard down among familiar faces. But Goffman showed that we are not relaxed, we are continually on alert for danger, in public encounters among strangers. The intricate etiquette he identified for these encounters provides mutual reassurance that we have nothing to fear from one another—and more fundamentally that order rather than chaos will prevail in chance street encounters.

If you want to test this proposition for street encounters, you can refuse to "dim your lights," as Goffman put it, and instead remained locked in eye contact until you are directly alongside the other person. You can try this, but I don't recommend it because this breach of etiquette will invariably be viewed by the object of your sustained gaze as an intrusive, hostile act. "Who are you staring at, buster?" is the most likely response before you get busted.

The possibility of physical assault may be the conscious account of the disturbing quality of this encounter. The basic fear in this seemingly small breach of street etiquette, however, is more than physical assault; the breach is a cognitive assault against our perceptions of the coherence of the universe. Goffman's prosaic examples of elevator and public street conduct reveal more than lessons for routine public encounters. These examples suggest a deep social purpose for these seemingly small details of public etiquette—that is, the existence of a tacit understanding that each of us needs to reassure himself or herself that we all will remain within the boundaries that mark our separate selves and that dangerous chaos will not materialize, notwithstanding the fragile foundation of those boundaries. We appease one another's fears so that we can carry on with the mundane tasks of everyday life. But the fears nonetheless lie just beneath the surface of awareness— which is why the simple act of refusing to break eye contact on a public street, the refusal to "dim the lights," is likely to engender a defensive response, maybe even an explosively hostile response.

Goffman focused his attention on social behavior. But it illuminates his account when we consider the individual psychological imperatives that find expression in these behaviors. Common conceptions of mental illness exemplify the breach of this conventional distinction. Thus schizophrenics "hear" imaginary voices that seem to be separate from them; thus people gripped by obsessive-compulsive disorders spend inordinate effort in controlling the world around them because of their incapacity to comprehend a self-controlling self. These are serious distortions of conventional behavior.

For our purposes of understanding the sources for common social relationships based on coercive subordination of others, it is most illuminating to focus on the garden-variety psychological mechanism of projection.[28] Projecting one's own attributes onto another person involves both the denial of any boundaries between the two people ("he embodies attributes of me") while at the same time insisting on clear boundaries between these two ("he is not at all like me"). This contradiction is embedded in the interplay of conscious and unconscious thinking. It becomes the basis for oppressive subordination when one group has sufficient motive and social power to assign its own feared or detested traits onto this vulnerable other group.

We can see the self-protective use of projection in the attitude expressed by Andrew Jackson, one of the most openly assertive subjugative presidents in our history—a man who constructed his popular reputation by virtually avowed genocide against Native Americans, and whose election to the presidency definitively marked the end of the founding generation's emancipatory era. In his 1830 address to Congress, Jackson offered this justification for forced migration of Native Americans: "Doubtless it will be painful to leave the graves of their fathers, but what do they do more than our ancestors did or than our children are doing? To better their condition in an unknown land our forefathers left all that was dear in early objects. Our children by thousands yearly leave the land of their birth to seek new homes in distant regions. Does humanity weep at these painful separations from everything animate and inanimate, with which the young heart has become entwined? Far from it. It is rather a source of joy."[29] This is a patent effort, as the political scientist Michael Paul Rogin has observed, "to impose the American experience of uprooting and mobility upon the Indians."[30] Jackson's deployment of the psychological defense of projection is revealed by his quick shifts from the question "Does humanity weep at these painful separations from everything animate and inanimate, with which the young heart has become entwined?" to his seemingly confident assertion "Far from it. It is rather a source of joy," to his ultimate conclusion that the Native Americans should be forced to experience this "joy." Jackson, that is, "first repress[ed] the intolerable experience, then project[ed] the experience onto the object, and finally separat[ed] or distanc[ed him]self from the object to fortify the defensive effort."

The psychological stress generated by the general American experience of uprooting or rootlessness was classically identified by Alexis

THIS WORD "REASON"

de Tocqueville in 1835. Speaking specifically of the individualist ethos in America, Tocqueville stated, "Not only does it make men forget their ancestors, but also clouds their view of their descendants and isolates them from their contemporaries. Each man is forever thrown back on himself alone, and there is danger that he may be shut up in the solitude of his own heart."[31]

There are of course many other plausible explanations for Jackson's brutal conduct toward Native Americans: greed for their lands, revenge for their real and imagined aggressions against whites, envy at their seemingly bucolic life style. These motives are not inconsistent with projection; but focusing attention on the psychological projective mechanism offers some illuminating lessons about the ameliorative possibilities for undoing the oppressions historically inflicted on vulnerable groups, such as Native Americans.

When we understand that oppression of others can be the psychological projection of the oppressor's undesired traits onto the vulnerable image of the oppressed, several consequences follow. We can first of all see why declarations of wrongdoing and simple commands by an external authority encounter obstacles when the negative view that oppressors have of the oppressed is itself based on their effort to avoid wrongdoing—to cleanse themselves of evil by seeing the oppressed as embodying evil forces that must be subjugated.[32] The command to stop the oppression because it is wrongful has rational force; but this formulation makes no reliable sense and has no impact on the oppressors when the underlying unconscious basis of their view of the oppressed as evil is already in the service of denying that they, the oppressors, are wrongdoers. These oppressors believe that their actions are not only necessary but also righteous.

The rational command from an authoritative source (such as a judge, a cleric, a legislator) that the oppression is evil can create cognitive dissonance, a sense of conflictual contradictions, in these oppressors. But unless the source of this conflict—the negative attitude of the oppressors toward themselves that is projected onto the oppressed—is addressed, the heightened sense of conflict arising from the external adjudicator's condemnation is likely to intensify

67

and lead to even more blame and condemnation by the oppressors of the oppressed. This dynamic lies beneath the historic pattern of oppressors' recoil against emancipatory impulses. When directly challenged, the oppressors' projective efforts can become more urgent and intense. The escalating oppression thus becomes endless.

Projection is a universal characteristic of human cognition. It is not inherently harmful and can establish the basis for empathy and fellow feeling among people. Harm arises when the projectors become rigidly committed to ascribing to vulnerable others their own characteristics that they regard as intolerable. Breaking down these rigid ascriptions and accepting rather than recoiling from the contradictory conjunction of separate and merged selves is the key to promoting relationships based on empathic fellow feeling, on reciprocally mutual respect among equals.[33]

The central characteristic of malign projection is one person's utter and unrelenting erasure of the other, a refusal to recognize the other as an independent agent. This refusal is a source of bitter conflict between the two. When the refuser has disproportionate social power over the other, this conflict is suppressed; but this subjugation inflicts great suffering on the victim and persistent, though unacknowledged and even denied, unease on the victimizer.

Can we design social institutions to promote a just resolution of this conflict? Is there a special role for the judiciary in pursuing this effort? Let us turn now to these questions.

five THE HEALTHIEST POSSIBLE SOUL

Slavery is the paradigmatic instance in American history of refusal to recognize the independent existence of another person. Its foundation on invidious racial distinctions is the hallmark of psychological projection by the subjugating whites onto the oppressed blacks. In a Message to Congress just a month before he signed the Emancipation Proclamation, President Lincoln said, "In giving freedom to the slave, we assure freedom to the free."[1] This statement rests on the proposition that enslavement is not just oppressive to slaves, it also harms oppressors. If oppressors can be brought to understand that any benefits of subordinating others are outweighed by the damage they inflict on themselves as oppressors, the obstacles to emancipation identified in the preceding chapter might be overcome.

We can glimpse the psychological cost engendered in the oppressors through a diary entry of a Southern plantation mistress, Mary Chesnut, during the Civil War:

> September 21, 1861. Last night when the mail came in, I was seated near the lamp. Mr. Chesnut, lying on a sofa at a little distance, called out to me, "Look at my letters and tell me about them."
>
> I began to read one aloud; it was from Mary Witherspoon—and I broke down. Horror and amazement was too much for me. Poor Cousin Betsey Witherspoon was murdered! She did not die peacefully, as we supposed, in her bed. Murdered by her own people. Her negroes.
>
> . . .
>
> September 24, 1861. . . . Hitherto I have never thought of being afraid of negroes. I had never injured any of them. Why should they want to hurt me? Two-thirds of my religion consists in trying to be good to negroes because they are so in my power, and it would be so easy to be the other thing. Somehow today I feel that the ground is cut away from under my feet. Why should they treat me any better than they have done Cousin Betsey Witherspoon?

Kate and I sat up late and talked it all over. Mrs. Witherspoon was a saint on this earth. And this is her reward.

Kate's maid came in—a strong-built mulatto woman. She was dragging in a mattress. "Missis, I have brought my bed to sleep in your room while Mars David is at Society Hill. You ought not to stay in a room by yourself *these times*." And then she went off for more bed gear.

"For the life of me," said Kate gravely. "I cannot make up my mind. Does she mean to take care of me—or to murder me?"[2]

In 1831, Alexis de Tocqueville generalized the lesson that Mary Chesnut's diary entry implied. Regarding pre–Civil War race relations both in the North and South, de Tocqueville observed: "Danger of a conflict between the blacks and whites of the South of the Union is a nightmare constantly haunting the American imagination. The Northerners make it a common topic of conversation, though they have nothing directly to fear from it. . . . In the Southern states there is silence; one does not speak of the future before strangers; one avoids discussing it with one's friends; each man, so to say, hides it from himself. There is something more frightening about the silence of the South than about the North's noisy fears."[3]

We can translate de Tocqueville's observation into the conception of psychic well-being in the vocabulary of psychoanalysis offered by Hans Loewald: "an optimal, although by no means necessarily conscious, communication between unconscious and preconscious, between the infantile, archaic stages and structures of the psychic apparatus and its later stages and structures of organization."[4] From this perspective, the pervasive and emotionally charged silence that de Tocqueville observed was not simply an unacknowledged disturbance in social relations between masters and slaves but also an individual intrapsychic failure of communication by the masters within themselves. In Loewald's words, the masters were afflicted by "a caricature of ego and id in irreconcilable opposition" rather than a "healthier . . . communication and interplay between the world of fantasy and the world of objectivity, between imagination and rationality."[5]

We might characterize this goal of achieving "communication and interplay . . . between imagination and rationality" as an effort to promote friendship between previously opposed forces in one's mind. This formulation draws on the parallels between social conflict and internal psychological conflict in individuals. It can deepen our understanding of why oppression is harmful to the oppressors. Rigid commitment to projective fantasies based on the establishment of firm boundaries between self and other harms the oppressors because they must engage in "a continuing effort to defend against the intolerable [intrapsychic] experience" that their projective imposition on the subordinated group was unconsciously intended to conceal from themselves.[6] Ending this repressive silence and openly admitting to oneself the fears that lead to the oppression of others is the basic technique of individual psychotherapy in working toward its goal of emancipation from self-oppression.

The oppressors have a powerful psychological stake in denying the fragility of their sense of social order, but that fragility explodes into view in times of undeniable social disruption. This was the impact of the Civil War on a slaveholder like Mary Chesnut. The sense of threat is not only unavoidable but even inclined toward magnification by the very fact that efforts to eliminate the threat cannot succeed. The threat must be tolerated rather than effaced; but toleration is precisely what the oppressor cannot tolerate. Hence the escalating burden of the efforts by the oppressors to maintain their hierarchically superior status.

I do not mean to diminish the depth of oppression experienced by the subjugated groups. But if we attend to the suffering that the oppressors inflict on themselves, we identify a motive that, if somehow brought to conscious awareness among oppressors, might serve as an impetus to replace subjugation with emancipation. How might this goal be approached?

Socrates tried to teach this lesson to his interlocutor Callicles in the *Gorgias*. Socrates insisted that it is better to be the victim than the perpetrator of injustice. Callicles mocked Socrates for his embrace of victimhood, but Socrates vividly portrayed the countervailing cost to the perpetrator of his tyrannical behavior. He analogized the oppressor to a man with a persistent itch who is driven to endless scratching, to a man who persistently tries to fill a sieve with water, and finally to a man without friends who can trust no one and must endlessly fear that others will follow his example by degrading him.

Socrates chose to be a victim rather than a perpetrator because, he insisted, only the victim can attain "the healthiest possible soul." This is a harmonious state of intrapsychic friendship, a state that is unavailable to the perpetrator of injustice, the man like Callicles who oppresses others in the impossible pursuit of controlling the uncontrollable forces in his own mind.[7]

It is sobering that white Southern slaveholders did not relent from unjustly subordinating fellow human beings but fought murderously until they had been subjugated by Northerners. It is sobering that Socrates failed to dissuade Callicles from his oppressive course. (Callicles was an actual person in Plato's time; he became a notorious tyrant.) But even so, Socrates pursued a pedagogic methodology that offered hope of demonstrating to Callicles the intertwined virtues of friendship with his own mind and with others, the possibility of "the healthiest possible soul."

Socrates attempted to engage Callicles with an offer of an empathic relationship, of friendship among equals. He extracted a promise from Callicles that the two of them would persist in conversation until they had found common ground. Callicles ultimately reneged on this promise and mockingly dismissed Socrates's advice. But Socrates never withdrew his offer of empathy, his visible commitment to serve Callicles's interests rather than his own. And he never stopped trying to persuade Callicles rather seeking submission from him. Even after Callicles had definitively withdrawn from engagement, Socrates persisted in seeking an empathic connection. Thus, at the very end of the dialogue, Socrates poignantly pleaded, "Let us follow this, I say, inviting others to join us, not that which you believe in and commend to me, for it is worthless, dear Callicles." Socrates's last words invoked an empathic connection to "dear Callicles."[8]

In American social history, Callicles's voice has been heard more often and more forcefully than the words of Socrates, his unheeded benefactor. But there is a way for us today to follow Socrates's path—a way in particular that might show oppressors what Socrates tried to demonstrate to Callicles, that he was injuring himself by subjugating others. Courts can lead this pedagogic endeavor.

Judges, of course, are not psychotherapists. They do not explicitly interpret unconscious forces underlying social conflicts as psychotherapists regularly do. But judges should be guided by appreciation of the psychological forces at work in social and legal conflicts. This is the spirit in which we seek to identify similarities in psychological and legal practice. The fundamental similarities are not in what judges or psychotherapists say but in what they do, in the processes upon which they rely in pursuing their goals of transforming the relationships between hostile groups of people or in one person's mind hostilely divided against itself. Exploring the processes of psychotherapy will lead us to identify parallel characteristics of litigation that can be used by judges to guide the oppressors to recognize and relent from the psychological erasure they have inflicted on the oppressed—in a word, to promote a re-cognition of the subjugated groups.

First of all, both litigation and psychotherapy involve recollections of past events (sometimes long past and sometimes recent). The goal of this recollection is to bring conflict-ridden outside events into the courtroom or the consulting room in order to make them available for discussion and evaluation as a purposeful alternative to thoughtless repetition in action of those events.

Second, these recollections take place before a person who was not involved in the past events, the judge or the therapist. This person in particular provides a protected, orderly setting for recollection of disorderly and often disturbing conduct and thoughts. In psychotherapy, the therapeutic consulting room is a "holding" site, as the British psychoanalyst D. W. Winnicott has described it—"holding" both as a place of affection and a place of restraint. In this space, the psychotherapist offers an unaccustomed sense of safety to the patient. The peacefully hushed setting of the courtroom, presided over by a black-robed judge elevated on a dais above the warring litigants, provides the same sense of "holding," especially in extending unaccustomed protection to the subjugated group.

Third, on some occasions in therapy the patients do not acknowledge the depth or even existence of inner conflict. The safe space provided by the therapist and adroit, carefully timed interpretations offered by the therapist as she listens to the patient's narrative can promote conscious reflection on conflicted matters that the patient might prefer to keep away from attention. Litigation by oppressed groups presents comparable settings and occasions for acknowledging buried social conflicts. In these circumstances, oppressors may insist that there was no conflict with the oppressed, that the oppressed acquiesced in their subjugation because they always presented "happy faces" and the appearance of conflict only arose because of "agitation by outsiders."

This apparent acquiescence by the subjugated is typically false; its appearance is fundamentally a reflection of oppression rather than a refutation and arises from the powerless vulnerability of the oppressed. Just as the therapist facilitates patients' acknowledgment of their unconscious conflicts by offering a deliberative alliance, so too the judge offers oppressed litigants a protected site for open acknowledgment of past oppression in their relationship. This admission can itself be a liberating enactment by the oppressed litigants; it can also prompt the oppressors to acknowledge their own wrongdoing.

Fourth, both litigative and psychotherapeutic processes focus on the past not for its own sake but for the purpose of charting a course for future conduct. The goal of evaluative discussion of the past is to work toward remedial changes that are needed to convert hostile aggression into respectful friendship within the patient's divided mind. This conversion is the central ambition of psychotherapy: not so much to resolve or dissolve internal conflicts as to talk about them and talk to them, to help the patient to become acquainted with and ultimately comfortable with his internal conflicts. The therapeutic goal is to transform the patient's hostile, divided mind into friendly interaction in which the patient takes personal responsibility for the conflict that he had struggled to ascribe to others.

One way of describing this gradual process is that the patient is helped to develop empathic relations among the conflicting rational and irrational forces in his mind. Similarly, the most effective remedy to address hostile subordinating social relations is by invoking empathic identification between the previously warring litigants. This appeal to empathy in both litigation and psychotherapy involves bringing the unconscious connections of both parties into conscious awareness, effectively diminishing or even dissolving the conscious relationship of hierarchic distance that had existed between them.

In psychoanalytically based therapy, this goal of developing patients' empathy for warring elements in their own mind is approached by the therapist's empathy for those "crazy, fearful" thoughts. The therapist embodies empathy by displaying a fearless attitude, a willingness to hear anything that might emerge from the patient's mind, any association no matter how aversive it may appear to the patient or to the therapist. As the therapist displays friendly acceptance of these aversive ideas, the patient comes gradually to feel this friendship, this direct connection, with previously hostile elements of his own mind.

Here is an apparent difference between the therapeutic and litigative settings. In therapy, the patients are actively encouraged to say anything that occurs to them. In litigation, the parties are restrained by etiquette to avoid epithets that demean one another. Even so, mutual hostilities that were openly expressed outside the courtroom can readily reappear in barely sanitized versions. Moreover, as much as patients are urged to speak freely and spontaneously, this is not easy to accomplish; etiquette often serves as a self-constraint in therapeutic settings.

Fundamentally, however, this difference in rules of etiquette is less important than the structural similarities. In both therapy and litigation, the distanced (and often violent) hostility between oppressed and oppressors becomes a subject for internal discussion as an alternative to unexamined outside actions. In this controlled setting, exploration can become mutual, more than a stereotyped exchange across previously fixed battle lines—whether that battle has been waged between the parties or within the divided mind of a single party. The possibility thus presents itself in both therapy and litigation of replacing hostility with empathic recognition.

Fifth, fearless willingness to listen to and to discuss anything, no matter how aversive, is often described as a nonjudgmental attitude on the part of the therapist toward the patient. By definition, a judge is not supposed to be nonjudgmental; she is a judge. But there is a deeper similarity between the therapist and the judge that this verbal differentiation obscures. The judge is committed to be impartial between the contesting litigants, not choosing sides until the conclusion of an open deliberative process but committed throughout to do justice between the parties.

"Justice" is not the goal that a psychotherapist usually invokes, but her commitment to assisting the patient toward a new attitude to the warring portions of his mind, toward a relationship of mutual acknowledgment and respect, is in fact judgmental. The psychotherapist's judgment favors a just—that is, a mutually respectful—outcome to the war waged by the patient against his own mind. This is what Hans Loewald meant in observing that the goal of psychoanalysis is "to appropriate, to own up to, one's own history . . . to be responsible for our unconscious, [which means] to bring unconscious forms of experiencing into the context and onto the level of the more mature, more lucid life of the adult mind."[9]

In the same way that a psychotherapist assists the patient in coming to recognize without fear or hostility the previously warring portions of his mind, so too a judge can self-consciously attempt to lead the warring litigants to recognize each other without fear or hostility. In both settings, the essential technique toward this end is to keep talking—but in a new format, presided over by an impartial person (the therapist or judge) who "holds" the parties together in Winnicott's sense, who maintains order and guarantees safety as the hostilities repeat themselves (but this time only in evaluative talk rather than unexplained and therefore unjustified action).

The verbal interpretations of law by the judge or of the patient's intrapsychic conflicts by the therapist are significant; these interpretations set the terms of the conversation between the parties and are properly subject to close scrutiny by them. The goal of the psychotherapist's verbal interpretation of the patient's unconscious thought processes is to promote a calm acknowledgment by the patient of undesired elements in his own mind. This goal, one might say, is to supplant conflict and aversion in the patient's divided mind with agreed resolution of those conflicts.

The judge makes verbal interpretations of the law. On its face, this is different from the psychotherapist's appeal to the patient's agreement as the path toward resolution of conflict in the patient's divided mind. It might appear by contrast that the judge simply announces the law and imposes it on the losing parties without regard to their agreement. But this ignores a deeper sense that the judge is also committed to soliciting the agreement of the losing litigant in particular. Judges typically issue opinions justifying rather than simply announcing the winner and loser. This typical judicial conduct reflects the systemic legal norm that judges should attempt to persuade rather than invoke unreasoned authority.

Legal interpretation is aimed at identifying communally shared meaning of the text (or if the judge uses discretion in choosing among many possible meanings, that this exercise itself is based on a communally agreed standard). In effect, the judge instructs the losing litigants that there is an agreed communal meaning to the law and that they have wrongly interpreted that meaning. The litigants may refuse to acquiesce in the judge's reading, just as the patients might refuse to acknowledge the correctness of the therapist's interpretation. But in both cases, judge and therapist embrace the premise that they are employing interpretative standards that are based on agreed communal standards and that the litigants or patients should in principle share this agreement.

The safe space provided by the judge or therapist facilitates respectful conversation, whether between the opposed parties or within the conflicted mind of the individual patient. Whatever is said is important, but it is more important that the conflicts (between the litigants or within the patient's divided mind) are expressed in hostile words rather than angry actions.

Sixth, in this "holding" space, the judge or therapist introduces disruptions in carefully modulated dosages to the established oppressive actions that the litigants or patients had inflicted. Just as the judge disrupts by overturning laws or official practices that underwrite the subjugation imposed by the oppressors, so the therapist does the same by calling into question the patient's conscious justifications for actions that mask his irrational, self-defeating motives. In both cases, this disruption of the control exercised over the socially subjugated group or the irrational forces in the patient's psyche is the necessary path toward the ultimate goal that the conflicting litigants or the conflicted patient should take responsibility for building a new relationship with one another or within one's psyche.

This is the reason to favor judicial remedies that command future interaction between the warring litigants but visibly leave open the possibility that they will accept responsibility for themselves to frame a new mutually respectful relationship on agreed, not externally imposed, terms. This possibility is sidelined if the judge insists on hierarchic command over the litigants' future interaction; the judge should instead press the litigants to directly interact with one another rather than relate primarily to the judge. There is a properly limited role for the hierarchical command mode, but only insofar as it is aimed at compelling future interactions among the hostile parties that might reveal to them their underlying commonalities.

The prospect of future interaction by the oppressor with subjugated groups or by the conflicted patient with the repressed elements in his psyche typically is not welcomed by the oppressor and the patient; their own sense of identity and safety can depend on domination of the oppressed group or the repressed idea. The disruptive interventions required for the judge to unsettle this repressed social relationship or for the therapist to unsettle the patient's repressed ideas therefore carries some likelihood that renewed subjugative efforts will follow.

The forces that press toward this regressive result can be understood through the psychological construct set out in the previous chapter. The oppressor or the conflicted patient conceives himself as the "self" in command of the subjugated "other." The judge or the therapist seeks to dissolve this rigid distinction between "self" and "other." The judge presses the conflicting litigants toward acknowledging a shared rather than hierarchically opposed self-identity; the therapist attempts to move the patient toward recognizing and embracing the conflicting elements in his own mind rather than ascribing undesired elements to others.

Calling into question the customary psychological defenses of the oppressor and the conflicted patient readily inspires in them intensified fear of those impulses and their projective targets. The attempt to emancipate the conflict-ridden litigants or patients from their struggles with one another and within themselves can be understood as impelling them toward confronting the boundless selves that offer no distinction between "self" and "other." Acknowledging the existence of this boundless self loosens the exclusive grip of rationality, of self-control.

Carried to extremes, this grip is symptomatic of a disordered mind—whether the extreme is expressed as exclusive control exercised by the bounded rational or the boundless irrational self. It is easy, however, for litigants or patients to imagine that disorder can be controlled by self-enforcement of rigid separation between the bounded and boundless selves. Relaxing this self-regulation can readily be experienced as a frightening, aversive act. Attempts by judges or by therapists to change the relationship between parties at war with one another or within themselves must accordingly proceed with care and psychological acuity.

The goal in these efforts might be characterized as the action Socrates took, as pursuit of the "healthiest possible soul," or, in psychotherapeutic terms, as pursuit of mental health. But nothing is lost in translating this goal to the pursuit of respectful acknowledgment between the conflicting forces of rationality and irrationality, between the bounded and boundless selves. This translation into the pursuit of mutual respect between conflicting external and internal combatants points to the difficulty of the emancipatory task. The judge or therapist calls the conflicting parties to account when they are not proceeding with mutual respect for one another or for their own divided selves. But the judge or therapist acting alone cannot ensure mutual respect. The individuals in conflict must deliberate between or within themselves to come to this result.

The parties may, of course, fail in this pursuit of mutual respect; one or the other may indeed disdain this goal. The judge or therapist may identify responsibility in one or both parties for this failure. But the direct interaction of the parties in conflict is the key toward a future relationship of mutual respected equality among or within themselves.

There is a seventh parallel between the processes of litigation and psychotherapy, which may at first glance appear to be a fundamental difference between them. It might be said that litigation is a public event while psychotherapy is intensely private. In fact, however, both are public events that have private—that is, internalized—psychological meanings. The very act of entering psychotherapy is to "go public" with inner psychic conflict. Struggles that the entering patient had waged in isolation from others becomes converted to a public event by the fact that they are shared with the psychotherapist.

Freud classically described the psychotherapist's role as holding a mirror before the patient in which he comes to recognize and understand himself. This conception is essentially private in the sense that the therapist disappears so that the patient can see himself alone. Freud's psychoanalytic successors have rejected the idea of a vanishing act, instead understanding the therapeutic process as a collaboration working toward a narrative of the patient's emotional life that ultimately feels "right" to both the patient and the therapist.

Litigation engages a wider cast—not just the judges and litigants but a considerable audience, especially for controversial litigation. Those who constitute this extended audience might appear to be passive spectators, but they become more active as they witness the litigation and identify with one or another of the protagonists. Just as the individual patient can come to recognize himself, to both confirm and reorder his own dramatic narrative in collaboration with the therapist, so too can the litigants and the wider audience interact with the judge.

Here, however, we encounter a fundamental weakness common to psychotherapist and judge. Psychotherapists cannot cure their patients; they can only guide them toward recognizing the source of their psychological difficulties. The psychotherapist has no power to command change; unless the patient takes responsibility for his own psychological well-being, no change will occur. The judiciary has access to many coercive impositions that psychotherapists lack. These coercive tools may be deployed to impose a truce between the warring parties. This respite from open conflict may indeed purchase peace. But these forced interventions are second-best solutions. They are likely to be only temporary. Even if the truce line holds for some considerable time, it nonetheless still falls far short of accomplishing the fundamental goal of transforming hostile social or intrapsychic relationships to mutually respectful interaction.

The centrality of this goal for Footnote Four interventions was revealed by the Supreme Court's identification of the basic wrong inflicted by racially segregated schools. The wrong was not simply state use of racial classifications. The injustice was the use of race segregation to demean blacks, to deny them equal respect. As Chief Justice Warren put it in his opinion for the Court in *Brown I*, "to separate [black schoolchildren] from others of similar age and qualifications solely because of their race generates a feeling of inferiority as to their status in the community that may affect their hearts and minds in a way unlikely ever to be undone." This "feeling of inferiority" would not be undone if black students could only obtain admission to all-white schools when escorted by armed soldiers.

Both the judge and the therapist can approach the transformative goal by eschewing efforts to exercise subjugative force to end the conflicts between the parties or within their divided minds. Put another way, both the judge and the therapist must recognize their ultimate powerlessness to resolve the conflicts that appear before them, their dependence on the conflicted parties to take responsibility to forge relationships of mutual respect that supplant the previous hostilities between and within them.

Freud himself notoriously erred by invoking essentially authoritarian remedies for psychological conflicts. He understood the unconscious psychological roots of his patients' self-injurious conduct but in his early work failed to see the best path by which patients could address these roots. He thought that rationality provided the therapeutic tool for this purpose, that informing patients of the existence of their unconscious conflicts and distortions would be enough to lead them to self-control. That is, they would obey his scientific authority over them by accepting his instruction to exert rational self-control over their irrational impulses. Freud thereby failed to acknowledge the deep stubbornness of unconscious defenses and was misled by his own overvaluation of rational discourse premised on objectivity.[10] The judge makes the same error if she simply proclaims "the law" and expects the parties to accept her superior authority.

This was not Socrates's way. Socrates did claim superior knowledge to his students at the beginning of his pedagogic endeavor, but paradoxically, he explicitly based his superiority on his conviction that he knew nothing while his students were falsely confident that they possessed firm knowledge, at least about everything that mattered to them. His goal was egalitarian in the sense that he endeavored to bring his students to his same state of acknowledged ignorance. Socrates sought to accomplish this through interactive questioning—always respectful, sometimes teasing, always designed to match their different capacities for comprehension, sometimes modeling through his behavior as well as his words.

Callicles's ultimate withdrawal from conversational exchange was the signal of Socrates's pedagogic failure—not only his failure to persuade Callicles but more pervasively the termination of the process by which learning could occur. At the beginning of their encounter, Socrates had specified that he would converse only if Callicles agreed to remain engaged until they had reached mutual agreement. The unilateral (and openly disdainful) withdrawal by Callicles violated his prior commitment. This in itself was wrongful. But there was an even more fundamental injustice inflicted by Callicles's withdrawal. The insistence by Socrates on this one prior promise before beginning his discourse with Callicles arose from his commitment to mutually respectful conversation as the foundation for a moral communal relationship. Callicles's unilateral withdrawal from conversation denied the existence of any communal relationship with Socrates. This is the fundamental reason that his withdrawal was unjust. Callicles thus acted consistently with his general willingness to inflict injustice.

Socrates did not, however, construe Callicles's wrongdoing as a justification for him to inflict a reciprocal injury. Socrates, that is, did not retaliate by withdrawing from a communal relationship; he attempted to remain respectfully engaged with Callicles. Socrates thereby acted consistently with his general willingness to be a victim of injustice rather than imposing injustice. After Callicles unilaterally withdrew from conversation, Socrates proceeded to deliver the longest uninterrupted speech in the entire dialogue, ending with his appeal to "dear Callicles." Though this engagement ended in failure, it demonstrated the core of Socrates's pedagogic methodology: that teaching can only take place in dialogue and only succeeds if it leads to mutual agreement.

Success is, of course, not guaranteed. But continuous interaction among individuals promotes in all of them alternating interior experiences of predominance between objectivity and subjectivity, conscious and unconscious forces, cognition based on conflicting premises of bounded and boundless selves. This is the psychological basis for egalitarian social relationships. Egalitarianism is not a fixed state; it is an experience of interactive alternations of competing forces among and within individuals. Rigid fixity among these forces—with some people always seeing themselves and being seen as subjugators and others as subjugated—is constructed on a psychological falsehood. As Socrates understood, this is an endless, inevitably escalating and unsuccessful pursuit in which enslavement of others is also an enslavement of oneself.

The psychotherapeutic practice of pedagogy—as Socrates put it, the development of the healthiest possible soul—attempts to replace efforts of fixed self-control with egalitarian conversation among the psychic forces within oneself. Unlike psychotherapeutic teachings, Socratic pedagogy does not avowedly attend to the setting in which dialogue takes place; but to the same effect, Socrates eschewed a monologue and placed the dialogue as such at the center of the pedagogic enterprise.

The judicial undertaking toward realizing the protective promise of Footnote Four, of emancipating vulnerable groups from subjugative authority, can find guidance from combining the psychotherapeutic and Socratic principles of pedagogy—by providing a safe space in which litigants are obliged to transform their hostile, disrespectful actions into a conversational interchange in a courtroom where the conflicting parties are required to treat one another with equal mutual respect.

The egalitarian conception of moral discourse appears on its face to be antithetical to the judicial role in the American constitutional scheme. Conventional legal doctrine appears built on a clearly fixed hierarchical ladder—the written Constitution at the top, judicial interpretations of the meaning of that document just a half-step below (and in practical terms, even superior to the written text because the Constitution is virtually impossible to amend and judges' interpretations are effectively final), and the rest of us obliged to obey the Constitution as interpreted by the Supreme Court.

For most of American history, the Supreme Court has insisted on this hierarchy—most emphatically in the long interval between the end of the Civil War and 1938, when the Court routinely overturned federal and state economic regulatory measures. This doctrinal hierarchy appeared to remain intact after 1938, even though the beneficiaries of the Court's protection shifted. But in spite of its intentions, the Court occasionally found itself drawn to a more egalitarian conception of its authority, a more conversational rather than apodictic mode.

The most dramatic and virtually avowed occasion for applying this new conception of judicial authority has been the Court's efforts to eliminate the Jim Crow regime, the legal structure of white supremacy. *Brown v. Board of Education* launched the most ambitious use of judicial authority in the Court's entire history; the vast scope of that undertaking pressed the justices to move outside the conventional depiction of their supreme authority. Even so, the justices did not clearly acknowledge this development; indeed, they may not have understood what they were doing or the implications of this revised conception toward egalitarianism for the rest of their responsibility.

The goal of this chapter is to bring into view the ways in which the Supreme Court's challenge to the Jim Crow regime implicitly reflected a novel, egalitarian conception of its authority, and the superiority (both as a matter of developmental psychology and of democratic principle) of this novel conception, not only as applied in race relations but also as applicable to the entire docket of the Supreme Court.

The Court's first glimpse of a new conception of its authority arose implicitly in the conjunction of the two decisions in *Brown v. Board of Education.* The Court's 1954 opinion in *Brown I* looked almost like the conventional exercise of judicial subjugation of wrongdoers. The Court struck down the entire regime of Southern race segregation, essentially overturning the constitutional approbation of "separate but equal" racial facilities that dated from *Plessy v. Ferguson* fifty-eight years earlier.[1] But even though the Court boldly proclaimed that "separate is inherently unequal," it nonetheless softened the customary timbre of its authoritative pronouncements by mentioning but not explicitly overruling *Plessy.* The Court instead ascribed its abandonment of *Plessy* not to its own authority but to the supposedly scientific findings of "modern [psychological] authority" that segregated black school children did not feel equal to whites in status or self-regard.

The Court's explicit citation of psychologists' work in its opinion has been widely criticized on the ground that the Court should have relied only on legal principles of equality rather than appealing to sources outside its acknowledged expertise and social function. Perhaps the critics are correct, if only on instrumental grounds, that the Court was less persuasive to the general population or legal academics than if it had invoked legal doctrines rather than misty popular psychology. But *Brown* was not an ordinary case.

In its previous assertions of judicial supremacy, the Court had pursued an essentially negative agenda; that is, the justices repeatedly overturned federal or state laws based on alleged constitutional norms. A vision of social relations as essentially based on individual freedom to enter or refrain from any involvement with others lay behind the Court's vetoes. By contrast, Chief Justice Warren's identification of the psychological harm inflicted on black children by public school segregation was more ambitious than simply vetoing racial separation laws. Warren's avowed goal was to transform race relations, to remedy the "feeling of inferiority" imposed on school children by the Jim Crow regime. Black and white people were inescapably entwined in a social relationship; race segregation could not be adequately understood as a choice to refuse any relationship with blacks, as simply an exercise of freedom of association by whites or blacks.[2] Race segregation was a relationship in which whites demeaned blacks. *Brown* properly held that this relationship violated constitutional norms of equality and that the relationship between whites and blacks had to be transformed into mutual respect as equals. The Court's explicit reliance on psychological premises outside its ordinary conceptual framework and conventionally conceived authority signaled the novelty of its affirmative vision of social relations.

The second *Brown* opinion, issued in 1955, differed more openly and fundamentally from a conventionally styled authoritative decision than *Brown I*. When a court defines a constitutional right in a conventional context, it then proceeds to enforce it for the benefit at least of the complainant in the case at hand and often for an entire class of which the complainant is representative. In *Brown II*, however, the Court delayed enforcement of the black schoolchildren's proclaimed constitutional rights for an indeterminate time. *Brown II* did not even attempt to guarantee that the individual students who were parties in *Brown I* (not to mention the other black students currently restricted to segregated schools) would ever benefit from their proclaimed constitutional right.[3]

The vague, seemingly indefinite enforcement delay propounded in *Brown II* has been the subject of considerable controversy, both on principled jurisprudential grounds and on practical grounds as inviting disobedience. Perhaps immediate enforcement would have led to quicker compliance; in any event, the campaign of massive disobedience in the Southern states of the former Confederacy was not forestalled as some justices had clearly hoped in opting for delayed enforcement.

There was, however, a principled basis for adopting the delay that is not typically seen by current commentators. In *Brown I*, the Court declared that the current relationship between Southern blacks and whites, based on race segregation, was constitutionally invalid; in its *per curiam* opinion in *Brown II*, the Court assumed the invalidity of the current regime but left open the range of possible remedial actions. In other words, *Brown II* announced that the future relationship between blacks and whites could not be based on race segregation laws, but the decision ostentatiously left the affirmative future terms of the relationship open to deliberation between the conflicting parties.

Brown II did set out some illustrative subject matter for future deliberation ("problems relating to administration, arising from the physical condition of the school plant, the school transportation system, personnel, revision of school districts and attendance areas ... and revision of local laws and regulations").[4] But the Court said nothing more substantive than these illustrations.

More important, *Brown II* implicitly challenged the local federal district judges to act with visible impartiality in presiding over the parties' conflicts regarding the terms of future black/white relations. The complainants urged that the Court appoint a special master to oversee implementation precisely in order to avoid the likelihood of racist bias by local district judges; the justices were, however, unwilling to assign enforcement oversight to a twentieth-century version of the Northern carpetbaggers who had traveled South immediately after the Civil War to protect freed blacks against retaliatory reprisals by defeated white Confederates. The justices were instead intent on enlisting local federal district judges, as representative Southern white notables, to model law-abiding behavior for the Southern white populace generally.

Some judges accepted this challenge, especially judges on the Fifth Circuit Court of Appeals; most district court judges, however, were hostile to the *Brown* endeavor, some quite openly so. The justices were thus generally disappointed in their hopes. Nonetheless, they had a clear justification in democratic theory for their enforcement delay.

The Court was attempting, on the one hand, to remedy the breach of democratic principle by the pervasive exclusion of blacks from legislative representation and the race-based prejudice against them that would deprive them of effective self-protection in any event, even if the Court could somehow propel them into participation in electoral politics. On the other hand, the Court was attempting to respond to the expressed will of the whites who constituted the majority in most of the Southern states even if blacks had been fully represented in legislative forums. *Brown II*, in effect, tried to work toward these contradictory goals by creating mini-institutions in the federal district courts where blacks and whites could directly and peaceably express their grievances toward one another—a public interaction that could not occur in the established political institutions because of the wrongful race prejudice of the whites.

Though the justices did not think in these terms, these local judicial hearings could work as the equivalent of the psychotherapist's holding space where hostile actions are transformed into reflective deliberation. Moreover, the proceedings were implicitly designed to take place in the way that Socrates envisioned moral deliberation to occur, as conversational engagement rather than socially isolated declamation. This was the Court's ideal. Observance of this ideal might be more likely to obtain compliance from wrongdoers than condemnatory moral pronouncements; but this is uncertain, as we have seen in Socrates's failure to persuade Callicles and in the Supreme Court's failure to persuade the Southern white resisters. Whatever its instrumental consequences, the very idea of moral deliberation requires commitment to persuasion by all participants. Disdain for persuasion and corresponding reliance on forced compliance was at the core of Callicles's wrongdoing and of the injustice inflicted by the Jim Crow regime on Southern blacks. This violation of principle cannot be cured by greater force. Such invocation, regardless of its effectiveness, reiterates the original injustice.

There is a difficult dilemma here. If a relationship based on coercion is inherently immoral, how can the victims of this coercion forcibly turn the table on their oppressors without themselves creating an immoral relationship based on coercion? This is what Socrates implied when he insisted that it was better to be a victim than a perpetrator of injustice.

Some people claim that this dilemma can be avoided by distinguishing between the offensive, unprovoked use of force and its defensive invocation. At first glance, this appears an attractive possibility; but it quickly comes to difficulty not simply in specifying criteria for distinguishing between "just" and "unjust" wars but in identifying the appropriate judge to draw this distinction in specific instances of social conflict. In the American constitutional scheme, the Supreme Court claims this adjudicative function. But unless the judge only attempts to persuade and refrains from invoking coercive force, the dilemma cannot be avoided.

The dilemma can, however, be directly acknowledged. The temptation in the American constitutional scheme is for the Supreme Court to conceal this dilemma with overblown rhetoric about its suitability for identifying the wrongdoer and the consequent propriety of forcing obedient submission. When the Court engages in this common bluster, we might say that it is cutting the Gordian knot engendered by this dilemma rather than patiently and modestly attempting to unravel it.

The enforcement delay in *Brown II* came close to a visible acknowledgment of the dilemma involved in any use of coercive force in a society committed to the democratic principle of mutually respected equality. In 1958, four years after *Brown I*, the Court dramatically enacted this dilemma in *Cooper v. Aaron.*[5] We addressed aspects of the Court's decision in chapter 1; we must now excavate deeper into it.

In its opinion, the Court issued the most extravagant rhetorical demand for unquestioning obedience in its entire history. The very extravagance of its demand, however, revealed more of its practical weakness, its dependence on the voluntary assistance of others, than its unassailable independent power.

The immediate background of the case clearly underscored this weakness for the justices themselves, even if their high-flown rhetoric obscured this reality from popular view. In particular, the justices had limited practical enforcement power because they knew that they could not count on Eisenhower's support. First of all, they lacked legal authority for ordering the president to deploy military force on their behalf; the Constitution identifies him rather than courts as commander in chief of the military. Furthermore, some at least of the justices had personal reasons to doubt Eisenhower's sympathies. In 1954, when Chief Justice Warren had just been appointed to the Court and oral argument in *Brown* was pending, Warren was invited to dinner at the White House and found himself and his wife alone with the Eisenhowers and another couple, Mr. and Mrs. John W. Davis. As Eisenhower clearly knew, Davis was the attorney representing the Southern states in the pending *Brown* argument. This impropriety was amplified when after dinner, as the three men retired to a separate smoking room, the president put his arm around the chief justice and said to him, "These are not bad people. All they are concerned about is to see that their sweet little girls are not required to sit in school alongside some big overgrown bucks."[6]

Perhaps at the time, Warren kept this personal knowledge of the president's views to himself. But the other justices were vividly aware of their limited support in the federal legislature. The most senior members of Congress were virtually all from Southern states and historically had wielded their considerable political power to block any consideration of civil rights legislation, especially relying on the filibuster rules that permitted unlimited debate in the Senate unless sixty-seven votes could be mustered. In 1956, nineteen senators and eighty-two representatives had issued a so-called Southern Manifesto condemning the Court's decision in *Brown* and vowing to use "all lawful means to bring about a reversal . . . and to prevent the use of force in its implementation." Among the signatories were the entire congressional delegations from Alabama, Arkansas, Georgia, Louisiana, Mississippi, South Carolina, and Virginia.

In its 1958 opinion in *Cooper v. Aaron*, the Court ostentatiously ignored this challenge to its authority in Congress and gave no hint of any awareness that the president's support was in any way begrudging. Nonetheless, this background ironically intruded into its opinion. The Court conjoined its most exalted historic claim for its own authority with an almost visible, almost intentional disclosure of its weakness in protecting this authority.

The Court's weakness appeared not in what it said; its opinion was filled with "hoopla" about its own authority—a description that one justice privately invoked in urging even "more hoopla" than he had seen in an early draft of the opinion.[7] The weakness was more apparent (though unintentional) in the format of the Court's opinion at its very outset.

Before John Marshall's reign as the third chief justice, Supreme Court justices had typically written separate opinions without any corporate identification. Marshall introduced a new practice of denominating Court opinions as such, with authorship ascribed to one justice as "delivering the opinion of the Court" (most frequently in Marshall's day, the chief justice alone spoke for the Court). This is still common practice (except that when no author is identified, though a majority supports the ruling, the opinion of the Court is designated "per curiam.")

Cooper v. Aaron dramatically broke from this tradition. At the head of its opinion, all nine justices were listed individually as joint authors. This novel identification has never yet been repeated; at the time, it was undoubtedly intended to underscore the Court's unanimity in response to the gravity of Arkansas governor Orval Faubus's challenge to the Court's ruling in *Brown II* by ordering national guardsmen to bar the entry of nine black students to a previously all-white school in Little Rock. But like the rhetorical force of their explicit command for obedience, this listing of shared authorship carried an implication of protesting "too much"; instead of confidently speaking as a corporate institution as they had always done, in this case the justices presented themselves as nine individuals. This was an unintended but implicit admission that the Court was after all composed merely of nine men—as if, like the Wizard of Oz, the justices were tearing away the curtain from their Leviathan-like appearance to reveal just nine men huffing and puffing in order to inflate themselves with "hoopla."

The second revelatory break with tradition appeared at the very end of the Court's opinion. By 1958, three of the justices who had decided the unanimous ruling in *Brown I* had left the Court. The

Cooper opinion, however, announced that the three new justices were "at one" with their predecessors and that *Brown v. Board of Education* was unanimously reaffirmed. This reaffirmation was not requested by any of the parties. It too appears to be an effort by the justices (suggested by John Marshall Harlan, one of the new members) to bolster the Court's corporate appearance of unquestionable authority.

Nonetheless, the reaffirmation implicitly and unintentionally pointed to a serious limitation in the Court's actual authority. If on this occasion the new justices affiliated themselves with their predecessors, the explicit act of reaffirmation pointed to the fact that the new justices were not obliged to approve of all or any prior rulings. The Court may claim authoritative subjugation over the entire citizenry, but it has no such authority over its own members. Moreover, the Court's ability to rule over the entire citizenry is dependent on the life span of its members and the will of the president and senators who nominate and confirm their successors. The supposedly unquestionable authority of interim sitting justices is thus dependent on their survivors, who are free to question that prior authority as they might choose.

An implication of diminished or doubtful authority thus might arise from the unusual aspects of *Cooper v. Aaron*. Paradoxically, however, the Court's display of weakness can be understood as an indication of great moral strength. The Court's self-portrayal in this case affirmed the justices' respect for the equal authority of one another. It is a striking depiction of the egalitarian rather than the subjugative mode of social authority, a visible enactment of democratic principle.

In psychological terms, the Court's opinion in *Cooper v. Aaron* enacts the conjunction of contradictory forces that we have identified in the alternations between bounded and boundless selves. The Court's traditional claim of hierarchic supremacy on the face of its opinion in *Cooper v. Aaron* is an echo of individuals' bounded assertion of impermeable invincibility, of rational self-control mirrored by claimed control over others. The Court's implicit demonstration of egalitarianism—its admission of weakness unless equally respectful individuals freely come into agreement—acknowledges mutual dependence and a corresponding willingness to refrain from attempting to exercise coercive authority over one another. In *Cooper v. Aaron*, the Court resisted the impulse to remain rigidly in control—or put another way, of trying to arrest the psychological alternation between claims of omnipotence and acceptance of dependence, of power and powerlessness over self and others.

In their behavior, if not in their verbal account of that behavior, the justices modeled the democratic practice of moral deliberation among equals in the sanctified setting of the judicial process. They also dramatically demonstrated the violation of democratic principle committed by Governor Faubus by comparison with their own conduct. Faubus's fundamental violation was not in his refusal to bow to the Court's authority. His violation was in attempting to subjugate his opponents—both the justices and the segregated black schoolchildren—in street combat rather than accepting the Court's invitation in *Brown II* to pursue agreement in court proceedings conducted on the egalitarian premise of shared mutual respect.

If he had obeyed this democratic imperative, Faubus would have been limited in the kind of objections he was entitled to raise. Specifically, he would be required to invoke reasons that could plausibly be persuasive to his opponents. Unexplained assertions of disagreement are not acceptable in any setting as a matter of democratic principle. Elected officials might claim a right to unreasoned opposition because they base their legitimacy simply on popular approval. Whatever the principled strength of this claim (nugatory in my view), it clearly has no applicability in judicial proceedings. Reasons must be given in court, both by the conflicting litigants and by the judges.

To be sure, the explicitly given reasons may be nothing more than masks, but they are required masks in judicial proceedings at the least. This may be a recipe for hypocrisy. But as La Rochefoucauld observed, hypocrisy is the homage that vice pays to virtue. Faubus may be insincere, but the very format of a courtroom confrontation presses him to formulate his objections in a way that invites reasoned rebuttal by his adversaries, followed by a re-rebuttal by him . . . and so on. In other words, whether he prefers it or not, the very setting—

the "safe, holding space" of the courtroom—prompts Faubus to honor at least the appearance of a moral deliberation, a conversational exchange as Socrates practiced it.

Of course, there is no guarantee that agreement between the opposed parties will emerge. But there is no chance that moral deliberation of any sort will emerge from a street confrontation with armed force deployed by one or the other disputants. Faubus's disdain for this endeavor violated a different, and I would say more profound, obligation than his disobedience to a specific court order. He chose to ally himself with the tyrant Callicles, who unilaterally refused to engage in conversation and thereby denied any moral relationship with or obligations toward his opponents.

The practice of moral deliberation—modeled in what the justices did more than in what they said in *Cooper v. Aaron*—is not simply more conducive to peaceful order than street confrontations. This practice is the only path that addresses a central difficulty at the core of our constitutional regime—the tension between the legitimate authority of majority rule and the legitimacy of court-enforced protection of minority rights. Nothing but unanimous agreement among previously opposed parties is adequate to resolve this tension. Typical judicial opinions assert that judges can find the proper balance between these two imperatives of deferring to majority rule and guaranteeing minority rights. In fact, these imperatives almost always overlap in competition with one another rather than coexisting in clearly dichotomized boxes. Judges can't impose the proper balance on contesting parties; there is no externally determinable balance between incommensurate claims. Only the complainants themselves can properly arrive at this balance.

Judges can, however, assist this process—not simply by presiding over deliberative interchanges among the parties themselves but by purposefully and skillfully intervening in discrete aspects of disputes. The goal of these discrete interventions should never be to conclusively resolve the dispute; it should only be to influence the future course of interchange among the parties. In other words, the goal should never be to end conversational interchange among the disputing parties but instead always be to promote further interchange by identifying and clarifying possible paths that might be likely to lead them toward agreement. Unanimous consent is the only outcome that satisfies the democratic premise requiring mutual recognition of equal moral stature.

Some argue that provision of reasons for disagreement is not required in popular voting, that an arithmetic majority is entitled to rule without giving reasons or attempting to persuade rather than electorally overwhelm its opponents. This is a commonplace definition of democratic rule, but it is a profoundly misguided understanding of the egalitarian premise required by democracy. John Hart Ely, most notably among constitutional scholars, maintained that in implementing *Carolene Products* Footnote Four courts should restrict themselves to "representation-reinforcing" measures in order to provide full access of vulnerable groups to legislative deliberations. But ensuring accurate representation in elected institutions is not adequate to solve the underlying problem of democratic principle in addressing the tension between majority will and minority rights.

That problem can be seen in the shortcomings of the majority rule principle itself. Majority rule inflicts legislative losses on the defeated minority, but some theorists maintain that this is consistent with the constitutional guarantee of equality because prior to any election every individual has an equal chance of casting the deciding vote. This is indeed equality among all voting participants; but it is equality only from an *ex ante* perspective. From an *ex post* perspective, after the ballots have been cast and winners and losers are clearly designated, the equal status of the losers becomes problematic. Equality is only attainable for the members of the minority if they have a realistic opportunity to become winners in the next iteration of electoral participation. For such groups, the erstwhile winners have reliable motives to treat the current losers with equal respect. But there are some groups who are permanent losers; either because of their small numbers or their diffusion among electoral districts or majority distaste for them, these groups are disabled from protecting their equal status in a regime where they are always an isolated minority group in legislative institutions.

Footnote Four is responsive to this flaw in democratic theory. Blacks have been the paradigmatic victim of this shortcoming in the American experience. Their complete exclusion from any recognized participation in democratic interaction was vividly portrayed by Chief Justice Taney in the *Dred Scott* case. He observed that all blacks, whether free or slave, were considered "beings of an inferior order . . . altogether unfit to associate with the white race . . . and so far inferior that they had no rights which the white man was bound to respect." This permanently devalued status persisted in the Jim Crow regime for at least a century after emancipation, and we are still struggling to transform the relations between blacks and whites to mutual recognition as equals. Blacks are not the only permanent losers in the American system, but they are the most vivid representatives of the failure of democratic principles in our communal life.

The political scientist Robert Dahl has pointed to a related shortfall in the egalitarian premise of majority rule—that is, the guarantee of "one person, one vote" doesn't adequately account for differences in intensity among various groups vying to become a majority.[8] If members of one group believe that victory regarding one issue is of life-and-death importance and another group is indifferent on this issue, why should each group be awarded equal votes in determining the outcome? This disproportionate commitment can be remedied by legislative logrolling, with the intensely committed group offering support on some different matter of intense concern to the otherwise indifferent group. But this remedy depends on the willingness of each group to make alliances with one another. This problem is not solved by the formalist guarantees of legislative access that Ely envisions, but it is amenable to the judicial scrutiny envisioned by Footnote Four.

It is misleading to describe this special judicial role, as Alexander Bickel classically asserted, as a "counter-majoritarian difficulty"; this role is required by democratic theory to address a shortcoming of majority rule, a "majoritarian difficulty" in democratic theory. However much majority rule may satisfy the equality norm from an *ex ante* perspective, nothing but unanimity will formally vindicate the equal status of each individual from an *ex post* perspective; and there is no basis for preferring one perspective over the other in defining the demands of democratic principle.

Unanimity is of course an impractical if not an impossible rule for political organization. But this reality does not lead to the conclusion that dissent can be reconciled with democratic theory. Rightly understood, dissent—any individual's dissent—is inconsistent with the democratic principle of equality, and everyone who purports to be governed by this principle is obliged assiduously to seek unanimity rather than easily turning away from sustained mutual deliberation in pursuit of this goal.

Even the specially protective judicial role envisioned by Footnote Four encounters practical difficulty in dealing with small numbers of dissenters. The baseline for democratic principle is individualistic; any persistent dissenter is vulnerable to disregard and oppression. But the "discrete and insular minority" identified by Footnote Four is a group phenomenon, if only because of the practical infeasibility of the courts taking on the vast task of protecting every disaffected individual among the American population.[9] The existence of even a single dissenter is a warning signal that can trigger a sustained inquiry about the practical extent of this dissent. The absence of dissent is a social ideal, an expression of respect for freedom of conscience by insisting upon individual consent to any political arrangement— in short, a necessary pursuit even if this goal is rarely achieved in practice.

Explicit endorsement of the legitimizing function of unanimity has been a recurrent factor in American social history. The Founding Fathers in particular regarded unanimity as the guiding norm for all political institutions.[10] The enshrinement of majority rule has, however, displaced the generalized unanimity rule from the Jacksonian era onward. Nonetheless, until very recently, the unanimity principle remained visible in the conduct of the Supreme Court.

Throughout the nineteenth century and the first half of the twentieth, Supreme Court justices customarily achieved unanimity. One measure of this valuation was the common practice among the justices about dissenting votes. Dissents were considered legitimate, if regrettable; but once an individual justice recorded his dissent, he typically acceded to the majority view in future applications, notwithstanding his persisting belief that the original result was incorrect. Proper judicial conduct thus required the initial dissenter to publicly display his acquiescence in the prior majority ruling. Before 1938, the purpose of the justices in suppressing persistent dissent among them was inextricably linked to their embrace of order for its own sake. After 1938, unanimity was sought specifically in race segregation cases; at the same time, however, unanimity was virtually abandoned as a generalized institutional pursuit.

Between 1801 and 1940, the Court ruled unanimously in approximately 90 percent of its decisions; during Harlan Fiske Stone's tenure as chief justice from 1941 to 1946, dissent rates suddenly escalated to 45 percent, and this proportion has remained above 50 percent ever since.[11] Moreover, restricting attention to self-described dissents understates the growth of openly avowed discord on the modern Court. Separate concurring opinions often convey deep disagreements even when all the justices concur in the ultimate result;[12] in 1935, concurring opinions were filed in only 2 percent of decisions, compared to 35 percent in 1994 (dropping to 24 percent in 1995).[13]

In the entire history of the Court before 1938, the Court's predominant presentation of unanimity among the justices conveyed the sense that they were always united in principle and already committed to the unquestionable maintenance of social order before deciding any specific dispute. After 1938, in those declining proportion of cases where it was actually achieved, unanimity conveyed a different message—that the justices may have been divided when they first confronted a given case but that they had subsequently deliberated their way toward consensus.

This was preeminently true of the race segregation cases. Between 1940 and 1973, the Court self-consciously worked hard and actually succeeded in achieving unanimity.[14] In his memoirs, Chief Justice Warren described one deliberative technique that the justices deployed to reach this goal. Three days after conclusion of oral argument regarding *Brown* in 1953, the Court met in conference, but Warren urged that no formal vote be taken on the ground, as he put it, "that when a person announces he has reached a conclusion, it is more difficult for him to change his thinking."[15] For some three months, "Warren pursued a strategy [in which] the cases were considered over lunch and from time to time informally discussed at the Court's regularly scheduled conferences."[16]

Some modern justices occasionally assert the legitimizing implication of unanimity. Most notably, the plurality opinion of Justices O'Connor, Kennedy, and Souter justified their unwillingness in 1992 to overrule *Roe v. Wade* on the ground that, although they might have voted differently when the case first was decided a generation earlier, the very process of constitutional interpretation "calls the contending sides of a national controversy to end their national division by accepting a common mandate rooted in the Constitution."[17] This Burkean paean to the Constitution as a transcendently "common mandate," reflecting a continuing relationship between the past, the present, and "generations yet unborn," ironically attracted the votes of only three justices. Indeed, most contemporary instances of Supreme Court decisions seem inattentive to, and even disdainful of, efforts to find consensus among the justices or to offer this effort by implication as a model to be emulated in society at large.

Supreme Court decisions today typically appear to be radically individualistic enterprises, as if the justices were ready to vote on the cases at hand without first deliberating among themselves or even hearing oral argument. The justices' low evaluation of deliberative efforts to persuade one another is vividly conveyed by the vitriolic charges that are frequently set out in opinions displaying their unresolved disagreements. Thus, for one recent example, the Court's decision in 2014 limiting the presidential appointment authority was resolved by unanimous vote, but this appearance of unanimity was exploded by the five-to-four vote regarding the rationale for these limitations. The minority opinion in that case was written by Justice Antonin Scalia, whose caustic rhetoric is notorious; he referred to the majority justices as engaging in "linguistic incongruity," "absurd results," "fumbling," and "judicial adventurism," and he concluded: "[N]o reasonable reader would have understood [the constitutional provision at issue] in the majority's . . . sense" and "I can conceive of no sane constitutional theory" that might support the majority's position.[18] In another example, decided in 2015, Scalia accused the Court majority of "quite absurd . . . feeble argument" that was "interpretive jiggery-pokery [and] indefensible."[19] Yet another example in 2015 was Scalia's dissent in the same-sex marriage case, characterizing Justice Kennedy's majority opinion as "pretentious . . . egotistic . . . incoherent"; perhaps reaching an apotheosis of insult, Scalia asserted, "I would hide my head in a bag" rather than join Kennedy's opinion.[20]

A generous Court analyst might be inclined to disregard Scalia's barbs on the ground that they were unique to his personal constitution and in any event he was well known as gregarious and likable off the Bench. But this tolerance of his public rudeness must somehow account for the fact that several of his colleagues not simply concurred in his result but explicitly joined in his dissenting opinions.[21] This kind of public exchange does not display deliberation or mutual respect either within the Court or within the increasingly divided American polity.[22] Indeed, the polarization of the justices appears to be mirroring the parlous state of the polity generally. This demonization of political disagreements is at war with the egalitarian ethos of democracy. Rather than reflecting it, the Supreme Court should visibly work against this contemporary distortion of democratic political practice.

Judicial protection of scorned minority groups, the visible pursuit of unanimity in the polity generally, the use of judicial commands only to compel hostile groups to interact with one another rather than ratifying the imposition of repressive order on losers—these are the central characteristics of the judicial role that have the greatest promise to vindicate the democratic ideal of equal respect, of "liberty and justice for all." Achievement of this ideal serves the interests of everyone, most notably including those who by their subjugative efforts to control others are locked in continuous even though masked conflict with themselves.

PART 2

Protecting Vulnerable Groups in Practice

The process for judicial interventions that protect vulnerable groups should promote interactive, mutually respectful deliberations among the conflicting parties. Judicial orders that simply demand obedience and leave no space for further deliberations among the parties and with the judge are antithetical to this goal. No ready-made formula can regulate judicial conduct toward this end; strategic calculations are required that depend on specific contexts of the disputes. The prelude and aftermath of the Supreme Court's judgment in *Brown v. Board of Education* provide one illustration of these strategic judgments. The following chapters provide further illustrations, some honoring this process and others disserving it.

seven **ENSLAVING CRIMINALS**

Slavery is the paradigmatic American example in American history of wrongful subjugation. It inflicts "social death" by radically erasing the independent identity of the slave.[1] State infliction of the death penalty imposes the same subordination. It destroys the possibility of any future relationship with the murderer, any possibility of his rejoining an egalitarian democratic relationship with others. The death penalty thus involves the same violation of democratic principle that Chief Justice Taney committed when he asserted in *Dred Scott* that all blacks were "beings of an inferior order . . . altogether unfit to associate with [others]." State killing in response to a murder does not redress the murderer's injustice, it compounds it. By democratic principle, the death penalty must be abolished.

The question is thus not whether American society should be emancipated from infliction of the death penalty but how—and specifically, the proper judicial role in accomplishing this goal. For fifteen years, between 1968 and 1983, the Supreme Court pursued this goal, though apparently without any clear understanding of the process it had initiated. After 1983, a Court majority abandoned this enterprise. This emancipatory interval was ended.

During more than a half century before 1968, the Court had dealt with details in the operation of the institution such as approving electrocution as a means of killing,[2] establishing a right to appointed counsel in capital cases,[3] and forbidding racial discrimination in capital jury selection.[4] In 1968, however, the Court accepted a case challenging exclusion of death penalty opponents from capital juries and thereby implicitly raising concerns about the legitimacy of the death penalty itself.

The prevailing state rule was to exclude not only committed abolitionists but also doubters. In *Witherspoon v. Illinois*,[5] the Court overturned this blanket disqualification. In a majority opinion by Justice

105

Potter Stewart, the Court noted the growing public debate about the death penalty—its supporters, the Court suggested, were a "small and dwindling minority"—and it ruled that potential jurors who had "conscientious or religious scruples against its infliction" could not be excluded "simply because they voiced general objections to the death penalty." The only exclusionary ground approved by the Court was for those "who stated . . . that they would not even consider returning a verdict of death." The three dissenting justices (Hugo Black, John Marshall Harlan, and Byron White) complained that a jury thus constituted would almost never impose the death penalty and that the Court in effect had endorsed the abolitionist movement. Indeed, Justice Stewart's opinion favorably cited the statement by a prominent abolitionist commending opposition to the death penalty because of empathic fellow feeling with the convicted criminal—"there but for the grace of God go I."

Witherspoon was, however, indirect in its opposition to the death penalty. The ruling was not intentionally designed to initiate public debate about the merits of the death penalty but designed to promote this conversation in the anonymous privacy of the jury deliberations. Just as the Court's early race segregation decisions in the late 1930s and 1940s implicitly conveyed the justices' discomfort but refrained from a frontal attack on the Jim Crow regime, so too *Witherspoon* did not directly assault the institution of the death penalty but suggested the justices' disapproval and narrowed its application.

In 1970, just two years later, the Court accepted review of a second death penalty case, which raised more direct and extensive objections to the death penalty as such. The petitioners in *Maxwell v. Bishop*[6] argued that all existing death penalty statutes were constitutionally invalid because they failed to specify substantive standards to guide jury sentencing discretion and because they did not procedurally separate guilt determinations from sentencing, thereby deterring defendants from testifying before the jury. If the Court had agreed with these objections, state legislatures would not have been prohibited from enacting new statutes with explicit sentencing standards and bifurcated procedures; such a ruling would, however, have disrupted the existing system and given visibility to the claims of unfair treatment by death-sentenced felons—a popularly disfavored group by any measure.

In 1970, moreover, there was an additional similarity between the litigative challenges to the death penalty and Jim Crow laws. The NAACP Legal Defense Fund had been the principal architect of the litigation that had pressed the Court to move incrementally from invalidating specific implementation of race segregation laws to its global assault in *Brown*. Beginning in 1963, Legal Defense Fund attorneys turned their attention to the death penalty, especially on the ground of racial discrimination in its application. By 1970, the LDF had come to a position "of unquestioned prominence" in general litigative challenges to capital punishment.[7] It was committed to the same strategy that it had pursued in attacking Jim Crow—to support a sustained, skeptical judicial scrutiny of the detailed operation of the death penalty, which over time promised to lead the Court to abolish the entire institution. In its scrutiny of the death penalty as in race relations, the Court thus had repeated access to a junior partner who could help it coherently organize critical review of the death penalty.

After oral argument in *Maxwell v. Bishop*, a majority of the justices appeared ready to require these changes.[8] This tentative Court majority did not, however, hold firm. While the decision remained pending, Justice Abe Fortas was forced to resign from the Court and was replaced by Harry Blackmun, who had written the Court of Appeals judgment in *Maxwell*. The Court accordingly decided that *Maxwell* was not suitable for considering large systemic issues and effectively dismissed the case by remanding it for consideration of jury exclusions in apparent violation of *Witherspoon*.

The Court, however, immediately accepted another case raising the same systemic issues, and in 1971 it decided *McGautha v. California*,[9] holding that specific statutory standards were not required, because death sentencing was an inherently and properly discretionary exercise that could not be constrained by "boilerplate" abstractions and that while bifurcated procedures might be a good idea, they were not constitutionally required. Rather than launching an evaluative, interactive conversation with state legislatures, the *McGautha* majority conclusively resolved the procedural issues on the basis of their independent, socially isolated, supreme authority.

Justice Brennan dissented passionately from this ruling, observing that no legislature had even tried to draft rational standards that might guide jury deliberation. It was not clear, Brennan claimed, that a rationalizing effort would inevitably fail; but if it did fail, Brennan stated that he would be forced to conclude that the death penalty was inherently inconsistent with the rule of law and had to be constitutionally invalidated. The intensity of his dissent (joined by Justices Marshall and Douglas) revealed an underlying pathos. By 1971, when *McGautha* was decided, the Warren Court had almost disappeared as a result of the 1968 election of Richard Nixon on a platform opposing "judicial activism." The imminent reversal of its legacy was ironically signaled by Nixon's replacement of Earl Warren by Warren Earl Burger as chief justice.

This immediate prospect of a transformed court had a clear impact on Justice Brennan's jurisprudence. His 1971 dissent in *McGautha* was vintage Warren Court—a bold proclamation of high principle joined seamlessly to an incremental remedial process that held open the possibility of elaboration and revision. The unspoken backdrop of this vision was patience and a long perspective on judicial success in protecting minority rights. By 1972, this backdrop had been shredded; four Nixon appointees had joined the Court and the card-carrying survivors from the Warren Court—Justices Brennan, Douglas, and Marshall—seemed beleaguered. For Justice Brennan in particular, his customary instincts to join bold principle with cautious implementation seemed out of place.

In the opinion Brennan prepared for the Court's next encounter with the death penalty, he was all passion and no caution. The case was *Furman v. Georgia*,[10] and the Court granted certiorari limited to one issue: whether the death penalty was substantively "cruel and unusual punishment" proscribed by the Eighth Amendment. A direct Court decision on this issue—whether for or against—would not have signified the beginning of an exploratory interaction between the judiciary, state legislatures, and the general public. Instead, this issue would be conclusively resolved.

According to his later testimony in a *Harvard Law Review* article, Brennan grimly anticipated that a Court majority would decide that the death penalty did not violate the Eighth Amendment and that that would be the end of any judicial contribution to the ultimate invalidation of capital punishment.[11] The apparent premise of Brennan's dissent in *McGautha* was that the death penalty could be incrementally improved; but the fact that the *McGautha* majority had turned away from this pursuit led Brennan—or perhaps more accurately, liberated Brennan—to reveal his deep conviction that capital punishment must be entirely abolished and that judicial interpretation of the Constitution should accomplish this result.

Brennan worked with his clerks during the summer of 1971, even before oral argument in *Furman*, to prepare what he expected to be a lone dissent. The most difficult interpretive problem that Brennan faced in writing his opinion was the explicit acknowledgment in the Fifth Amendment that the death penalty could be imposed so long as "due process" was observed. The *McGautha* majority had rejected systemic challenges to the processes by which the penalty was imposed, and Brennan was not content in *Furman* with simply repeating his "due process" dissent. How, then, could he justify substantive use of the Eighth Amendment to condemn capital punishment when the Fifth Amendment explicitly approved the death penalty as such? Brennan tried to surmount this problem by writing an extensive opinion elaborating a complicated analytic structure built upon the few even arguably relevant cases that previous Courts had decided. It was a thoughtful and original analysis.

Originality is not ordinarily a prize-winning category for judicial opinions, but Brennan was not writing an ordinary opinion or even an ordinary dissent. He appeared to have abandoned any effort to persuade his immediate colleagues. Even his closest colleague, Thurgood Marshall, had stated in the conference deliberations on *McGautha* that he could not vote for the constitutional abolition of the death penalty. Brennan spoke to a distant future like the lone dissent of the first Justice Harlan in *Plessy v. Ferguson* lamenting that "the thin disguise of 'equal' accommodations [in the administration of the death penalty] will not mislead anyone, nor atone for the wrong this day done."

After circulating his dissent within the Court, however, Brennan learned that he was not alone. The first indication was no real surprise. Justice Marshall had secretly worked on his own dissent during the summer, and at the beginning of the fall he presented it first to Brennan (as a gift for his best friend, he said)[12] and then circulated it to the other justices. But soon thereafter, three other Justices (Stewart, White, and Douglas) circulated opinions that in effect constitutionally invalidated all extant death penalty statutes, apparently because of their random application. The opinions of these three confusingly left open whether this flaw was an inherent or a remediable feature of capital punishment.

A five-person majority thus amazingly coalesced in overturning all of the extant death penalty laws. Stewart and White had concurred in the *McGautha* majority, and it was difficult to reconcile their votes in *Furman* with their prior views. Stewart, however, had written the Court's opinion in *Witherspoon*, suggesting sympathy for the abolitionist perspective while including fence-sitters in capital juries; perhaps his apparent contradiction between *McGautha* and *Furman* reflected his own ambivalence. White, on the other hand, had dissented in *Witherspoon*, arguing that states that endorsed the death penalty were entitled to choose single-minded supporters to implement the state policies. White's position was thus difficult to understand; in any event, there was a Court majority, and Brennan was not a lone dissenter but a member of that majority.

If the Court had then followed its long-established procedures, the senior justice voting with the majority would assign the task of writing a majority opinion. (The chief justice has this responsibility, but only when voting with the majority; in this case, Burger dissented, along with the three other Nixon appointees.) Douglas was the senior justice in the *Furman* majority; in his separate opinion, he suggested that the cumulative votes of the majority amounted to a repudiation of *McGautha*; and it is conceivable that a majority opinion could have been written that simply reversed that ruling even though it had been decided only a year earlier.

There was no opinion for the Court, however, when the result in *Furman* was announced. Even more unusually, none of the majority justices concurred with one another. All instead spoke alone. State legislators reading the aggregation of opinions in *Furman* were left on their own to decide whether their death penalty statutes were conclusively forbidden or potentially salvageable and if so, then by correcting exactly what errors. The death penalty jurisprudence in *Furman* could not have been further from the self-consciously shared effort in *Cooper v. Aaron* fourteen years earlier to construct a unanimous judgment uniting past and current justices. (It was, moreover, revealing that in 1971, the year before *Furman* was decided, the Court's commitment to unanimity during the preceding thirty-one years in school segregation cases was ended by dissents from two of the new Nixon appointees, Justices Powell and Rehnquist.)

The cacophony of the Court in *Furman* thus gave a considerable opening for state legislatures to respond. But *Furman* was not conceived by the justices as an initial gambit in an ongoing conversation, as a respectful solicitation of opposing views. *Furman* arose unintelligibly from the rubbled tower of Babel.

This was a jurisprudential error. The *Furman* majority should have reversed *McGautha* and thereby launched an extended conversation with state legislatures identifying particular shortcomings in the administration of the death penalty and considering whether these flaws, individually or taken together, ultimately led to the conclusion that capital punishment inherently could not be made fair and had to be entirely abolished. In particular, Justices Brennan and Marshall should have withdrawn their opinions, originally drafted as dissents, and recast their views in this interactive, evolutionary format. This is not because the Constitution could not plausibly be construed to abolish capital punishment but because this constitutional interpretation in 1972 was too sudden, too novel, injudicious.

In chapter 6, I set out reasons why democratic principle requires this extended mode of decision making, this extensive passage of time, in preference to abrupt pronouncement from hierarchic superiors. Visible solicitation of and respect for others' views are necessary elements in all democratic decision making. This is especially important in judicial practice because of a difficulty that lies beneath judicial decision making. In interpreting the commands of the Constitution, judges are obliged to set aside their "merely personal" views and rely on fundamental communal values. Elected officials are also prohibited from using public office to pursue personal gain. But in theory at least elected officials are constrained by the wishes of their constituents to set aside personal bias in favor of public values. Moreover, the immediate connection between elected officials and their constituents at least presumptively suggests that their actions are based on communal values.

This does not mean that judges are required to construe majority enactments as invariably reflecting fundamental communal values. But a judge can too easily imagine that he is hearing the voice of the constitutional authors in construing fundamental values when in fact he is hearing nothing more than echoes of his own voice. The social isolation of life-tenured judges heightens this risk, and the risk is multiplied by the universal psychological difficulties that I described in chapter 4 of distinguishing between self and other.

Justice Harry Blackmun, dissenting in *Furman*, cited the difficulty of distinguishing between his personal revulsion toward the death penalty and his judicial obligation to enforce impersonal values. He misconstrued the consequences, however, that follow from this difficulty. It is a warning sign against rather than a settled reason for always concluding that personal and communal values cannot be differentiated—any more than the psychological difficulty of distinguishing self from other means that the distinction can never be drawn. The distinctions between personal and communal morality as well as between self and other cannot be derived from isolated ruminations. The distinctions can be drawn only through intense social engagement with others.

Blackmun himself ultimately concluded that he could sufficiently distinguish between personal and official morality to justify determining that the Constitution required abolition of the death penalty. He came to this conclusion, however, only after an extended—and I would say, excessive—lapse of time. For ten years after he dissented in *Furman*, Blackmun regularly voted to affirm death sentences, though he almost invariably failed to give any reasons for these votes. In 1983, he suddenly dissented in a series of cases, with almost explosive rhetorical force: "[T]his is too much for me";[13] the Court's affirmation is "too much for me to condone";[14] the Court's ruling "does the rule of law disservice."[15] Blackmun subsequently moved to regularly opposing aspects of death penalty administration, most frequently in dissent. Finally, in 1994 Blackmun declared his commitment to constitutional abolition of the death penalty.[16] Yet this declaration came just a month before he retired from the Court, as if to acknowledge his continuing difficulty in distinguishing personal from official morality by speaking in his official capacity virtually at the same moment he relinquished this status.

Judicial observance of the distinction between personal and public values is not an easy task. There are, however, better alternatives than those that Blackmun or Brennan and Marshall chose. Blackmun acknowledged the difficulty in his *Furman* dissent but then was almost entirely silent and consistently voted in support of the death penalty for the next decade; another decade passed before he finally seemed satisfied that his opposition to the death penalty had become more than a personal preference. Virtually at the moment that he announced this judgment, however, he retired into private life.

If Blackmun was too slow ("too much deliberation, too little speed," as the Court observed regarding race segregation), Brennan and Marshall were too speedy. Their abolitionist opinions in *Furman* recited reasons that looked suitably impersonal; but they were too much alone. They underscored their isolation in subsequent capital cases by issuing opinions in some nineteen hundred cases, including every denial of certiorari, with the identical language.[17] Their opinions seemed formulaic, as if they were entering keystrokes for macros in their word processing programs rather than engaging in a reasoned dialogue with legislative proponents of the death penalty.

Immediately after *Furman*, thirty-five legislatures enacted new versions of the death penalty. Some specified substantive standards for jury sentencing, some of which were more stringent and others less stringent. Some new statutes separated guilt and sentencing proceedings. Some purported to eliminate jury discretion altogether by mandating death sentences for specified crimes. These cases came to Supreme Court review in 1976. Brennan and Marshall refused to accept any of these statutory revisions on the ground that the death penalty was constitutionally invalid on its face. Three other justices— Stewart, Powell, and Stevens (who had replaced Justice Douglas)— formed an alliance voting to uphold some, but invalidating aspects of most, of the new enactments.

This triumvirate held together for the next seven years. During this time, no Court majority emerged in these cases; instead, all of them were decided by patchwork pluralities—Brennan and Marshall voting to overturn all death penalty statutes, White and three of the Nixon appointees voting to approve all, and the three allied justices approving some and disapproving others. It was as if the three allies had resuscitated *McGautha* by giving particularized scrutiny to the detailed operation of death penalty statutes rather than considering their constitutional validity wholesale.

In this scrutiny, the aggregation of justices' votes led to several results: barring the death penalty for any offense except murder,[18] and then only in cases of those who actively intended to kill;[19] providing unlimited opportunities to present mitigating evidence to the sentencing jury;[20] and assuring access for the defendant to all information before the sentencer.[21] Of the fifteen capital cases fully argued and decided on the merits by the Court between 1976 and 1982, all but one resulted in a reversal or vacating of the death penalty.[22] In effect, the plurality results could be viewed as exposing one flaw after another, progressively leading the Court toward assessing the constitutional validity of the entire capital sentencing enterprise in the light of these multiple flaws. There was no Court as such at work in these decisions; but even so, this progressive review process suggested that the plurality justices were educating themselves—and educating the public by example—regarding the possibility that the death penalty was systemically unsupportable, for reasons that reflected more than the justices' personal distaste.

During all of this time, several federal district courts had imposed a nationwide moratorium on executions, on the ground that the Supreme Court had undertaken a detailed scrutiny that might possibly lead to invalidation of the entire enterprise. This moratorium had several consequences. First, it guaranteed that no one would be executed while the systemic validity of the death penalty remained unresolved. A context was thus established that permitted calm case-by-case deliberation rather than frenzied, unrelated review of individual sentences that, if imposed, might have inflicted irreparable individual injustice. Second, the moratorium was first established in 1967, just before the Court decided *Witherspoon*, the jury exclusion case. By the time *Furman* was decided in 1972, executions had been suspended for almost six hundred death-sentenced convicts. The Court's unexpected, erratic invalidation of all pending death sentences in *Furman* might have reflected some justices' distaste at the prospect of mass killings that would otherwise have occurred. Justice Marshall specifically acknowledged ("[C]andor compels me to confess," he wrote)[23] that he was influenced by revulsion at the prospect of mass executions. Did this confession reveal a "public judicial" reason for averting these executions or was it "merely personal"?

In the ordinary application of the death penalty for almost a century before 1972, executions had taken place out of public sight— behind prison walls and in very early morning hours.[24] The cumulation of executions after five years' suspension gave more public visibility to the enterprise, and itself served as a confrontational test not only for the justices but also for members of the general public regarding their knowing support for capital punishment as opposed to their unacknowledged acquiescence. By 1982, the incremental case-by-case judicial scrutiny initiated by the three-justice plurality had led deeper and deeper yet into publicly revealing fundamental difficulties in the death penalty statutes enacted in the wake of *Furman*.

At this juncture, however, a new Court majority came together and abandoned this pursuit. In 1983, the newly constituted majority began its retreat by restricting availability of federal habeas review of state death penalties.[25] This new majority emerged because Sandra Day O'Connor had replaced Potter Stewart, and she virtually always voted to uphold state death penalty statutes, and because Justice Powell changed his vote recurrently to favor suppressing rather than visibly promoting misgivings about capital punishment.

The Court's retreat was underscored by its 1985 decision in *Wainright v. Witt*.[26] In that case, the Court revisited its initial foray into the death penalty issue when in 1968 it had mandated inclusion of jurors notwithstanding their reservations about the death penalty so long as they would "make unmistakably clear" that they would not "automatically" vote against it. In *Witt*, the 1985 Court "modified" this substantive standard to permit more rigorous exclusion of reluctant jurors. Even more important, the Court altered the procedure for review of juror selection; in direct appeals from federal court sentences, appellate judges were instructed to pay "deference . . . to the trial judge who sees and hears the juror," and in federal habeas reviews of state sentences the trial court's juror exclusion was given a "presumption of correctness."

The procedural aspect of *Witt* dramatically testifies to the new attitude on the Court. During the previous decade, the willingness of a Court majority to narrow the applications of capital punishment had been mirrored in an extraordinary number of invalidations by federal appeals court judges. Judicial findings of wrongful juror exclusion had been a fecund source of reversals; but this was only one example of a proliferation of reversals by federal judges. Thus Justice Marshall observed in a 1983 opinion that "of the 34 capital cases decided on the merits by Courts of Appeals since 1976 . . . the prisoner has prevailed in no fewer than 23 cases, or approximately 70% of the time."[27] State appellate court reversals were similarly high. For example, the Florida Supreme Court reviewed 247 death sentence cases from 1972, after *Furman*, until March 1984; of these, 116 (or 47 percent) were set aside. Overall, according to a 1982 study, from 60 to 75 percent of defendants sentenced to death obtained reversals at some point in their appeals. By comparison, this is roughly ten times the reversal rate obtained in noncapital federal criminal appeals and almost one hundred times the reversal rate for general felony convictions in California.[28]

One way to interpret these data was offered by Justice Rehnquist in a 1981 dissent: The Supreme Court's "constant . . . tinkering with the principles [governing death sentencing] since 1976, together with the natural reluctance of state and federal habeas judges to rule against an inmate on death row, has made it virtually impossible for States to enforce . . . their constitutionally valid capital punishment statutes. . . . Given so many bites at the apple, the odds favor petitioner finding some court willing to vacate his death sentence."[29] There is, however, another interpretation—that the Supreme Court's "tinkering" had created new occasions for state and federal appellate judges to review the operations of the capital punishment enterprise and thereby see themselves as direct participants rather than passive bystanders in the operations of that system. The fact that considerable numbers of these judges found themselves reluctant "to rule against an inmate on death row" testifies to the existence of an attitude that had been submerged in abstract deliberations about the death penalty—an unaccustomed attitude of empathic fellow feeling. As Justice Stewart had observed, there was "a shuddering recognition of a kinship" even with criminals sentenced to death.

Between 1968 and 1983, the Supreme Court was thus engaged in the social process I have described generally by which vulnerable groups have been emancipated from subjugation. *Witherspoon* in 1968 was a barely visible disturbance, while *Furman* in 1972 was a seismic disruption of the existing subordinative relationship. These rulings were the prelude to reiterative interactions in various public deliberative forums. In these deliberations, the customary definitive boundaries between the dominant and subordinated groups were blurred, enhancing the possibility that empathic fellow feeling would arise.

The interventions by lower-court judges were one instance of that process—but only because the Supreme Court left considerable discretion to these judges, rather than imposing strictly subordinating commands. Their remarkably high reversal rates in capital cases thus provided testimony about their acceptability that was more direct and more revelatory of contemporary attitudes toward the death penalty than abstract public opinion polls. The judges' attitudes were not the final word, but they were relevant to the Supreme Court's own deliberations about the "cruel and unusual" character of capital punishment.

Rather than cultivating interactive conversation with state and federal lower-court judges, however, the new Supreme Court majority devised new procedural means to close down appellate courts' involvement in the administration of the death penalty. Just as they had limited appellate court scrutiny of jury exclusions by proclaiming the trial judges' determinations as presumptively correct, so the justices narrowly confined the availability of habeas corpus review of state actions. In 1984, the Court made clear that it would not promote effective assistance of trial counsel.[30] Heightened standards of effectiveness would increase the likelihood that a multitude of ameliorative possibilities would be raised in litigation. But the Court closed off future deliberations by virtually explicit approval of shoddy lawyering (and by corresponding unwillingness to insist that states increase the funding and administrative structure for legal representation at trial, on appeal, and in federal habeas proceedings).

The shift from exploring to concealing inequities in capital punishment intensified in two decisions rendered immediately after *Witt*. In 1986, a Court majority dismissed extensive evidence that death-qualified juries, culled of jurors doubtful about their support of capital punishment, were more inclined to convict criminal defendants than juries selected in noncapital cases. If the jury selection process systematically favored guilty verdicts, this would violate the constitutionally guaranteed presumption of innocence.[31] In *Lockhart v. McCree*, the Court dealt with this possibility by exaggerating shortcomings in the evidence presented at trial; but even more egregiously, the Court proceeded to assume the correctness of the evidence but concluded that the state was not required to empanel juries that equally represented all social viewpoints of "Democrats and Republicans, young persons and old persons . . . and so on."[32]

This argument is patently fallacious. The question at stake is not whether a jury must be representative of the general population, it is whether the state would be constitutionally permitted to purposely exclude from the jury Democrats or young people or people inclined toward sympathy for criminal defendants. If the federal district court's empirical finding of guilt bias in capital juries were flawed, this should have led the Court to remand the case for further evidentiary exploration, not to a conclusive dismissal no matter what evidence might exist.

If, on the other hand, the guilt bias finding were accepted, this would once again (as in *Furman*) invalidate all existing death penalty statutes; but (unlike the immediate sequel to *Furman*) this inequity could be readily remedied by providing separate juries to determine guilt and sentencing. This two-jury scheme would be cumbersome, since the prosecution would need to repeat the substantive evidence to the separate sentencing jury (the only death-qualified jury); indeed, it would seem that an entire retrial would be necessary, since the sentencing jury's decision for or against death could properly be influenced by the strength or weakness of the proof of guilt. By demanding this remedy to protect the constitutionally based presumption of innocence, the Supreme Court would have intensified its searching conversation with state legislatures. Once again, the Court would require a substantial reorganization of the capital punishment scheme; and once again, the Court would be forcing states to decide whether the added cost and effort was worth the benefits of retaining the death penalty. The Court would not, however, have answered this question. It would have required state legislatures to answer this question for themselves.

A year after deciding *Lockhart v. McCree*, the Court was presented with extensive evidence about another aspect of the administration of the death penalty—whether racial bias was influencing sentencing decisions. When the Legal Defense Fund first became involved in death penalty litigation, the LDF attorneys suspected racial bias but could not conclusively prove its existence. None of the majority justices in

Furman asserted the existence of racial bias (though Justice Marshall alone mentioned its likelihood); and prosecutors responded to *Furman* by increasing the proportion of whites subjected to capital trials or convicted of death. On the face of the system, it was difficult to document race discrimination; but a costly and intensive empirical investigation was launched by opponents of capital punishments, and its findings were presented to the Supreme Court in *McCleskey v. Kemp*.[33]

The new evidence forcefully demonstrated bias hidden in the interstices of the system, notably in the fact that death sentences were disproportionally imposed when whites rather than blacks were victims, when blacks killed whites as opposed to when whites killed blacks, or when killers and victims were of the same race. The investigators used a complex regression analysis to show that 6 percent of all death sentences could be explained only by the racial characteristics of the murderers and victims; and if the most heinous murders were excluded, involving torture, rape, or multiple victims, the proportion of death sentences attributable to race alone rose to 20 percent.

In 1987, a five-person Supreme Court majority dismissed this evidence, while "assum[ing] the study [was] valid statistically." The Court concluded that the study inherently "[could] only demonstrate a *risk* that the factor of race entered into some capital sentencing decisions." In other words, the Court would accept only evidence of actual bias in specific cases, not simply a statistically demonstrated probability of bias. Though the Court did not admit this, it was demanding proof that was virtually impossible to achieve; and even if racial bias were shown in the motives of some prosecutors or some sentencing jurors, this would have no systemic impact, even though the evidence presented in *McCleskey* showed systems-wide probability of bias that could be corrected only by systemic reforms rather than individualized inquiry on a case-by-case basis. The *McCleskey* Court thus relied on the same strategy that it had followed two years earlier in *Witt* and the previous year in *Lockhart:* that is, to close off judicial inquiry into the fairness of the capital punishment system by imposing an insurmountable burden of proof on any complaints.

If the Court had accepted the evidence of racial bias presented in *McCleskey*, it is more difficult to see remedies than in *Witt* or *Lockhart*. Appellate court scrutiny of individual juror exclusions would likely be effective for enforcing *Witt;* and, as noted, separate juries for guilt and sentencing determinations would solve the problem in *Lockhart*. But if case-by-case inquiry into the racial biases of individual jurors is an inadequate systemic remedy, what reformation could exclude racial bias except the wholesale abandonment of juries in making sentencing decisions? The statistical evidence implies, moreover, that racial bias is also present in jury decisions about guilt. This was not the focus of these evidentiary studies, but it would be surprising if investigators found pervasive racial bias in capital sentencing and yet discovered no evidence of such bias in guilt determinations (whether in capital or noncapital cases).

Justice Powell, the author of the Court's opinion in *McCleskey*, clearly saw this implication if the Court gave any credence to the evidence of racial bias in capital sentencing. He wrote for the Court, "McCleskey's claim, taken to its logical conclusion, throws into serious question the principles that underlie our entire criminal justice system. . . . [I]f we accepted [McCleskey's] claim that racial bias has impermissibly tainted the capital sentencing decision, we could soon be faced with similar claims as to other types of penalty." If the "principles that underlie our entire criminal justice system" can only be sustained by refusing to engage in rigorous statistically based inquiry regarding possible inequities in that system, then what are those principles?

The quick succession of *Witt*, *Lockhart*, and *McCleskey* marked the end of the Supreme Court's commitment to sustained critical inquiry into the death penalty. Since then, a Court majority has ruled that the death penalty could not be imposed on people with mental retardation or juveniles; but these special categorical exemptions don't force state legislatures to reexamine fundamental systemic aspects in the administration of capital punishment. The Court has also recently endorsed a narrowly framed exemption from time limits on federal habeas corpus review for death-sentenced prisoners who claim that they are "actually innocent."[34] Public discomfort about the death penalty has recently increased because of exonerations of convicts on death row (some 151 people since 1973)[35] and the increasing frequency of these claims based on new scientific capacity to analyze genetic materials at crime scenes. The Court's constrained invitation for pursuing such claims in federal habeas proceedings offers a limited forum for amplifying these flaws. The Court's conduct for the past thirty years, however, provides little hope that "searching judicial inquiries" will occur.

Of the many obstacles that blocked serious attention to flaws in the capital punishment regime, one in particular seems to me substantial and offered in good faith. That is the concern that judges hostile to, or even simply uncomfortable with, the death penalty were motivated more by personal revulsion than by adherence to constitutional principle. This speculation is based on two bits of evidence. The first is the especially intense emotional reaction to death that is common to the human condition. Judges inevitably share some measure of this aversion. This can be a basis for a judicial conclusion that purposeful infliction of death is so disturbing that communal principles forbid it. But this heightened discomfort about death as such also affects the judges personally in a way that is not provoked by other issues that regularly come to their official attention.

There is a paradox here, of course: the belief that "death is different" can readily support a judgment that communal standards demand more stringent treatment at the same time that this belief provokes judges to conclude that their misgivings arise more from personal aversion than from communal principles. This paradox can cripple the capacity for judgment.

Justice Blackmun in particular never relented from but never resolved his attempt to distinguish his "merely personal" revulsion and his official disapproval of capital punishment. Moreover, he set an implicit example for his colleagues Justices Stevens and Powell. Stevens had persistently supported critical inquiry into the workings of the death penalty throughout his judicial tenure, but he publicly announced his conviction that the death penalty should be abolished only immediately after he retired from the Court. Powell had been ambivalent throughout his tenure—first dissenting in *Furman*, then joining the three-person plurality in critically scrutinizing the death penalty for some eight years, and then withdrawing from this position and refusing to sustain further inquiry until he retired from the Court. In a *New York Times* op-ed, Powell specifically repudiated his vote in *McCleskey*, dismissing evidence of racial bias; but this editorial opinion was issued only after he was no longer eligible to write Supreme Court opinions.

If Justices Blackmun, Stevens, and Powell gave too much attention to the difficulty of distinguishing personal from official morality, Justices Brennan and Marshall gave too little. These two were not disabled by the difficulty they perceived in separating personal and judicial values. It is not clear, however, that they saw any difficulty. They were willing to invoke entirely novel constitutional interpretations to overturn long-established institutional practice—and to do so abruptly, even in the face of recent Court decisions such as *McGautha* that apparently accepted the constitutional validity of the death penalty. Their opinions appeared, at least, to confuse personal values and communal morality and thereby undermined the public legitimacy of their efforts.

How, then, can judges successfully navigate this narrow track dividing private and communal morality? Some guidance can be found from extending an analogy I invoked in chapter 5—another parallel between litigation and psychotherapy. In my previous discussion, I stressed process similarities between the two endeavors. In attempting to separate personal from public values, we can find a substantive parallel.

Psychotherapists use a different vocabulary to characterize this effort—not separating personal and public values, but therapists distinguishing between their personal struggles and their patients'. The professional depiction of this difficulty is "countertransference." This designation is the counterpoint to the patient's inclination to the same confusion (professionally described as "transference"). By the psychotherapeutic understanding, this confusion—this projective identification of therapist and patient—cannot be wholly eliminated.

This confusion is built into every individual's cognitive structure; it is reflected in the difficulty I have discussed of distinguishing between "self" and "other." The answer, from a psychotherapeutic perspective, is not to draw rigid distinctions but instead to acknowledge the difficulty and open oneself to alternating experiencing of bounded and boundless selves.

There are many ways that psychotherapists approach this goal. The most illuminating technique for identifying parallels with judging is the psychotherapist's practice of interpreting the patient's unconscious motivations. Freud's initial practice was apodictic; Freud proclaimed the "correct interpretation" and explained the rejection of that explanation by his patients as psychological resistance on their part, as a pathological expression. This interpretative practice reflected his view that he had successfully distinguished between his personal attributes and his patients'. Indeed, Freud conceptualized psychoanalysts as entirely setting aside their own personality and serving as a passive mirror from which their patients could see themselves and their unconscious mind.

Freud's authoritarian attitude toward psychotherapeutic interpretation was an egregious mistake. He retreated from this attitude in his later publications, and among the most prominent of his current successors his authoritarianism has been thoroughly discredited in practice. Instead of announcing socially isolated, hierarchically superior pronouncements, modern psychotherapists offer interpretations in an admittedly tentative manner—as a subject for further exploratory conversation between the therapist and the patient, not as the "last word" uttered by a delphic oracle. Through the extended exploration that follows every interpretation, both the therapist and the patient induce each other to search for possible distortions that may have arisen between them—possible confusions of self and other, of "transference" and "countertransference."

Psychotherapists do not share all of their thoughts, all of their "personal" confusions, with their patients, because this could significantly interfere with the capacity of the patients to explore their own projective identifications, their own confusions about the therapist's identity. But the process itself, the preference for tentative interpretations that must be confirmed or discarded in further reiterative conversation, provides a framework for therapists to reflect on their confusions even without directly discussing them with their patients.

In the Supreme Court's tangled death penalty jurisprudence since 1968, the self-awareness of the justices about the sources and significance of their attitudes toward death as such was only rarely evident. Their commitment was either wavering or nonexistent for clarifying the possible confusion between private and public values through dialogic interaction with legislators and, through them, with the general public. Yet in 2015, an open critique of the death penalty suddenly and surprisingly emerged in the United States Reports.

In *Glossip v. Gross*, a five-person majority turned away a challenge to the methods of execution by administration of drugs.[36] Four justices dissented, but Justice Breyer, joined by Justice Ginsburg, wrote an extensive opinion calling for reexamination of the constitutional legitimacy of capital punishment. "Rather than try to patch up the death penalty's legal wounds one at a time," Breyer opined, "I would ask for full briefing on a more basic question: whether the death penalty violates the Constitution."

Breyer cited numerous uncorrected and apparently uncorrectable flaws in the administration of the death penalty: "lack of reliability, the arbitrary application of a serious and irreversible punishment, individual suffering caused by long delays, and lack of any penological purpose" as well as evidence that innocent people had been executed or threatened with imminent execution, and that the entire system was warped by racial discrimination. Breyer concluded, "I recognize that in 1972 this Court, in a sense, turned to Congress and the state legislatures in its search for standards that would increase the fairness and reliability of imposing a death penalty. The legislatures responded. But, in the last four decades, considerable evidence has accumulated that those responses have not worked. Thus we are left with a judicial responsibility. . . . I believe it is highly likely that the death penalty violates the Eighth Amendment. At the very least, the Court should call for a full briefing on th[is] basic question."

During Senate hearings on his confirmation in 1993, Breyer had observed that the constitutionality of the death penalty was a settled issue in the Court's jurisprudence. Twenty-three years later, he (along with Justice Ginsburg) has come to a different conclusion.

With the execution in Florida of John Spenkelink in 1979, the twelve-year judicially imposed national moratorium was ended. This event was the first clear indication that a Court majority was abandoning the interactive process to which Breyer alluded of judicial challenges and legislative responses. Between 1979 and June 19, 2015—a week before Breyer issued his separate opinion—1,411 people convicted of felonies were executed. Virtually all of these executions occurred after some review, if only summary, by the justices of the Supreme Court. It may be that their own participation in this process finally pressed two of the sitting justices in 2015 to their reexamination—thus joining the three retired justices in their retrospective repudiation and their two predecessors, Justices Brennan and Marshall, in their persistent protesting vigil.

It is not enough to say, as Justice Scalia asserted in his response to Justice Breyer's opinion, that the Founding Fathers assigned conclusive responsibility for evaluating capital punishment to popularly elected legislatures. These institutions are bound by the Constitution to observe the basic principle of democracy—to treat everyone with equal respect. The text of the Fifth Amendment does indicate that its authors did not consider the death penalty to be intrinsically impermissible. But the Fourteenth Amendment's guarantee of equal protection introduced a possible contradiction with the Fifth Amendment's apparent acceptance of capital punishment. The later amendment in effect pulls to the surface a self-contradiction within the text of the Fifth itself. The Fifth Amendment holds that "no person . . . shall be deprived of life . . . without due process of law." This text does not consider the possibility that experience might demonstrate that "due process of law" cannot effectively be provided in the actual administration of capital punishment. Thus understood, the Fifth Amendment does not provide a clear answer but instead presents a choice between continuance of the death penalty and observance of due process of law. The authors of the Fifth

Amendment did not understand that they had enacted an oxymoron; but if subsequent experience demonstrates this proposition, if subsequent generations are forced to choose between the death penalty and guaranteeing due process, then the relevant amendments—specifically the Fourteenth Amendment—give priority to due process.

I suggested at the beginning of this chapter that the humanity of those subjected to slavery and the death penalty is equally erased. The Thirteenth Amendment makes a tight connection between these two inflictions; it banned slavery "except as a punishment for crime whereof the party shall have been duly convicted." That is, the Thirteenth Amendment directly acknowledges that the state may enslave a person "as a punishment for crime." This authorization is a more direct endorsement of the death penalty as a permissible punishment than the Fifth Amendment, which insists on "due process of law" that has proven to be unattainable.

Only three years elapsed between the ratification of the Thirteenth Amendment (in 1865) and the Fourteenth (in 1868). But the latter amendment is a more generalized and deliberate embrace of equality for all people than the former. The Thirteenth Amendment dealt only with slavery and involuntary citizenship; the Fourteenth assured citizenship for everyone born or naturalized in the United States, and guaranteed to every citizen the same "privileges and immunities" and to "any person . . . the equal protection of the laws."

The Fourteenth Amendment also repeats the oxymoron in the Fifth, that the state may "deprive any person of life" so long as this deprivation is consistent with "due process of law." As a matter of textual interpretation, imposing slavery as a criminal punishment is approved by the Thirteenth Amendment but forbidden by the Fourteenth; and the death penalty is permitted by the Fifth and Fourteenth Amendments only on conditions that are now proven to be unattainable. Two currently sitting Supreme Court justices have resuscitated the dialogic process that leads ineluctably to this result: a clear understanding that the death penalty violates the guarantees of the Eighth Amendment against cruel and unusual punishment and the Fourteenth Amendment for equal protection of the laws.

There is another way, moreover, by which a convicted felon is made nonexistent in contemporary America—not only by killing him but by inflicting a kind of "civil death" (which is the term the sociologist Orlando Patterson used to describe slavery). Many specific inflictions of permanent invisibility of convicted criminals can be identified. These inflictions take place, moreover, in a general social context in contemporary America. That context is the abandonment since the mid-1970s of the so-called rehabilitative ideal.

In itself, imprisonment of convicted felons removes them from any mutually respectful, equal interchange with others. But this removal was not avowedly permanent so long as the professed goal of imprisonment was more than punishment, more than physical confinement for the sake of deterrence—so long, that is, that imprisonment was linked to state efforts at rehabilitation. In actual practice, the promise of rehabilitation was hypocritical. Inadequate financial resources were dedicated toward vindicating this promise; the promise itself, though frequently reiterated after the turn of the twentieth century, was patently hypocritical. But even so, the promise was "politically correct," and this social etiquette constrained the social impulse to permanently extrude convicted criminals. In the 1970s, the rehabilitative ideal was widely criticized not only as hypocritical but also as a cosmetic disguise for the imposition of worse punishments than would otherwise be inflicted. Thus "soft-on-crime" liberals joined with hard-nosed, if not hard-hearted, conservatives to disavow rehabilitation.

This disavowal may not have caused the escalating practices of banishment that has occurred in America since the mid-1970s; but it is indisputable that such escalation has occurred since that time. Opportunities for education and job training along with the presence of mental health professionals on prison staffs have dramatically declined, even disappeared, while the draconian quality of imprisonment and its aftermath have increased.

It is notable that this increasingly harsh subjugation falls with special weight on black prisoners. Blacks are disproportionately represented in the prison population generally. (In 2000, black men were incarcerated at 7.7 times the rate of white men; by 2009 this racial disparity had narrowed to 6.4 times that of white men—a significant decline, but still a considerable disparity.)[37] But although this disparity suggests the lingering impact of the old racially based subordination, it is clear that all blacks as such are no longer predominantly viewed as socially scorned outcasts; the presidency of Barack Obama is proof enough of this proposition.

Convicted criminals have, however, always been targets for special social scorn. Since the mid-1970s, convicted criminals have been treated as "civilly dead" and excluded from fully human status in a multitude of ways, with very real practical impact. Thus a sharply increased rate of imprisonment occurred between 1971 (when a total of four hundred and fifty thousand were incarcerated, a figure of 143 per hundred thousand of the population) and 2005 (when 2.19 million were incarcerated, a figure of 742 per hundred thousand of the population). Since just 1990, the average length of prison sentences has increased by 36 percent; and in 2015 forty-one thousand people in the United States were serving life sentences without the possibility of parole. Even for prisoners with fixed terms, their permanently subordinated status persists. Thus, notwithstanding the expiration of their prison term, no one convicted of a felony is entitled to vote in any U.S. state.[38]

The exclusion of prisoners from human eligibility for interaction is especially pronounced in the extensive use of solitary confinement. The typical mode of this confinement is to lock the prisoner alone in a small, bare cell for twenty-three hours each day (with one hour respite for solitary exercise in an outdoors cage). Both inside the cell and in the outdoor cage, the prisoner is essentially denied any eye contact with other human beings, including guards. The typical justification for this extreme isolation is to protect others—guards or other prisoners who were attacked or threatened—or, less frequently, to protect the prisoner himself from others. This can be a justifiable reason for separating the prisoner from others. But the extreme conditions of the isolation are not necessary for these purposes and cannot be justified.

Prolonged and often even relatively short-term solitary confinement typically induces psychoses—involving infliction of self-injury, smearing of feces, destruction of the minimal cell furnishing. In chapter 4, we explored the reasons that interaction with others is a necessary element for producing and sustaining a sense of personal identity, of a distinct self, in every human being. The extreme isolation involved in solitary confinement assaults and ultimately disintegrates the prisoner's identity as a human being. This impact is virtually identical to the psychological impact of waterboarding suspected terrorists, a tactic that has been widely condemned as torture because it induces a sensation of imminent death by drowning. The extreme isolation involved in current practices of solitary confinement produces the subjective experience of personal disintegration, which is another way of dying. Prisoners may be separately confined from others—but not under conditions that assault their existence as recognized human beings.

Those who are convicted of sexual offenses are also treated as degraded species of humanity. They are subjected to lifelong public registration and banned from living in most residential neighborhoods, especially where any contact with children is even a remote possibility (even if the convicted offense did not involve children). Moreover, in new statutes enacted in twenty states since 1990, sexual offenders at the expiration of their prison terms are vulnerable to subsequent lifetime confinement. These commitment statutes provide a dramatic illustration of the cycle I have identified generally of oppression of vulnerable groups based on fear of disorder, emancipation following some social crisis, and then new or renewed oppression.

Between 1935 and the mid-1950s, twenty-six states and the District of Columbia enacted statutes aimed at so-called criminal sexual psychopaths.[39] These statutes generally required a finding of mental illness and provided indefinite civil commitment "until cured." In practice very few of those committed were ever released; in 1969, Chief Judge David L. Bazelon of the District of Columbia observed that the statutes promised rehabilitative treatment but added, "Notoriously, this promise of treatment has served only to bring an illusion of benevolence to what is essentially a warehousing operation for social misfits."[40] Two years earlier, in 1967, the U.S. Supreme Court had overturned one such state statute on narrow due process grounds.[41]

In the succeeding twenty years—during the most recent dominance of the emancipatory impulse on behalf of vulnerable groups—most state criminal sexual psychopath laws were invalidated by courts or repealed by legislatures. Though statutes remained on the books in thirteen states, they were no longer used in practice.

But in 1990, the emancipatory moment as applied to sexual offenders had conclusively ended, and a new wave erupted of sexual offender civil commitment statutes; by 2013, such statutes had been enacted in twenty states.[42] Under these statutes, commitment follows if an individual is judicially found to have "serious difficulty in refraining from sexually violent conduct or child molestation if released."[43] No finding of mental illness as such is required. Commitment is indefinite, and no treatment or any promise of treatment is provided in the confinement institutions.

By 2007, some forty-five hundred sex offenders had been civilly committed nationwide, and only some 10 percent of those had been released. In some states, confinement is virtually endless; for example, after Minnesota enacted its commitment statute in 1995, by 2013 670 people had been confined and only one had been released.[44] In 1997, in a case from Kansas, the U.S. Supreme Court upheld the constitutionality of these new, avowedly and exclusively custodial statutes.[45] Thus criminals generally, and sexual offenders in particular, currently have inherited the status that homosexuals occupied until very recently—the status, that is, of being a different, diseased, and dangerous breed deserving exclusion from the human community.

Though criminals have always been scorned and quarantined, the contemporary status of criminals in the United States has thus taken a new turn. In the old modality, criminals were not permanently banned but were assumed to be redeemable and potentially eligible to rejoin the human community. This was the promised implication of rehabilitative treatment programs. The promise itself, though often ignored, was a marker that criminals were not an indelibly different species of humanity. The commitment to rehabilitation was hypocritical; but this hypocrisy was, as La Rochefoucauld put it, "the homage that vice pays to virtue."

Today in the United States, however, the promise of rehabilitative treatment is no longer extended to prisoners; they are indelibly a different breed, and this status degradation is no longer seen as a vice that should be disguised.[46] We have finally come to rigorously embrace the proviso in the Thirteenth Amendment that slavery is abolished except for prisoners who have been duly convicted of crimes.

There is special contemporary danger from this derogatory status imposed on prisoners. We have recently developed the capacity to observe the functioning of living brains, and in the next twenty years our capacity to change brain structure in order to control social conduct will most likely increase dramatically. The enlistment of science in the quest to control ourselves and others has a long and destructive history—from the lobotomies inflicted on disturbed and disturbing people during the first half of the twentieth century and eugenically motivated sterilizations to ensure "racial purity" to less grotesque but empirically unsupportable proposals to control violent conduct by destruction of small portions of the convicted criminal's brain.[47]

In future years, as our knowledge of brain function deepens, the temptation will increase to use various forms of psychosurgery and related interventions to control antisocial conduct. Coercive use of these interventions might seem justified because candidates have an "abnormal brain" that distorts their decision-making processes. Or these interventions might be restricted to "voluntary" deployment, disregarding the devaluation that these "abnormal people" impose on themselves in response to the fear and revulsion they inspire in others.[48]

These possibilities are worrisome, especially in light of the abuses that have historically been inflicted by medical scientists in the service of social control. Our past history of false promises—of self-deception and deception of others—is a basis for great caution in advancing yet new promises. But we must also take care that, in the name of skeptical caution, we do not turn away from violent criminals by withholding treatment from them that would welcome their return to full membership in the human community.

As with other oppressed groups, the goal for social response to convicted criminals should be to cultivate opportunities for mutually respectful relationships. There is better reason to fear and confine convicted criminals than the oppressive inflictions on other scorned groups that are motivated by nothing more than projection of the fears oppressors have about themselves. Even so, this psychological impulse is at work in some aspects, at least, of social regulatory attitudes toward criminals. To guard them and us against yielding to this impulse, we must apply some reliable marker in order to differentiate deserved from undeserved subordinations of criminals.

The key differentiation is the permanence of the subordination imposed. An avowedly temporary subordination does not definitively rule out the possibility that the criminal can be restored to a mutually respectful relationship with others. This restoration need not be automatic; because of their past behavior, criminals can justifiably be required to show some clear evidence that they deserve reinclusion in ordinary social relations. Demanding such assurance is not inconsistent with social acknowledgment that the confinement and subordination are temporary. Courts should oversee the actual processes available for parole to ensure that the promise of possible release is not chimerical. To this end, courts should mandate appointed attorneys for effective representation of prisoners in release proceedings.

Infliction of the death penalty is not the only indicator of a permanent, irremediable, and irreconcilable exclusion of the criminal from even the possibility of a restored relationship with others; so too is the imposition of life imprisonment without possibility of parole, the permanent disqualification of convicted felons from voting, and indefinite solitary confinement. Courts should hold all of these practices unconstitutional because they permanently extrude convicted felons from even the possibility of recognized, mutually respectful interaction with other people. Such definitive constitutional ruling is the necessary precondition for judicial promotion of future interactions. To this end, assurance of effective appointed counsel is necessary to represent convicted felons in all aspects of their subordinating confinement—not simply regarding the initial conviction[49] and parole hearings but also conditions of confinement, alleged probation or parole violations, restoration of voting rights, and the multiple barriers to reentry into civic life, such as housing restrictions and job discrimination. Unlike the global permanent extrusions that should be held unconstitutional, specific deprivations imposed on convicted felons during or after their prison term can be justified in various ways. The goal of courts in these contexts is to provide forums in which convicted felons are able to contest the reasonableness of the deprivations imposed on them—or, in other words, to engage in a recognized, extended, mutually respectful exploration of their grievances.

eight **RESPECTING SAME-SEX RELATIONS**

Blacks were the initial group, and are still the paradigmatic group, that attracted judicial protection following the promise of *Carolene Products* Footnote Four. Gays and lesbians moved into the forefront of judicial attention only during the first decade of this century. Both groups have historically been subject to powerful degradations. There is a close kinship between Chief Justice Roger Taney's characterization of all blacks, whether slave or free, as "beings of an inferior order" and Chief Justice Warren Burger's observation, in upholding its criminal status, that same-sex sexuality was "a disgrace to human nature [and] a crime not fit to be named." For both groups, the Supreme Court has invoked norms of equality and dignity in order to overturn such devaluation.

The most intriguing similarities are, however, in the process by which the judiciary has worked its way toward this remedial attempt. For most of American history, the Supreme Court purposely contributed to the degradation of both groups, of blacks until the 1940s and of gays and lesbians until the beginning of this century. When the Court resolved to change the status of both groups, a similar path was taken.

For blacks, the first interventions did not frontally assault the deep insult inflicted by "separate but equal" racial facilities but instead gradually mounted an attack over a decade and a half. Thus, in 1938 the Court did not question the validity of segregation but only required states to provide racially separate graduate education within their own borders, rather than paying tuition for blacks to enroll in other states. Step by step the Court subsequently overturned racial exclusion practices in interstate bus travel, in electoral primaries, in housing—and only then took direct aim at the principle underlying racial exclusion in 1954.

The Court delayed for a considerable time, however, before applying the antiracist premise of *Brown* to invalidate miscegenation laws enacted by Southern legislatures as part of the Jim Crow impositions on black people. In 1956, the Supreme Court refused to overturn a Virginia law forbidding marriage by a man and woman of different races. Eleven years later, in a case aptly named *Loving v. Virginia*, a unanimous Supreme Court invalidated this law on two grounds: denial of equal protection (an unsurprising application of *Brown v. Board of Education)* and violation of a "fundamental right to marriage" (a newly announced constitutional right).

The Court's delay in this ruling was widely understood to be strategic. In 1956, its ruling in *Brown* was under attack in Southern states as part of an alleged rapacious plot (as President Eisenhower had privately observed to Chief Justice Warren) to force "sweet little [white] girls . . . to sit in school alongside some big overgrown [black] bucks." By 1967, when the Court finally spoke in *Loving*, the Congress by an overwhelming vote had endorsed the antiracist premise of *Brown* in the Civil Rights Act of 1964 and the Voting Rights Act of 1965. (Indeed, just two months after the *Loving* decision, Thurgood Marshall was confirmed as a justice, the first black to have joined the Court.)

The Court's delay between *Brown I* and *Loving* was part of its strategic effort to enlist federal and state institutions in acknowledging the injustice inflicted on blacks and reshaping future race relations. The Court pursued this effort by retreating into silence; it spoke only twice about racial desegregation during some ten years after *Brown II:* in 1958 when Governor Faubus sent troops to bar the entry of any black schoolchildren to an all-white high school and in 1963 when a Virginia school board closed all public schools rather than accept even token desegregation. The actions of both Faubus and the Virginia school board did more than obstruct implementation of *Brown I;* they were blanket refusals to engage in any interchange in a courtroom rather than unreasoned conflict in the streets.

In these two cases, the Court acted to sustain a conversation about the morality of race segregation, not to impose its own resolution of moral conflict. This judicial restraint was at the heart of the indefinite compliance schedule accepted in *Brown II.* The Court did not rescind this schedule until 1968, after Congress had responded to its appeal by enacting the Civil Rights Act of 1964, the Voting Rights Act of 1965, and the Civil Rights Act of 1968.

In the 1960s, the proposition seemed unthinkable, even preposterous, that the Supreme Court might one day apply the fundamental marriage right to command state marital status for same-sex couples. At that time, same-sex sexual relations were not a basis for community licensure or celebration; they were a criminal offense in almost every state. In 2015, however, the Supreme Court proclaimed a constitutional marriage right for two men or two women on the identical terms traditionally available to mixed gender couples. The title of this ruling was *Obergefell v. Hodges*—not as obviously evocative as *Loving* but, even so, conveying a hint of the name of our forty-fourth president, born in 1961 to an interracial married couple in Hawaii at a time when their union was illegal in every Southern state that had been a member of the Confederacy.

The Court acted similarly only during the past decade or so in addressing the status of gays and lesbians. Before this time, a Court majority had in effect ratified existing subjugative relations between straights and gays. In 1986, by a five-to-four vote in *Bowers v. Hardwick*,[1] the Court refused to overturn state laws criminalizing sexual relations in a private home between two consenting, adult men. This refusal, moreover, was conveyed in overheated rhetoric that seemed to convey substantive approval of the criminal statutes. The majority opinion, written by Justice Byron White, revealed its underlying animus at its outset by characterizing the petitioner's claim as a "fundamental right upon homosexuals to engage in sodomy."

White's tendentious characterization was consistent with a broader purpose—that is, to ratify the state's treatment of homosexuals as unfit for relations with anyone, barring them not only from sexual congress with one another but also more fundamentally from any human intercourse. White betrayed this demeaning view of homosexuals with his observation that there is "no connection between family, marriage, or procreation on the one hand and homosexual activity on the other." He observed that "24 States and the District of Columbia continue to provide criminal penalties for sodomy performed in private and between consenting adults," and that, presumably by virtue of this simple head count of the states, any claim to associational rights for sodomists "is, at best facetious."

It is hard to imagine a more thoroughgoing dehumanization of gays and lesbians, but Chief Justice Warren Burger accomplished this in his concurring opinion. Burger justified his vote to uphold the criminal statutes on the ground that William Blackstone, the eighteenth-century English jurist, viewed homosexuality as an " 'infamous crime against nature [which was] an offense of deeper malignity' than rape, an heinous act 'the very mention of which is a disgrace to human nature, and 'a crime not fit to be named.' "[2]

In 2003, the Court overruled *Bowers* by a six-to-three vote in *Lawrence v. Texas*,[3] and it thereby initiated a new enterprise of promoting moral conversation between straights and gays by amplifying the voices of LGBTQ advocates—voices that had been suppressed by hostility from electoral majorities and the Court itself in *Bowers*. The new Court majority signaled this purpose in several ways.

First of all, the Court's action in overruling *Bowers* was presented with unusual emotional force. The Court proclaimed, "*Bowers* was not correct when it was decided, and it is not correct today. It ought not to remain binding precedent. *Bowers v. Hardwick* should be and now is overruled." It is rare that the Supreme Court ever directly overrules its past decisions; but it is virtually unprecedented that the Court reverses itself by essentially vilifying the prior ruling (especially when three justices who had decided the original case remained on the Court—Rehnquist and O'Connor, who had concurred in White's majority opinion, and Stevens, who had dissented).

Another aspect of *Lawrence* more visibly conveyed its emancipatory intention. This was revealed paradoxically in the apparent analytic disorder of the Court's opinion. In his dissent, Justice Antonin Scalia complained that the majority opinion revealed that "principle and logic have nothing to do with the decisions of this Court."[4] Scalia leveled this charge specifically at the Court's dictum that *Lawrence* "does not involve" the issue of same-sex marriage.[5] Beyond his complaint that the Court's ruling was an unacknowledged stalking horse for same-sex marriage, Scalia criticized the Court generally for lack of clarity and a clearly argued connection with past precedent, which, in his view, overwhelmingly supported state criminalization of same-sex sexual relations.

It is indeed difficult to identify from the Court's opinion the specific justification for overturning the Texas statute. Was the Texas statute invalid because it invaded the same-sex lovers' privacy rights as consenting adults acting in their home? Kennedy in his opinion invoked the privacy ideal, but he didn't clearly rely on it alone. He also characterized same-sex couples as seeking autonomy regarding "matters involving the most intimate and personal choices a person may make in a lifetime . . . just as heterosexual persons do"[6] (thus an equality principle) and asserted that criminalizing persons for engaging in same-sex sexual relations "demean[s] their existence [and] control[s] their destiny"[7] (thus a dignity principle). Do these expressions mean that "invasion of privacy" and "denial of equality" and "derogation of dignity" were independent, alternative grounds for invalidating the Texas law? Or are these criteria cumulative, requiring all of the grounds together in some combination to explain the Court's ruling?

Regarding the issue of same-sex marriage, privacy does not readily fit the claim for a publicly proclaimed marital status. Equality is a better fit, and dignity the best of all.[8] Are two out of the three possible rationales in *Lawrence* enough to invalidate state bans on same-sex marriage? If dignity was the central rationale for *Lawrence*, does this mean that states are barred from regulating all sexual encounters or barred only regarding those encounters in the context of a long-term, emotionally committed relationship? Is this why state prohibition of commercial sex, whether heterosexual or homosexual, is constitutionally permissible? Kennedy noted that the case did not involve commercial prostitution or claims for same-sex marriage. But what if the next case to come to court did involve one or the other? Kennedy's opinion leaves us adrift, with few hints at most for charting a future course. Oliver Wendell Holmes observed that all that was meant by "law" is a prediction of what judges will do. By this criterion, *Lawrence* is not law.

This is the basis for Justice Scalia's criticism of *Lawrence* as devoid of "principle and logic." A hierarchical conception of the Court's authority lies behind this criticism in this sense: that the Court is obliged to articulate principles that would guide future decision makers and preferably would provide explicit commands, specific "marching orders," for future, hierarchically subordinate actors, whether lower-court judges or elected officials.

Viewed, however, from a different perspective on judicial authority, from the egalitarian conception, *Lawrence* is a quintessential expression of law. From this perspective, the opacity of the Court's opinion is appropriate and even instrumentally essential. This is because the Court's proper role viewed through the lens of the egalitarian mode is to invite others to develop the full implication of its ruling. To pursue this end, the court must unsettle the past oppressive relationship and provide a public forum for waging the now openly disputed relationship between homosexuals and the state. But on its own, the court must withhold conclusive resolution of the dispute.

The *Lawrence* Court could have narrowed the scope of, or even closed off, future debate about the status of gays and lesbians by accepting Justice Scalia's critique to provide a comprehensive principle clearly sufficient for deciding *Lawrence* and any imaginable ancillary issues. Thus the Court might have rested solely on a privacy principle to overturn the statute while specifically holding that this principle had no application to claims for marriage, commercial sex, or even short-term sexual engagement in settings where they might be publicly observed. The Court did briefly refer to these issues, only to specify that they were not being decided but left open—implicitly, for future deliberation in some official forum. The Court was, however, virtually explicit in observing that those deliberations must lead to respect for the privacy, equality, and dignity of gays and lesbians—respect that they had not previously received.

Whatever the Court's intention, *Lawrence* set the stage for a transformation of social attitudes without assigning the principal dramatic role to itself. This apparently implicit invitation was accepted just five months later in a November 2003 ruling by the Massachusetts

Supreme Judicial Court. In *Goodridge v. Department of Public Health*, the court ruled that the state constitution required official recognition of marriage by same-sex couples. The court gestured toward *Lawrence* in this ruling; it observed that in *Lawrence*, the possibility of a constitutional right to same-sex marriage was "left open as a matter of federal law [and] the Massachusetts Constitution is, if anything, more protective of individual liberty and equality than the Federal Constitution."[9] *Lawrence* was thus not dispositive for the Massachusetts court, but it was not irrelevant. It was as if *Lawrence* had put the issue of same-sex marriage on the state judiciary's agenda, as if it had precipitated but not ended a new conversation.

Goodridge was the first state supreme court decision mandating same-sex marriage in the nation. Prior to the *Lawrence* decision, various state courts had addressed the issue and had come to more limited or even outright negative conclusions. Thus, in 1999 the Vermont Supreme Court had ruled that the state was constitutionally obliged to provide the same practical benefits to same-sex couples as it offered to mixed-sex married couples.[10] But the court explicitly endorsed a new status of "civil union" for same-sex couples that withheld the honorific title of "married" from them. A 1993 ruling by the Hawaiian Supreme Court had seemed to go further, holding that denial of marriage to same-sex couples presumptively violated the state constitution and remanding the issue to the trial court to give the state an opportunity to demonstrate an adequate basis for this denial (in the catchphrase of constitutional adjudication, to show a "compelling state interest" in this legislative denial).[11] Before trial on this issue began, however, the Hawaiian constitution was amended by popular referendum, which, in effect, overruled the prior judicial decision.

In its ruling, the Massachusetts court was itself virtually explicit in seeking to exercise its authority in collaboration with other state officials rather than by simply commanding their obedience. The court signaled this preference by staying the effective date of its ruling for six months to allow the state legislature "to take such action as it deem appropriate consistent with [the court's] opinion." In December 2003, the state senate passed a formal resolution asking the court "whether permitting civil unions with all the appurtenances of marriage, except for the nominal designation," would comply with its decision. In February 2004, the four-person majority responded that this would not suffice but would "assign same-sex . . . couples to second-class status." Immediately afterward, the governor of Massachusetts, Mitt Romney, called for an amendment to the state constitution that would overrule the court's decision. At the end of February, President George W. Bush advocated an amendment to the United States Constitution permitting state legislatures to recognize same-sex marriage but denying any federal constitutional entitlement or consequent judicial command for this recognition.

The Massachusetts Supreme Judicial Court could have invoked a command mode at the outset, ordering the state executive immediately to implement its reading of the state constitution. Instead the Court portrayed itself more modestly, as if it were initiating a conversation with the state legislature regarding the precise meaning of its ruling. When the state senate asked it to approve a less radical change from past practice, the court stiffened its resolve. But this delay in itself produced a significant public event. The revelation of the state senate's willingness to envision official recognition of same-sex coupling, albeit as "civil unions" rather than "marriage," was a significant retreat from the state's past hostility to all same-sex relations.

Hostility did not vanish, however, among all official actors, as evidenced by the proposals for state and federal constitutional amendments by Governor Romney and President Bush. These proposals were not enacted; but legislative silence, especially among state officials, was an unstated though unmistakable exercise of authority. That is, the failure of the Massachusetts legislature to overturn the court's state constitutional ruling could fairly be understood as acquiescence to the court's initiative in mandating same-sex marriage by the Massachusetts elected officials (and the public whom they represented).

This intentional acquiescence could not be ascribed to President Bush or to any federal officials, because the U.S. Constitution is virtually impossible to amend. But this is not true for state constitutions.

Massachusetts is unusually restrictive in this matter; amending the state constitution requires a two-thirds vote of both legislative houses and then repetition of this vote in the immediately subsequent legislative session, to assure explicit electoral deliberation about the amendment. Other states are more permissive; for example, the constitutions of both Hawaii and California were amended by a one-shot public referendum to reverse state court rulings recognizing same-sex marriage based on state constitutional requirements. Massachusetts provides more deliberative opportunities, but amendments are not impossible to achieve. This political reality could not be overcome by the justices of the Massachusetts Supreme Judicial Court; whatever their preference, they had no choice except to understand their exercise of authority as shared and interdependent with the state legislature and the populace at large.

This institutional interaction echoes the process by which emancipatory moments on behalf of vulnerable groups have appeared in our social history: that is, from disruption of the existing power structure built upon the subjugation of some by others (the Massachusetts court's constitutional invalidation of the discrimination against same-sex marriage); to the loosening of categorically scornful attitudes toward the vulnerable group (the Senate "trial balloon" promising to validate same-sex civil unions); to an unaccustomed widespread empathic fellow feeling toward the previously scorned group (the acquiescence through inaction of the Massachusetts legislature and public).

The immediately subsequent condemnations of same-sex marriage by the governor and the president signaled reactionary efforts to restore and even intensify the old subjugation-supporting social order. The emancipatory goal posited by the Massachusetts Supreme Judicial Court was accordingly only an early episode that might readily have been abandoned by other actors.

During the decade after the Massachusetts ruling, litigative claims for same-sex marriage were brought in different states by LGBTQ advocates, with mixed results. Thus the New York high court ruled in 2006 that its state constitution was not violated by the denial of marital status to same-sex couples,[12] and in that same year the New Jersey

Supreme Court held that civil unions were constitutionally mandated to vindicate the equality rights of same-sex couples but access to formal marital status was not required. In 2009, the Iowa Supreme Court unanimously ruled that its state constitution demanded marital status for same-sex couples (a ruling informally repudiated by the Iowa electorate's subsequent rejection of three justices in a retention vote—though in 2012 retention was approved for a fourth justice).

The workings of the egalitarian mode of authority was most directly revealed in the five-year saga between 2008 and 2013 regarding the status of same-sex marriage in California. As its process unfolded, the issue of the legitimacy of same-sex marriage was directly engaged by almost every imaginable institutional actor—state and federal courts, elected state officials, and the popular electorate. At the end of this circuitous journey, the federal constitutional right to same-sex marriage emerged victorious in California (but only in California). True to the dictate of the egalitarian mode, although the end result was clear it was impossible to identify a hierarchically superior actor who commanded this result. Instead there were multiple actors with different perspectives who took action at various stages of the controversy. At the end, rather like the conclusion of Agatha Christie's novel *Murder on the Orient Express*, every conceivable suspect took part in the assassination, and it was therefore impossible to assign exclusive responsibility to any one of them—or to deny responsibility to all of them

The saga began in May 2008, when the California Supreme Court ruled that access to marriage by same-sex couples was required by the state constitution.[13] Just five months later, the California voters by a narrow 52 percent majority adopted Proposition 8 amending the state constitution so as to overturn the state supreme court's ruling. In May 2009, the state supreme court held that Proposition 8 validly amended the state constitution, thus effectively accepting the reversal of its previous ruling.[14]

This result was not preordained. California precedent could have been cited by the court to require more than popular-referendum approval for constitutional amendments that effectively reversed substantial portions of the document.[15] For such matters, prior state rulings rejected one-shot popular referenda in favor of an alternative, more elaborate amendatory process that involved approval by legislative supermajorities followed by popular referenda. Though Proposition 8 dealt on its face with only one limited issue of same-sex marriage, a larger jurisprudential issue was involved. In its initial decision, the court ruled that homosexual persons were a *Carolene Products* Footnote Four "discrete and insular minority" whose socially disfavored status made them so vulnerable to popular disapproval that special judicial protection was necessary. The court's subsequent willingness to accept a popular vote hostile to this "suspect class"— moreover, a popular vote that had barely mustered a majority—makes nonsense of the court's prior ruling that as a matter of general constitutional jurisprudence, it was obliged to extend special solicitude to the vulnerable minority.

Thus, passage of Proposition 8 not only harmed a constitutionally designated "suspect class," but it also called into question the fundamental constitutional principle regulating the relationship between courts, popularly elected officials, and the electorate. The California Supreme Court reflexively fell back on a hierarchical conception of social authority by giving automatic deference (and the last word) to a referendum process that reduced issues to television sound bites. The court turned away from requiring a more deliberative process that, because of the supermajority provisions, was more protective of the interests of this vulnerable group.

The court was not obliged to ensure victory to this group by awarding hierarchical prevalence to its members; the court was, however, obliged to oversee the deliberative process to ensure a fair hearing for them. This required judicial amplification of their claims so that their previously suppressed voices could be heard. At its core, this means that the court should see itself as engaged in an iterative process, as part of an interwoven egalitarian relationship that transcends hierarchy.

Three days before the state supreme court deferred to Proposition 8, a lawsuit was filed in federal district court in the Northern District of

California, arguing that the same-sex marriage ban enacted by Proposition 8 violated the federal Constitution. The suit was brought by two attorneys, David Boies and Theodore Olson, who had not been active in LGBTQ litigation and had previously opposed one another in *Bush v. Gore* regarding the Florida vote count in the 2000 presidential election. This federal court filing was not welcomed by the organizations that had previously taken the lead in LGBQT cases and had assiduously stayed away from federal courts regarding the marriage issue.[16]

In process terms, however, the filing of this lawsuit points to an advantage of both state and federal litigation over other formats for advocacy as an instrument for building egalitarian interactions. Anyone can file a lawsuit and thereby demand some reasoned response; advocates in nonjudicial forums, whether elective institutions or popular media, can readily be met by nothing more than a wall of silence, which is another tactic for asserting unquestionable hierarchic authority.

In August 2010, the federal district court judge, Vaughn Walker, ruled that the California constitutional ban on same-sex marriage did indeed violate the federal Constitution. At this point the state's Republican governor, Arnold Schwarzenegger, and its Democratic attorney general, Jerry Brown, independently decided that the state would not appeal Judge Walker's ruling. An appeal was nonetheless filed by private parties who had been active in the referendum campaign advocating passage of Proposition 8. In 2012, the Ninth Circuit Court of Appeals accepted this appeal and affirmed Judge Walker's ruling on its merits,[17] but a year later the U.S. Supreme Court reversed on the ground that the private-party appellants lacked standing to sue.[18] The net result of the Supreme Court's decision was to vacate the Ninth Circuit's ruling on the merits of the federal constitutional claim and to leave intact Judge Walker's original ruling because, in effect, the appropriate state officials had refused to appeal it.

Who then bore final responsibility for overturning the California ban on same-sex marriage? In one sense, the last word goes to Judge Walker, the federal district court judge; but this was only by default, since the state governor and attorney general chose not to appeal his ruling. In making this choice, were the two state officials registering the will of the people of California? They were elected representatives of the people and in this sense were responsive to the popular will. But the voters had clearly (if by a narrow margin) registered their preference on this specific issue by enacting Proposition 8. There was thus no single "voice of the people" involved in the federal lawsuit; there were instead competing voices, all claiming superior though conflicting authority to represent the popular will.

Though the various actors certainly did not self-consciously intend this, there could have been no better demonstration of the egalitarian conception of social authority than this saga. The interdependent conception could, however, have been aborted in the final act by the U. S. Supreme Court if that tribunal had ruled on the merits of the claim, whether for or against the constitutionality of bans on same-sex marriage—a ruling that would have applied not only in California but also nationwide. (Judge Walker had jurisdiction—the authority to "speak the law"—only in California, and his ruling is final there because of the procedural quirk that no valid appeal was filed. His ruling is suggestive as an interpretation of the federal constitution but not dispositive for other federal district or state court judges.)

On the same day that the U.S. Supreme Court issued its ruling in the California case, it decided another case regarding the constitutional status of same-sex marriages. In that case, *United States v. Windsor*,[19] the Court issued a definitive ruling that the federal Defense of Marriage Act (DOMA) violated the Constitution. DOMA provided that federal law would not recognize marital status in same-sex couplings even if the couples had been validly married under state law. This statute was enacted by Congress in 1994, when no state recognized same-sex marriages but just one year after the Hawaiian Supreme Court had cast doubt on Hawaii's marriage ban.

On its face, the Court's ruling in *Windsor* might look like a hierarchical exercise of authority; the U.S. Supreme Court authoritatively declared DOMA unconstitutional and left no room for further debate. But in fact DOMA was only one facet of the larger issue about the status of same-sex marriage. While the statute had considerable financial implications for same-sex couples formally married under state law, the statute itself did not directly address the underlying question whether any state was obliged to recognize same-sex marriages. (Another section of DOMA, not addressed in *Windsor*, considered whether any state was obliged to recognize same-sex marriages validly entered into in another state. DOMA provided that there was no such obligation. This provision, like the ban on federal recognition, certainly reflected hostility to same-sex marriages but did not bar any state from endorsing them.)

The Court's action in *Windsor* was not a neutral act regarding the status of same-sex marriage. Justice Kennedy's opinion for the Court had the same fundamental characteristic as his opinion ten years earlier in *Lawrence v. Texas:* though the end result was clear, the reasoning supporting this result was unclear and open to multiple interpretations that might or might not subsequently be relevant to the Court's resolution of the overarching constitutional claim for the right to same-sex marriage. On one side, Kennedy's opinion set out a narrow basis for overturning DOMA that would have no direct relevance to the overarching claim; he said that marriage was traditionally reserved for state regulation and on that ground the federal government violated federalism principles by refusing to recognize same-sex marriages approved under state law. But more broadly, Kennedy criticized DOMA for its hostility to same-sex marriage as such and appeared to rely on this hostility as an independent ground for overturning the statute. As with *Lawrence*, the Court's ruling in *Windsor* was somewhat inscrutable, a significant contribution to an ongoing national conversation but not the final word.

The open-ended quality of Kennedy's opinion distinguishes it from the rigorously logical structure that characteristically arises from the premises of the hierarchical command mode. By contrast, Kennedy's opinion was more free-form and suggestive rather than dispositive. Kennedy's evident sympathy for the same-sex couples, already apparent in his *Lawrence* opinion, spoke to his empathic identification with them. He invited a similar empathic response, but this invitation is much more in the format of a question than a command. Unlike a command, this question could be answered only by further interaction between the citizenry, officials in state and national fo-rums, and the Court's justices themselves. One might say that Ken-nedy's opinion is more like a dream of future harmony between same-sex couples and the rest of the community than a command-ment favoring same-sex couples over their antagonists.

However much Justice Kennedy's disposition in *Windsor* and *Law-rence* illustrates the egalitarian conception of judicial authority, it is reasonably clear that Kennedy in particular did not embrace this con-ception. In the Ninth Circuit case where the Supreme Court acted consistently with this conception by denying standing (and giving dispositive significance to the California elected officials, the gover-nor and attorney general, in their acceptance of same-sex marriage), Justice Kennedy dissented. It thus appears that he was ready for the Supreme Court to speak the final word about the constitutional sta-tus of same-sex marriage, notwithstanding that the issue was still the subject of passionate debate and dramatically shifting attitudes in the country at large.

In 2013, three federal courts of appeal—for the Fourth, Fifth, and Tenth Circuits—affirmed district court rulings in favor of a constitu-tional right to same-sex marriage. The Supreme Court denied cer-tiorari review of those cases in October 2014. The jurisprudential effect of these denials was to require recognition of same-sex mar-riage in all the states within those circuits, thus increasing from nine-teen to thirty-five the number of states where same-sex marriage was available. Even so, the Supreme Court persisted in its own silence, and same-sex marriage remained unavailable in fifteen states.

The three appeals courts were in agreement among themselves, and thus the conventional rule was not violated that the Supreme Court should resolve conflicting lower-court decisions. This denial of certiorari was unusual, however, in light of the remaining unavail-ability of same-sex marriage in fifteen states; there was a conflict among the states notwithstanding the agreement of all the federal appeals courts that had thus far ruled on the constitutional issue. In this matter, the Supreme Court's silence was an unmistakably deliberate act.

The Court never offers any explanation for denying certiorari review. Occasionally the reason can be glimpsed when individual justices dissent from this denial. But no Justice spoke on this occasion. Moreover, Supreme Court rules specify that only four justices must concur in order to grant certiorari. Accordingly, at least six of the justices must have decided against review of the three ruling circuit courts. Perhaps the six (or more) were uncertain about the voting inclinations of their colleagues or even themselves and hoped that the rulings of more federal appellate courts, more public debate, and the moral sympathy inspired by more same-sex marriages in two-thirds of the states would influence those inclinations. Whatever the reason, the Court's silent denial of certiorari meant that the constitutional issue would remain without definitive resolution for some additional time.

Just one month later, a panel of the Sixth Circuit Court of Appeals ruled (by a vote of two to one) against the existence of a federal constitutional right for same-sex marriage. Now there was an apparent conflict among the circuit courts, which accordingly presented the classic reason for Supreme Court intervention. The Court indeed did grant certiorari in this case and, in June 2015, proceeded in *Obergefell v. Hodges*[20] to rule, by a five-to-four vote, in favor of a constitutional same-sex marriage right.

There was an alternative path available to the Supreme Court that would have delayed and perhaps even rendered unnecessary this definitive ruling. It was not clear that *Obergefell* represented a true conflict with the other federal circuit court rulings for which the Supreme Court had denied review. *Obergefell* was a ruling by a three-judge panel on the Sixth Circuit, with one of the judges dissenting. The Sixth Circuit is, however, composed of thirteen judges, and the full court is authorized by statute to vacate three-judge panel decisions on its own motion, even if the litigating parties had not requested this *en banc* review. It would have been conceivable for the Supreme Court to grant certiorari in *Obergefell* and, rather than proceeding to decide its merits, to remand the case to the full Sixth Circuit with a suggestion—not a command—that the appeals court consider whether to proceed to *en banc* consideration.

This would have been an unconventional disposition, though no more peculiar than the Supreme Court's earlier action denying certiorari in the three consistently favorable rulings on same-sex marriage. Indeed, the underlying achievement of a remand in *Obergefell* would have been similar to the practical effect of the certiorari denial in these previous cases. The Supreme Court would have invited even more participation than had already occurred in the preceding deliberations in state courts and legislatures and, more recently, in some thirty federal district courts and eight courts of appeals.[21]

Between 2006 and 2014, seven state legislatures endorsed civil union status for same-sex couples providing state benefits formally equal to mixed-sex couples but without the honorific designation of marriage. In 2009, the Vermont legislature endorsed same-sex marriage as such, thus becoming the first state to authorize this by statute rather than as a result of a state court ruling; two months later, the New Hampshire legislature did the same. In 2010 the Connecticut legislature endorsed full marriage, enlarging on its state court ruling that favored civil union. In New York, notwithstanding the ruling of its supreme court that same-sex marriage was not required under the state constitution, the state legislature approved same-sex marriage in 2011. In 2012, Maine, Maryland, and Washington State approved same-sex marriage by popular referenda. In that year, Minnesota voters rejected a state constitutional amendment forbidding same-sex marriage, which was followed in 2013 by a legislative act authorizing it. Also in 2013, the legislatures of Rhode Island, Delaware, Hawaii, Illinois, and New Mexico approved same-sex marriage.

Thus, as of January 2014, seventeen states and the District of Columbia had endorsed same-sex marriage, three by state courts' constitutional rulings, twelve by independent legislation (one of which, California, resulted from elected officials' refusal to appeal a federal district court ruling based on the U.S. Constitution) and three by popular referenda. Seven states had provided for civil unions, and twenty-five states had withheld both marriage and civil union status from same-sex couples. Moreover, in 2011 the U.S. Congress repealed the "don't ask, don't tell" rule that had barred openly gay and lesbian people from military service. This litany of successes was not unbroken during this time, but the dominant story has been increasing acknowledgment by the straight majority of the claims of gays and lesbians for respect as equal participants in communal life. There have thus been extensive interactive deliberations. But even so, deciding whether "enough" interactions have occurred is not amenable to clear-cut determination. The question is complicated because of the nature of the LGBTQ claim for state recognition of marriage. This is not a claim for privacy, to be left alone, to be free from state intrusion. This is a claim that state institutions should publicly celebrate same-sex marriage just as it celebrates mixed-gender marriages. Equality and dignitary considerations could justify judicial invocation of the Constitution to force state recognition of same-sex marriages. But stating the issue in these terms does suggest that voluntary acceptance of this celebration is more consistent with its social meaning, even among same-sex couples, than forced acknowledgment.

Especially if the justices knew, or even suspected, in considering *Obergefell* that the Court was poised to decide for a constitutional right to same-sex marriage by a sharply divided vote, the majority justices might have understood that the legitimacy of their position would have been enhanced by widespread support in endorsement in other tribunals. Favorable rulings in federal courts would not connote voluntary acceptance as had resulted from state legislative approval or state judicial rulings (because of the relative ease of the state constitutional amendment process). But if the central goal of the Supreme Court is to promote widespread participation in deliberative institutional forums, especially to protect vulnerable Footnote Four minorities by amplifying their effective voices in those deliberations, then the Court should actively and imaginatively create these opportunities.

Promoting deliberative participation takes time. Some argue that delaying the availability of constitutional rights to same-sex couples is itself a denial of those rights, just as earlier critics found fault with the *Brown II* delay in guaranteeing access of black students to nonsegregated schools. This criticism, however, relies on a constricted conception of constitutional right. If the right appears recognizably full-blown, it might make sense to condemn any delay in its application. But rights only emerge this way if constitutional rights arise through hierarchical imposition by socially isolated interpreters. If constitutional rights don't leap from Zeus's head but properly emerge through an extended participatory deliberation, then the passage of time is an essential element in the unfolding of this process.

Thus withholding access from same-sex couples to marriage in states subject to the jurisdiction of the Sixth Circuit while permitting access to couples in states where same-sex marriage is already approved is not a denial of constitutional rights to Sixth Circuit couples. The constitutional right is in the process of emerging; at the most, it has not yet blossomed into full expression. Similarly, during the effective era of *Brown II* the constitutional wrong may have been clearly established, but the remedy for this wrong could emerge only in a deliberative process conducted over time. The affirmative right was inchoate until this process took place.

Questions of timing become a central concern in applying the egalitarian mode of authority. These questions do not arise in the hierarchic command mode; if the sovereign rules over all that he can see, there's not much reason to delay decision making in order to solicit others' views and engage in a collaborative enterprise. If, however, the justices explicitly understand the importance not just about what they say but when and how they say it, there are formal doctrines available for them to employ. (Here is another parallel with psychotherapeutic attention to the timing and techniques of interpretation—a concern that is expressed in the necessity for "therapeutic tact.")

Judicial attention to timing has two related doctrinal formulations—ripeness and abstention. Ripeness recognizes that some issues are not sufficiently well developed—not "ripe" for adjudication—even though they can be abstractly fitted into a conventional jurisdictional framework. This doctrine has more academic than explicit judicial recognition; in particular, the constitutional law scholar Alexander Bickel placed the ripeness idea at the center of his jurisprudence.[22] The abstention doctrine is more commonly invoked by judges; it applies to relationships between federal and state judicial processes and enjoins federal courts to withhold judgment from certain issues because they are better suited, at least for initial consideration, by state courts.[23]

Many Supreme Court cases illustrate the uses of these doctrines. For example, in 1990 the Court in effect decided in the *Cruzan* case that mentally competent individuals have a federal "constitutionally protected right" to refuse lifesaving treatment.[24] In reaching this result, the Court referred to numerous state court cases decided during the previous fifteen years addressing this issue on the basis of state law. In finding a comparable federal right, the Court did not formally rely on state court rulings but nonetheless held that this past history was highly informative in reaching its own judgment on this issue. Similarly, the Court cited state cases on the criminal responsibility of mentally retarded people[25] and minors younger than sixteen in reaching its own judgment on the federal constitutional status of these individuals.[26]

In these cases and many others like them, the Supreme Court did not explicitly claim that it was obliged to follow state court results, nor did it rely on those decisions as formally binding on federal constitutional claims. Nonetheless, the Court regarded the prior state court rulings as relevant to its own rulings and, in effect, shared authority with them. The Court implicitly recognized that the issue was more "ripe" for decision because of the prior state rulings; or put another way, the Court abstained from decision making in order to permit prior state consideration. Neither the ripeness nor the abstention doctrine requires federal court deference to state processes; the doctrines are available if the federal judges understand the reasons why this deference—at least for some extended period of time— would serve the interests of a just result.

The Supreme Court's extended silence between *Lawrence* in 2003 and *Obergefell* in 2015 was not primarily a self-conscious choice by the justices. Advocates on behalf of LGBTQ people purposefully kept away from federal judicial forums for many years. This mistrustful avoidance was overcome by the Supreme Court's *Windsor* decision in 2013. At the same time, however, the Court itself appears to have embraced strategic silence in denying standing to the appellants in the California Proposition 8 case, *Hollingsworth v. Perry*, and even more clearly in 2014 when it denied certiorari review in four courts of appeals judgments upholding a constitutional right to same-sex marriage. The contrary ruling by the Sixth Circuit panel finally impelled the Court to act in 2015. The triumphant proclamation of the constitutional ruling in *Obergefell* thus emerged. But this climactic event should not obscure the fact that the interval between *Lawrence* and *Obergefell* not only had strategic value but, for at least part of that time, was also purposefully chosen by a majority of the justices. Thus a path was marked for future deliberative processes in the formulation of constitutional protections for vulnerable, subjugated groups.[27]

Nonetheless, the legitimacy of constitutional interpretation cannot depend on majority approval. Facilitating an extended deliberative process is an important goal; but achieving this goal cannot mean that courts should wait indefinitely for popular majorities to form. The shadow of brutal subjugation continues to oppress LGBTQ people, notwithstanding their recent success in state courts and legislatures. Voluntary recantation of this oppression is obviously desirable. But courts are especially required to promote corrective emancipatory efforts. Delay can be strategically justified to serve this goal, but it cannot override this goal.

It would be wrong for the Supreme Court permanently to refuse any ultimate declaration of a constitutional right to same-sex marriage. The four dissenting justices in *Obergefell* took this erroneous position, arguing that legislatures alone are properly authorized to proclaim such entitlement. Elected officials must not be left free, however, to permanently withhold the honorific status of marriage to same-sex couples. For LGBTQ people, availability of marital status is not simply legislative refusal of an incidental benefit. State action visibly withholding approval of same-sex intimate relationships fundamentally refuses recognized human status to LGBTQ people because of the centrality of same-sex intimacy to their social identity.

Refusal of marital status to LGBTQ people strikes directly at their recognized capacity to engage in intimate human relationships, in the same way that ownership of slaves was a pervasive deprivation of human self-possession. The core indignity imposed by slavery could not be remedied by a compensatory salary. The core indignity was the ownership of one human being by another, the utter effacement of slaves' entitlement to recognized freedom in choosing a life course—employment, marriage, child rearing, domicile—for themselves.

It would be preferable to have same-sex marital status endorsed by majority legislative votes and popular recantations of past wrongful inflictions on LGBTQ people. It would be appropriate for courts to delay ultimate proclamation of a constitutional right while promoting mutually respectful interactive deliberation between oppressed and oppressors. These are legitimate strategic considerations, but ultimately these considerations must not exclude a principled proclamation by the Supreme Court that fundamental constitutional rights are at stake in the availability of marriage for same-sex couples. Respecting these rights is not a legislative option but a constitutional obligation. By this recognition, "our constitutional ideal of equal justice under law is thus made a living truth."[28]

nine ABORTION: PRIVATE AND PUBLIC CONSIDERATIONS

Abortion first appeared on the Supreme Court's docket in 1970. A District of Columbia statute outlawed abortions except where necessary to "protect the health or life" of the pregnant woman. A physician, convicted of performing an illegal abortion, argued that this statutory standard was unconstitutionally vague. If the Court had accepted this (entirely plausible) claim in *United States v. Vuitch*,[1] it would have invalidated the abortion restrictions then in force in forty-six states. The Court could thus have unsettled the subordination of women implicit in restrictive abortion laws without itself conclusively settling the abortion dispute. This ruling would not have prohibited any state from restricting abortion, but any restrictions would have required new legislation in almost every state. The Court would not have drafted a new statute but would have challenged all states to devise their own. An iterative process would have been initiated in which states might or might not enact new restrictions that the Supreme Court might ultimately approve or again find insufficiently precise. In this iterative process, the effective power of women would have been enhanced.

In 1970, substantial numbers of women were already newly aroused about their subordinate status, regarding abortion restrictions and a range of other issues, with fervor that had not been seen since the 1920 enactment of the Nineteenth Amendment guaranteeing women's suffrage.[2] In the mid-1960s, a second Feminist Movement had been launched, but in *Vuitch* the Court was apparently unaware of the social significance of this new advocacy or of its opportunity to give unaccustomed amplification to women's voices, which could have helped to overcome the silence that had been imposed on them by their subordinated status. Overturning abortion laws for vagueness would have promoted an interactive process in which courts were important participants but not the sole or even central authoritative speaker.

The Court in *Vuitch*, however, squandered this opportunity. It upheld the abortion statute by a five-to-four vote and itself clarified the District of Columbia statute by construing "mental health" as included within the statutory reference to "health," rather than remanding the issue to the legislature. The Court committed the same error in *McGautha v. California*, decided during the same term, when it refused to require more precise substantive standards in death penalty statutes. During the next two years, the Court's response to these two issues then wildly diverged. Instead of the confusion and fractionation in *Furman* that followed regarding the death penalty, on abortion a clear Court majority took command of the entire abortion dispute. In *Roe v. Wade*,[3] decided in 1973, the Court (by a six-to-three vote) not only invalidated all existing state restrictions but also prescribed its own detailed standards, which, it claimed, satisfied all constitutional requirements.

The Court, moreover, acted in a way that betrayed its misunderstanding of the issues at stake in the contemporary abortion debate. Justice Harry Blackmun, writing the opinion for the Court, nodded toward the women's claim for a personal privacy right; but, as he reiterated several times, Blackmun relied primarily on the doctor's right to practice medicine as he saw fit without state interference (and Blackmun several times used this gendered depiction, speaking of "the physician [and] his pregnant patient").[4]

In subsequent cases, the Court caught up with the advocates for women's rights and abandoned the formulation of a "doctor's right," instead relying exclusively on the women's privacy claim.[5] This new reliance, however, itself reflected the Court's wholesale embrace of the hierarchic command mode in the abortion dispute.

There were, moreover, grounds other than the privacy right that the Court could have offered to invalidate the state abortion statutes. These alternative grounds are intrinsically more coherent as applied in the context of abortion. Moreover, the privacy rationale rests on a hierarchic conception of social authority, not simply regarding the superior status of the Supreme Court but in all social relations. The privacy doctrine generally is at odds with an interactional mode of shared egalitarian authority. The concept is thus jurisprudentially suspect.

Legal commentators since *Roe* have offered formulations other than privacy for depicting the wrongfulness of abortion restrictions, some favoring denial of "equal protection" between men and women, others specifying derogation of a woman's fundamental "right to dignity."[6] These alternative formulations are based on the existence of relationships. "Equality" is clearly a relational concept; it depends on the characterization of a relationship between A and B, whether hierarchical or horizontal, denying or affirming their equal status compared to one another. "Dignity" is also relational. Though not directly addressing whether A and B treat one another as equals, dignity makes no sense as a status accruing in the abstract, outside a social relationship. A can heap B with indignities or respect her claim to be honored with dignity; but B's claim for dignity is incoherent unless it is understood as directed at someone else, an A. By contrast, "privacy" is the negation of an interactive relationship.

Justice Louis Brandeis introduced the concept of the "right to privacy" into American constitutional jurisprudence. In his germinal dissenting opinion in *Olmstead v. United States*, however, he did not speak of privacy as such but instead extolled "the right to be let alone—the most comprehensive of rights and the right most valued by civilized men."[7] In one sense, the right to be let alone does describe a relationship, but it is characterized by willful separation from others, whereas "equality" and "dignity" depend on engagement with others. The core of the privacy ideal is best captured by defining it as the absence of or refusal to engage in a relationship.

Defined in this way, privacy is psychologically incomplete; it rests solely on the premise of the rational, bounded self—that it is possible and desirable to define oneself as wholly separate from others—and it denies the inevitable entwinement with others posited by the contradictory premise of the boundless self. By contrast, equality and dignity can readily be comprehended through both modes of cognition. The aspiration to be treated as an equal or with dignity depends on an underlying belief—or at least a hope—that harmony between

A and B is possible, no matter how conflictual their past relations have been. The privacy ideal rests on a contrary belief—that harmony is not desirable or, at least, not possible as a goal.

The demand for privacy is thus psychologically defensive. The wall that the privacy ideal erects between self and other is not a mutually satisfying settlement to conflict but more like a temporary truce between warring parties, an interlude between the inevitably renewed eruption of hostilities when, as it must, the contradictory psychological premise of the irrational, boundless self reasserts itself.

Some disputes are so deep rooted that nothing better is possible than a standoff, a mutually agreed suspension of open warfare. But there is an inherent instability in reliance on the privacy ideal, an instability that does not afflict the alternative conceptions of equality and dignity. We can see this instability by examining disputes where A invokes his right to privacy and the other conflicting party B invokes his right to equality or dignity. In effect, A says, "I want nothing from B but to be let alone from his intrusions and demands against me." B responds, "A is ignoring our long-standing history of inequalities and indignities that he has imposed on me, and his claim today to be let alone merely ratifies the unjust status quo."

In concrete terms, these were the conflicting claims advanced in the nineteenth century in the *Dred Scott* case[8] and *Plessy v. Ferguson*,[9] and recast in the twentieth century in *Brown v. Board of Education*. In *Dred Scott*, the Supreme Court sought to separate the hostile parties by withholding from the opponents of slavery any forum where they could pursue their complaints, both by negating the authority of Congress or the territorial legislatures to limit slavery and by barring blacks from access to federal courts. The Southern supporters of slavery were thus guaranteed the right to be let alone—without any acknowledgment that their claim for noninterference was from the perspective of their adversaries an imposition on them.

In *Plessy*, the Supreme Court was explicit that the right to be let alone was dispositive of the conflict about separate public facilities for blacks and whites. If there is to be any interaction between the conflicting parties, the Court observed, it must be on the basis of mutual agreement; in the absence of such agreement, separation—and the denial of any acknowledged relationship—must prevail.[10] This disposition wholly ignores the competing claim that requiring racially separate facilities was not the absence or the denial of a relationship between blacks and whites but a continuation of a past relationship that was intended by whites to demean blacks, and was understood as such by both races.

This characterization of *Dred Scott* and *Plessy* points to parallels with the economic liberty rulings that the Supreme Court issued in the late nineteenth and early twentieth centuries.[11] In all of these cases, there was conflict between those who sought to deny the existence of any relationship with their adversaries and those who insisted that there was a relationship, albeit an unjust one that had to be transformed. In the economic liberty cases, the Court endorsed the claim of capitalists to be let alone on the ground that they were the sole owners of the property in dispute. The Court thus ignored the workers' claim that they shared the enterprise, and that they had an ineluctable relationship with their employers derived from past interactions. The workers sought to enforce their relational claim by legislative action, which the Supreme Court overturned, in effect erecting a right to privacy that favored the capitalist employers by protecting the status quo from any "outside interference," notwithstanding the competing claims of workers to be "insiders" who deserved a recognized stake in the enterprise.

These uses of the equivalent of the privacy principle to resolve the disputes were unstable in fact. *Dred Scott* inflamed the controversy and played a significant role in precipitating the Civil War (in which the central dispute initially was between the Southerners, who insisted on withdrawing from a relationship with the North, and the Northerners, who claimed that the relationship persisted and could not justly be denied). *Plessy* bought peace for a time between blacks and whites, but the suppressed (though denied) conflict openly erupted after a half century and in many ways has not yet been resolved (though it has abated) another half century later. The economic liberty cases hardly produced even a temporary truce in hostilities between capitalists and laborers but was recast for the parties by the immense external shock of the Great Depression, which undermined the adamant resistance by employers to acknowledge shared stakes with employees.

The use of the privacy principle was also conceptually unstable. This instability is the core problem with the contemporary liberal invocation of John Stuart Mill's harm principle: "The only purpose for which power can be rightfully exercised over any member of a civilized community, against his will, is to prevent harm to others."[12] Mill's principle is psychologically obtuse. It presumes that two people are capable of refraining from harming one another because they conceive themselves as separate. The harm principle thus relies on only one cognitive mode (the rational bounded self), giving no recognition to the contradictory mode (the irrational boundless self). By the latter mode, one or both of these people conceive themselves as boundlessly entwined with one another so that the action of one necessarily impacts the other, whether for good or for harm.

Mill's harm principle is premised on both parties maintaining a clear separation between self and other. The principle expresses only one side of an argument and has no conclusive resolving force. A insists that, from her perspective, she has no relationship with B, but B insists that A is blinding herself to the existence of their relationship. There is no overarching principle available to resolve these contradictory accounts.

Privacy and the harm principle have been invoked in the abortion dispute, but their shortcomings are evident on the face of the controversy. If the fetus is regarded as a human being from the moment of conception, then the claim that the pregnant woman's decision is "private" and no one else has a recognizable stake in it is patently false; the fetus is a separate being in a relationship with its mother and has much at stake in her decision to abort or continue the pregnancy. The question whether or when the fetus is a recognized member of the human community, however, cannot be resolved. It is not a scientific question; scientists can only testify about when various developmental markers occur in the gestation of the normal fetus, but science cannot establish which marker or constellation of markers constitutes enough of a "full-fledged being" to warrant recognition as such.

Invoking the privacy principle as a way of thinking about the abortion dispute gives no coherent vocabulary for discussion among the disputants and therefore promises nothing more than an endless shouting match about incommensurate values. By contrast, understanding the dispute in relational terms—about the equality or dignity of women as compared to others—does point the disputants toward the possibility of a shared understanding. It is of course conceivable for abortion opponents to insist that fetuses deserve fully equal status or recognized dignity with their mothers. But this argument instantly offers a refutation, that even if the fetus deserves equality or dignity, the pregnant mother deserves the same. Unlike with "privacy," there is no temptation to fall back on incoherent formulas for determining when or whether a fetus is a human being.

Indeed, if the fetus is a human being, it might claim privacy, "a right to be let alone," as it matures enough to survive outside its mother's womb. This maneuver, however, obviously treats the mother as nothing more than a biological container. It strips her of human status and replicates the wrongful erasure that has historically characterized the subordination of women.

Equality and dignity are obviously deserved by both the mother and the fetus however it might be ranked on the spectrum of humanness, but debating their relative claims to equal treatment or dignified treatment invites a commensurate metric for comparison in a way that invocation of the privacy principle does not. The privacy claim depends upon making the conflict between maternal and fetal claims disappear by insisting a priori that the decision is "private," so that the fetus or the woman vanishes before the dispute begins. The equality and dignity claims invite discussion of the history of women's subordinate status, the role that abortion restrictions played in that subordination, and the remedial significance of shifting authority from doctors to pregnant women as a response to this demeaning social treatment. The privacy principle and its close cousin the harm principle give no room and therefore no impetus for considering this social history.

Abortion opponents may insist that this history is irrelevant, but they can't exclude it from conversational dispute by fiat, as the abortion supporters do when they invoke privacy as the justification for women's priority. The argument for the irrelevance of the past history of women's oppression, especially regarding abortion restrictions, is difficult to sustain when the dispute takes place regarding the comparative merits of the competing equality and dignity claims. Is there a past history of demeaning or subordinating impositions on fetuses as such? Perhaps so if we consider female fetuses or fetuses with significant mental or physical disabilities; and perhaps this history could justify state restrictions on abortions for gender selection or for narrowly perfectionist goals, but this justification would not extend to abortions for other nondiscriminatory reasons. Viewed through the lens of equality or dignity, the disputes about abortion availability would be about real matters that invite some common metric for deliberation rather than about empty abstractions regarding whether the fetus "exists" or not.

If the Court understands its authority as hierarchically commanding, then it makes no difference how it characterizes the abortion dispute. All of the characterizations array incommensurate values against one another and cannot yield definitive resolutions that don't depend at some level on question-begging assumptions. But by conclusively resolving the dispute, the Court missed the opportunity for inviting the disputants to directly confront one another, to characterize for themselves the reasons that they view the other as an oppressor and—most important—to decide for themselves whether they are able and willing to relent from what the other regards as oppression. If a mutually satisfactory accommodation is reached through this interactive process, both disputants can feel liberated. If the Court imposes conclusive victory for one and defeat for the other, only the victor feels liberated, but this emancipatory moment might be very brief indeed as the defeated party lashes out, impelled even more intensely by his heightened sense of grievance.

It may be that the end result of this iterative process is continued or even intensified conflict. On the ideological front, the pro-choice forces may unshakably insist that abortion restrictions, even those that appear reasonable on their face, are not offered in good faith but instead merely reiterate and reinforce the subjugated view of women that was dominant when the statutory restrictions were first enacted. On the practical front, the pro-life forces appear to confirm this diagnosis. For example, the restrictions ostensibly offered as health protections for the mother, requiring abortion providers to have admitting privileges with tertiary care hospitals, have had the impact of shutting down many abortion clinics, especially in rural areas.[13] Of course, it appears reasonable to insist on adequate training and facilities to protect the health of women seeking abortions. But the restrictions espoused and often legislatively achieved by pro-life opponents of abortion seem to reflect a barely disguised strategy for whittling away piece by piece at women's access to any abortions while hoping that the Supreme Court can ultimately be persuaded to overturn *Roe v. Wade*. Indeed, at the moment there are three justices who appear ready to overrule *Roe*.[14] The ultimate outcome depends on the politics of presidential elections and the longevity of the older, abortion-supportive justices.

Perhaps the roiling politics of the abortion dispute would have erupted no matter what the Court proclaimed in *Roe*. This claim has recently been put forward, with extensive documentation of social dispute about availability of abortion both before and after *Roe*.[15] This research may demonstrate that the Supreme Court was not responsible for the intense political polarization that has grown around the abortion issue since 1972. But even if the Court was not responsible for this polarization, it can be faulted for failing to shape its interventions in ways that facilitate direct interaction between the conflicting parties. Instead the Court consistently acted as if it was independently concluding the abortion debate. Although it responded to political opposition to *Roe* by announcing new standards that incrementally retreated from the sweeping strictures of *Roe*, the Court nonetheless still understood itself as the principal actor in dictating a proper settlement.

The 1972 Court was inattentive to the interactions that had only recently emerged in state legislatures. In particular, just two years before *Roe*, four state legislatures had approved women's free choice for abortions in the first trimester—in New York, Washington State, Alaska, and Hawaii. In addition, in 1968 the California legislature adopted an abortion reform whose standards were so permissive as to predictably amount to abortion on demand; in practice, between 1968 and 1972 this was the actual result.[16]

The new California bill neatly sidestepped the issue of the humanness of the fetus. In the bill's original form, abnormality of the fetus was one ground for permissable abortion. The governor of California objected to the dehumanizing implication of this ground and threatened to veto the bill unless that provision was dropped. Supporters of the bill observed that abortion permission in the new law based on the mother's psychological well-being would be sufficient to approve requests for abortion in response to fetal abnormality.[17] Thus amended, the bill was passed by the California legislature, and the governor signed it; in 1968, the governor of course was Ronald Reagan, who subsequently, as president, became the most visible and politically powerful leader of the pro-life forces opposed to all abortions.

Perhaps the Supreme Court was not responsible for the explosion of polarized opposition and the elevation of the abortion issue into a national political obsession that followed the decision in *Roe v. Wade*. *Post hoc* does not demonstrate *propter hoc*. But the Court should have cautiously attended to the possibility that its wholesale constitutional resolution of the abortion issue dramatically cut off opportunities for pro-life forces to fight for their convictions in political forums where they saw themselves as potentially potent actors. If the Court was not directly responsible for the open entry into public political debate by the Catholic Church immediately following *Roe* or the church's subsequent alliance with the Christian evangelical movement,[18] the possibility of an unprecedented breach in the church/state wall might have prompted the Court to act cautiously in not simply amplifying the previously suppressed voices but rather awarding them an apparently conclusive victory.

To be sure, pro-life forces did initially press for a constitutional amendment after *Roe;* but simple electoral arithmetic always makes this a virtually impossible goal to obtain. Realistically their only hope was trying to elect presidents committed to appointing justices intent on overruling *Roe* and praying that death would come soon to the life-tenured justices who had decided *Roe.* Forty years later, the anti-*Roe* forces do seem poised at the edge of victory. But in the long interim, the institutional frustration of the pro-life forces may have induced an escalated measure of anger and desperation to their quest.

Perhaps the abortion issue would have become central and trans-formatively polarizing in our political life regardless of what the Court might have done. Nevertheless, irrespective of its actual im-pact, the Court can be faulted for the way it intervened in the abor-tion issue. In *Vuitch,* the Court could have done nothing more than invalidate the statutes in all of the forty-six states with existing abor-tion restrictions. If and when legislators sought to reenact new re-strictions in response, courts would have given pro-choice women new political power; their newly aroused voices would have been am-plified, although victory over their adversaries would not have been assured. The means for initiating this process were within grasp, if only the Court had taken the path offered two years before *Roe*—that is, to declare void for vagueness the criminal prohibitions of any abor-tion "except to protect the life or health of the mother." This disposi-tion would have set the stage for a new and more equal interactive dialogue between pro-choice and pro-life forces without itself pre-emptively settling the dispute.

Roe was not, of course, the last word uttered in the controversy. Pro-life legislatures enacted numerous new restrictions that were re-peatedly challenged in court proceedings, sometimes leading to judi-cial invalidation of the restrictions and sometimes to approval. The conflicting parties were thereby drawn into confrontation presided over by judges who were ready to pronounce the final results. Both pro-choice and pro-life sides in the abortion debate were forced to see themselves as supplicants before the Court rather than as equal par-ticipants seeking to persuade one another. If the Court had understood the virtues of actively promoting dialogue, it could have purposely steered the parties toward legislative forums in which they interacted with one another, seeking common understanding. Instead the parties spoke past one another, aiming their persuasive efforts toward attracting the votes of five ruling justices.

Indeed, in practical terms, because of the polarized opposition in the Court regarding abortion, the litigants' efforts were principally aimed at one justice, Sandra Day O'Connor, whose single "swing" vote regularly determined the outcome in the abortion cases during her tenure from 1981 to 2006. Over more than two decades, abortion policy was thus decided for the entire United States by one person.

In legislative settings, the abortion opponents are not supplicants. They are entitled freely to threaten uncooperative legislators with retaliation at the polls, whereas no sane litigant would dare even to hint at impeachment efforts or otherwise show contempt toward a hostile (life-tenured) judge. In legislatures, moreover, the newly assertive women's rights movement could have protected its interests in freely chosen abortion by relying on the political tenet that adamant minorities can much more readily block hostile legislation than enact new laws. At the same time, the pro-life forces might muster enough legislative strength to extract compromises from (but not complete victory over) their pro-choice opponents. Perhaps the California model in its 1968 reform act could provide a meeting ground for the parties. Perhaps some other possibilities might arise.

The Court might participate in this unfolding interactive process from the sidelines in ways that stop well short of commanding total victory or defeat for either combatant. For example, three of the four legislatures endorsing freely available abortion in 1971 had restricted access to state residents. The fourth, New York, had no such limit and was available to any woman who could make her way to the state. Similarly, the new California statute that effectively enacted abortion on demand had no residency restriction. The Court could readily declare that prior residency requirements violated the constitutional right to interstate travel for a woman seeking an abortion in any nonrestrictive state. For this holding, the Court could have relied directly on its 1969 decision overturning prior residency requirements for welfare eligibility.[19] The Court could also have ruled on equal protection grounds that states were not free to deny welfare assistance for abortion costs if they provided financial support for other medical services.

With these two rulings, the Court would have established a framework to protect impoverished women's access to abortion even though some states persisted in reimposing clear restrictions. This national patchwork (where abortion is readily available in blue states but not in red states, as the polarized vernacular now puts it) would not satisfy the full demands of either pro-choice or pro-life forces. But it might be one result that emerges from engaged discourse among these combatants—a result that is not available to courts when they grandiosely propound a single constitutional rule for all states at all times.

In short, the Court in *Roe* failed to observe, or even to understand, the lesson of *Brown v. Board of Education*—that the Court should not see itself as supreme commander, as a Hobbesian Sovereign imposing its own conception of order on all combatants, but instead should self-consciously promote interaction between oppressors and oppressed in a way that might foster equal authority and mutual respect on both sides. The specific techniques for such interaction vary. In *Brown*, delay was the Court's chosen path, effectively setting the stage for enlisting others besides Southern whites and blacks to see their stake in this polar conflict and take new responsibility accordingly. In the LGBTQ and mental disability cases, delay was not a purposeful judicial choice, but it emerged adventitiously and has had the same interactive result. In *Roe*, by contrast, the Court saw itself as a hierarchically dispositive, socially isolated force; it ultimately relied upon an incoherent principle of "privacy" to impose in a single sweeping gesture its own resolution of the newly waged controversy between oppressors and oppressed women.

Social relations between blacks and whites in America is the paradigmatic and preeminently important context for the operation of Footnote Four, the judicial enterprise of protecting vulnerable groups. The Supreme Court was right in *Brown I* initially to identify and condemn in principle the devaluation of blacks embedded in racially separate public facilities, especially in schools, and then in *Brown II* to draw back in order to enlist the attention and stronger remedial capacities of other actors, both the federal Congress and the executive branch, federal district judges, and state officials. The Court failed, however, consistently to sustain this approach after its initial success in engaging other actors, especially in the Civil Rights Act of 1964, the Voting Rights Act of 1965, and the Fair Housing law in 1968. Indeed, in many instances the Court obstructed the newly established ability of blacks to find forums where the future terms of their relationship with whites could be peacefully and systematically addressed.

In drafting the Court's opinion in *Brown I*, Chief Justice Warren vowed that its tone would be "non-accusatory."[1] Warren achieved this literary goal, even going so far as charitably ascribing the approval of race segregation in *Plessy v. Ferguson* to the 1896 Court's "lack of psychological knowledge" rather than racial animus. Warren's rhetorical accomplishment was not matched, however, by practical success. "Massive resistance" was launched by white Southern political leaders from all the states that had made up the Confederacy. The white South generally construed *Brown* as a hostile act, a further battle in the continuing Civil War, waged explicitly for the "noble cause" of states' rights but silently for the perpetuation of black slavery.

The accusatory implications of *Brown* were dramatically underscored in the 1960s civil rights legislation enacted by defeating persistent Southern opposition, including the mustering of a two-thirds

Senate vote to overcome Southern filibusters. The overwhelming congressional majorities not only approved the substantive goal of ending race segregation but also provided new enforcement means that had not been available to the Court from its own authority. Thus Title VI of the Civil Rights Act of 1964 denied federal funds to any school district practicing racial discrimination and prescribed administrative means for enforcing this measure, while Title IV authorized the attorney general to bring desegregation suits on behalf of the United States, thereby ending the need to rely on financially strapped private plaintiffs. The Voting Rights Act of 1965 replaced discriminatory state officials with federal voting registrars, thus even more directly echoing the victorious Northern dispatch of the Freedmen's Bureau in 1865 to protect freed slaves immediately after the Civil War.

Following these enactments, the Court itself appeared emboldened to escalate judicial enforcement efforts, repudiating in 1964 the slow pace envisioned by *Brown II* ("delay is no longer tolerable"),[2] broadening its oversight efforts in 1968 ("racial discrimination [must] be eliminated root and branch"),[3] and in 1971 approving far-reaching remedies involving extensive busing between innercity and suburban schools and other specific efforts to spread the attendance of black and white school children equally throughout the school district.[4]

In 1973, the Court came to a new moment. For the first time, it addressed race segregation in a public school outside the former Confederacy, in a school district with no prior history of explicit statutes requiring racial segregation. Nonetheless, the Court found that the Denver school board had purposely manipulated the attendance zone for one school based on its racial composition and that this gerrymandering had general impact that justified systems-wide remedies. The South was accordingly no longer the exclusive focus of the Court's attention; *Brown* was no longer a direct reenactment of the Northern abolitionist condemnation of Southern slavery.

This did not mean that the Court had returned to Chief Justice Warren's goal of avoiding condemnatory accusations. To the contrary. The Denver case, *Keyes v. School District No. 1*,[5] apparently broadened the indictment to include any official deployment of racial segregation, whether in the South or in the North. The accusatory implication of this condemnation was the Court's insistence on intentionality.

Intentional guilt—*mens rea*, or a "guilty mind," in legalese—is the centerpiece of the legal system's precondition for moral blame and consequent punishment. In *Keyes*, the Court did not order the imprisonment of the offending school board, but the justices' intensive search of the record for evidence of the school board's intentional discrimination clearly signified a charge of blameworthy conduct. In its vernacular, the Court insisted on a radical distinction between *de jure* and *de facto* discrimination, limiting its condemnation and remedial interventions to race segregation imposed "by law" as opposed to discrimination "in fact" arising from other causes, such as private choice of residential neighborhood based on differential housing costs or even privately based on unavowed though implicit racism.

In the 1973 Denver case, Justice Lewis Powell offered a different approach. Powell was a recent Nixon appointee, the only white Southerner then on the Court, and he had been chairman of the school board in Richmond, Virginia, from 1952 to 1961. In a separate opinion, Powell urged that the Court redirect its attention away from past findings of intentional discrimination and toward contemporary school boards' inaction regarding systemic occurrence of race segregation. He observed that much contemporary race segregation, especially in the North, may not have been purposefully designed by school boards but was nonetheless passively tolerated. He maintained that the Court had been wrongly obsessed with the *de jure/de facto* distinction, that although this distinction differentiated Northern and Southern origins of racially separate public schools, racial separation was nonetheless equally characteristic of the two sections (and even more pronounced in the North because of belated Southern compliance with federal enforcement pressure). Powell urged the Court to relent from its search for past origins of wrongful segregation and concentrate instead on promoting the future commitment of blacks and whites in addressing the pervasive racial separation through the country.

The *de jure/de facto* distinction ultimately rests on the difference between active intention and passive omission of school board officials. Powell insisted that school boards open their eyes to the racially separatist consequences of their failure to consider the demographic implications of attendance patterns or school construction sites or parental economic capacity and willingness to leave public schools. Whatever the cause of existing patterns of racial segregation, Powell asserted, "there is a prima facie case that public authorities [are] sufficiently responsible" for perpetuating this separatism, so that they "must make and implement their customary decisions with a view toward enhancing integrated school opportunities." Failure to act may not be as morally blameworthy as intentionally designing a racially discriminatory school system, but bystanders are also blameworthy when they witness injuries and are capable of redressing them but do nothing.

From this perspective, the very process of litigation may precipitate the existence of a school board's obligation to "enhance integrated school opportunities." The conventional view is that the litigation provides a forum for determining the existence of past wrongdoings. Under Powell's regime, contemporary evidence mustered in litigation regarding present circumstances can in itself be sufficient to alert school boards to the existence of racial separation in public schools and consequently produce an obligation to take affirmative remedial steps.

In rejecting his proposal, the Court majority was apparently concerned that the lesser burden of moral guilt that Powell envisioned would lead to considerable weakening of support, among judges and within the general public, for extensive and stringent enforcement efforts. Powell fed this concern by stating that the responsibility he would impose on school boards would not include "extensive student transportation solely to achieve integration." Though Powell himself may have drawn this consequence, it would follow only because he entirely abandoned the *de jure/de facto* distinction. Borrowing the concept from tort law, one might say that Powell envisioned a "no-fault system," which would wholly replace fault-based litigation for automobile accidents or medical malpractice suits. But his proposal could readily be adapted to create a hybrid system: stringent enforcement consequences for intentionally imposed race discrimination and less stringent, though still conveying some blame, for discrimination tolerated but not initiated by school boards.

The Court has persisted to the present day, however, in requiring past intentionally imposed race discrimination as a prerequisite for judicial imposition of remedial measures. Intentionality is not (or at least not yet) required for legislative imposition of remedial measures; "disparate impact" on racial minorities, even though unintended, can be sufficient. The Court recently affirmed this difference in statutory as opposed to constitutional violations, though by a five-to-four vote;[6] the issue remains open, however, whether the Constitution permits legislative enactments that substantially dispense with past intentional wrongdoing while imposing liability for passive tolerance of race separation. Even if the narrow majority holds firm by constitutionally endorsing this legislation, it has nonetheless clung to the requirement of some moral blameworthiness by insisting that the "disparate impact" must have been directly "caused" by state action—thus appearing to entirely exempt race separation that arose through "private" choice (most notably, by changing residence to racially separate neighborhoods or removing their children from public schooling).

The Court's inability to dispense altogether with moral blameworthiness in assessing race separation has had two unfortunate consequences. One consequence is its ruling that school officials are not entitled voluntarily to adopt explicitly race-conscious remedies for racial segregation unless they have been directly guilty of past wrongdoing.[7] This holding is part of a campaign waged by some justices to forbid any use of race regardless of its emancipatory intent or effect. To this end, the Court appears poised to constitutionally disallow any use of racial criteria in admissions to higher education institutions, no matter what justification might be put forward for these policies. If a Court majority takes this step, it will ignore the probability that racial minorities will predominantly remain excluded from institutions of high prestige.⁸ Forbidding the inclusive use of racial criteria in order to remedy past subordination will thereby ironically promote the exclusion and subordination of racially identifiable groups.

The second deleterious consequence of the Court's fixation on moral blame is its insistence that judicially imposed race-conscious remedies must end even if unintentional race separation persists. Thus the Court has held that once a school system has achieved "unitary status," there is no justification for further judicial inquiry regarding the possibility of resegregation.⁹ This holding arises from the view that remedial responsibility must not be extended indefinitely; it may appear justified because it limits courts' authority to permanently displace local school authorities.

This ruling, however, ignores the role that continued litigation can play in providing a protected space where conflicting racial groups can deliberate as equals about the future of their social relationship.

Observing this limitation—distinguishing between judicial subordination of school board authority and judicial illumination of persistent subordination in race relations—is not easily achieved. The limitation requires considerable finesse and self-restraint by the judge (corresponding to the parallels I identified in chapter 5 between litigation and psychotherapy). The judicial task is not mechanistic but properly and necessarily involves judgment. In particular, judges must understand themselves as ultimately promoting equal deliberation among conflicting parties rather than imposing their own calculus of equality on the parties. This understanding is not alien to the judicial function; it is the core value that harmonizes the apparent conflict in democratic principle between majoritarian authority and protection of minority rights.

Given the stubborn histories of black subordination and the cyclic recurrence of oppressions after emancipatory efforts, the Court should acknowledge the need for indefinite concern regarding the future. To this end, it should have embraced the willingness of local school boards to foster racial interaction by purposefully drawing multiracial attendance zones, applauded the concern expressed by substantial majorities in Congress to assure unobstructed minority participation in elections, approved affirmative action plans devised by public and private colleges and universities to assure substantial minority group presence, invalidated state laws forbidding the use of affirmative action in the service of racial interaction, and extended protections to convicted criminals, especially by accepting Justice Breyer's proposal to reexamine constitutionality of the death penalty.

Courts today must guard against resurgence of the psychological forces that have repeatedly impelled subordination of vulnerable groups—not just blacks but also women, LGBTQ people, people with disabilities, and convicted criminals. These psychological forces impel some people to protect themselves by inflicting degradation on others; they are powerful and often difficult to detect. If I believe I can affirm my sense of righteousness by projecting (without conscious awareness) my destructive impulses onto someone else, it is easy for me to imagine myself as pure-hearted. After all, I am acting in compliance with the directive of my internal compass pointed toward righteousness. This self-justificatory attitude among oppressors is so common, so strong, and so much entangled with a conviction of goodness that it is very difficult for the oppressor to see his actions for what they truly are. Somehow the oppressor must be induced to see his mixture of motives, good and bad, honorable and dishonorable—and to accept full responsibility for what he is doing, one might say, with half his mind.

This is descriptively inaccurate, of course. All we can know is that our minds are fundamentally divided between two modes of cognition; but this doesn't mean that we are led to victimize others for our own shortcomings because half our mind draws firm boundaries with others and half draws no boundaries. In fact both modes of cognition can conspire together for me to impose my fears about myself boundlessly onto you while at the same time insisting that rigid boundaries separate bad you from good me.

How, then, can we be led to look honestly and fearlessly at our tangled psyches, our self-contradictory sense of ourselves? We must help one other to accomplish this—with empathic, imaginative tolerance for contradiction and patient persistence in offering help rather than self-righteously commanding obedience.

Judges can constructively help in shaping our social regulations, but only if they understand the need for this help. The goal for this pedagogic process is to liberate everyone—not only those enslaved by others but also those who enslave themselves in the effort to deny freedom to others.

eleven ORDERING MORAL DELIBERATIONS

There are two ways to describe the role of the judiciary in realizing the core constitutional guarantee of equal protection of the laws. One way is to view the judiciary as a calculator measuring the relative status of conflicting parties in order to assure equal substantive entitlements. This is the conventional view of the judicial function. It focuses attention on the judge and the metric of equality that she applies to decide among the competing claims of the parties.

The second way—the way I have urged throughout this book—is to shift attention from the judge and to redefine the equality guarantee as emerging from an interactive process among the parties, carried out under the judge's watchful observation. From this perspective, democratic equality is not so much an end state as measured by a judge, and much more a relationship of mutual respect among people in conflict with one another.

There is a substantive dimension to this second conception. The outcome of the parties' conflict may be so demeaning, so dismissive to one party that it readily reveals that the parties' relationship is not mutually respectful but oppressive subordination of one by the other. This determination requires a substantive calculation by the judge; but having found inequality, the judge is tasked not simply to announce this conclusion but instead to require the parties to resume their interaction, under the judge's continuing observation.

The core requirement of this second conception is not for the parties to satisfy the judge's conception of equality but to justify themselves to one another. This is the heart of democratic practice. This mutual self-justification occurs in popularly elected institutions as the conflicting parties struggle with one another and attempt to enlist allies. When one of the parties is excluded from this mutual interaction of self-justification, because of extreme vulnerability or "prejudice," as Footnote Four understood, this is a deformation of democracy that requires "more searching judicial inquiry." The corrective to this deformation is not for the judge to definitively impose her own calculus of equality but to direct the parties to engage in new interactions in which each treats the other with equal respect.

I have set out from American social experience and from individual psychological consideration the basis for hope that this disruption by the judge of the existing unequal relationship and the parties' supervised interactions on a different basis will lead to some new measure of fellow feeling among the disputants. This empathy is the foundational constituent of a democratic relationship. It is, however, a fragile foundation. Individual psychological structure, as revealed by the American social history of alternating eras of subjugation and emancipation, demonstrate this fragility. There are no ready-made formulas, but there are strategically imagined ways, as I have illustrated throughout this book, in which judges can foster the emergence of mutually respectful relationships.

It is tempting for judges to short-circuit this interactive process, to fall into the error Freud did when he analyzed the illness of his patients, announced the results to them, and considered them cured. Freud's psychotherapeutic successors have redefined their enterprise by focusing on their interactive relations with their patients and striving for the goal of enhancing the patients' own self-understanding and sense of responsibility. Judges are not psychotherapists, and the analogies between the judicial and psychotherapeutic enterprises are only suggestive. Nonetheless, judges should take some guidance by redirecting their sense of mission away from defining equal relationship in order to impose that definition on the parties in conflict.

The parties may be so locked in hostile interactions that no empathic connections ever emerge, however skillfully and persistently the judge attempts to lead the parties toward assuming responsibility for a different direction in their relationship. The judge can hold out the ideal of a democratic relationship. She can illustrate it in her own behavior. She cannot, however, impose it on others. The persistent disrespect of one or both parties signifies a defeat for democratic principle. The judge's attempt to impose this value rather than facilitate its emergence is itself a failure of democratic principle. Judges should not abandon this facilitative effort, but neither should they pretend that the failure of this effort was actually a victory for the observance of minority rights in a democracy.

Judges are not the only instruments through which democratic values based on empathic fellow feeling and mutual accountability can be fostered. I witnessed a successful instance of this process when sixty-seven members of the U.S. Senate voted to impose cloture to end the Southern filibuster against the Civil Rights Act of 1968. Here is how Vice President Hubert Humphrey, acting in his official capacity as president of the Senate, set the stage for one senator to revise his moral evaluation of himself and to embrace an empathic relationship with fellow citizens, though he had previously denied any connection with or obligation to them.

In 1968 I was legislative assistant to Senator Joseph D. Tydings, a liberal Democrat from Maryland. Tydings was skeptical of the possibility that the proposed Civil Rights Act would pass, and especially that sixty-seven votes could be mustered in the Senate to close down the inevitable Southern filibuster against the bill. Cloture had been voted by two-thirds of the Senate in 1964 and again in 1965 to enact the civil rights bills, but the Fair Housing provisions of the 1968 act were directed against Northern practices of residential discrimination against blacks, unlike the previous civil rights enactments, which were principally aimed at Southern practices. Where could sixty-seven votes be found in the Senate when the Northern senators would be voting against segregationist practices of their own constituents? Moreover, it seemed to Tydings (along with most politically savvy observers) that the mood of the country had changed between 1965 and 1968, that sympathy for black civil rights had waned and "white backlash" had set in. Accordingly, though Tydings supported the 1968 act, he nonetheless kept some distance from it, refusing to join other liberal senators (such as Walter Mondale, Ted Kennedy, and Jacob Javits) in the regular strategy sessions convened by Senator Philip Hart to explore ways of obtaining enough votes in the Senate to end the filibuster by Southern senators.

Tydings's misgivings were a boon to me because, rather than attend in person himself, he assigned me to sit in on these meetings. This was a heady experience for me, just four years out of law school. In addition to watching these senators interact, I also regularly saw Ramsey Clark, the attorney general, who attended all of these meetings. I vividly recall Phil Hart soliciting Clark's views on various matters and Clark's regular refusal to respond. "I am here," he repeatedly stated in his Texas drawl, "to tell you that the United States Department of Justice wholeheartedly supports your effort to pass this Open Housing Act, but I have no advice to offer you about the Senate strategy to bring this result about."

All of us in the room, senators and staff alike, knew the subtext of Clark's quiet presence. President Lyndon Johnson had thrown himself into the effort to pass the Civil Rights Act of 1964, principally aimed at public accommodations, employment discrimination, and school segregation, and the Voting Rights Act of 1965. But Johnson's political priorities had shifted between 1965 and 1968; the Vietnam War was centrally on his mind, and he was intent on allying himself with the powerful Southern plutocrats in the Senate rather than opposing them as he had done in 1964 and 1965. The attorney general's support was less than a substitute for the president's active lobbying; but Clark was intent on displaying whatever support he could convey. That was the meaning of his silent witness at the morning strategy sessions convened in Senator Hart's office.

At one meeting in late February, almost two months into the Southern filibuster, Senator Hart informed the group of a message he'd received from Vice President Humphrey about his conversation with Senator Bob Bartlett of Alaska. Though Bartlett was a liberal-leaning Democrat, he had not previously voted to end this filibuster of the 1968 act. In those days, filibusters brought all other Senate business to a halt, and Senator Mike Mansfield, the Democratic majority leader, informed us that he would permit one more vote at the beginning of March. Mansfield announced that if it was unsuccessful, exercising his authority to control the Senate agenda, he would withdraw the 1968 act from consideration so that the Senate could proceed to other matters. We were (tantalizingly and incredibly) close to two-thirds support in the Senate, but on the prior vote we were still six votes short. Where were they to be found? That was Humphrey's recruiting mission with Alaska's Senator Bartlett.

There were almost no blacks in Alaska, and the Native Americans in the state were apparently content to live apart from whites in remote villages. From Bartlett's perspective, therefore, the 1968 act was free from direct constituency pressure. This consequently meant that the bill was available for bargaining, and Bartlett told Humphrey that he had been promised by Senator Richard Russell of Georgia, the powerful chairman of the Senate Appropriations Committee, that Russell would ensure funding for improvements on the Alaska-Canada Highway that linked the state with the "lower forty-eight" and, moreover, that Russell would guarantee highly visible credit to Bartlett for the Al-Can Highway—but only if Bartlett would abstain from voting for cloture on the 1968 Civil Rights Act.

In the shadow of this alluring commitment, Bartlett informed Humphrey that there was no possibility of extracting a vote favoring cloture from him. Humphrey did, however, offer an alternative— that Bartlett would promise not to vote until Humphrey (as presiding officer) or the clerk of the Senate (responsible for vote tallies) told him whether his vote was essential for victory. Bartlett stated that even then he would refuse to support cloture: Russell's offer was too enticing to turn down, and he faced a difficult primary fight for his next reelection campaign, in 1970. Nonetheless, Humphrey urged Bartlett to delay his vote, and Bartlett agreed.

This was all that Humphrey could obtain from Bartlett. But Humphrey told Hart not to worry, that Bartlett would not want to be the defeating vote and that, if it came to that, he would support cloture. "I know my man," Humphrey said. Hart and the other liberal senators were skeptical.

The final voting day arrived on March 4, 1968. I was seated in the gallery (ordinarily staff members were permitted on the Senate floor, but today we were banished to the gallery). All the senators were in their seats except, so far as I could see, Bartlett. The voting began,

ORDERING MORAL DELIBERATIONS

and we saw that we were newly (and amazingly) joined by conservative Republican senators from New Hampshire and Vermont in the roll call. Following completion of the roll call, individual senators sought recognition, but several (who had previously opposed cloture, such as Margaret Chase Smith, Republican of Maine) were muffled in their votes. Most senators (along with us staff in the gallery) had no idea of the cumulative vote count.

When voting ended and the Senate chamber fell silent, Bartlett suddenly appeared at the door of the adjoining cloakroom and strode purposefully toward Humphrey and the clerk in the well at the front of the chamber. But Humphrey interrupted him. "Mister Bartlett," he called. Bartlett had not sought recognition, and he did not respond; instead he increased his speed toward the well. Again Humphrey called to him, "Mister Bartlett." Bartlett then paused and waved his arms in what looked to me like a negative gesture. I thought, "My God. He's going to vote 'no.'" A third time, Humphrey called to him. "Mister Bartlett." Then Bartlett stopped. He was silent for a moment. Then, almost inaudibly, almost seeming to choke, he said, "Yes."

Humphrey pounded his gavel on his elevated desk and proclaimed, "Cloture is voted." The entire chamber, both the Senate floor and gallery, erupted in cheers, and Humphrey let the celebration proceed for a long moment before bringing back order.

The next morning I called Bartlett's administrative assistant. "What went on with your boss yesterday?" I asked him. The AA responded, "When he returned from the floor, Bartlett said he had been confused. Humphrey had agreed that he would learn the vote total and have an opportunity to deliberate, but Humphrey violated their agreement by calling on him. Then, Bartlett told me, as Humphrey repeatedly called his name, he thought to himself, 'If I want to remain in the Senate, I should be a Senator. I can't trade justice for a highway. So I voted yes.'"

Bartlett had not been directly involved in maintaining segregated housing between blacks and whites. At most, he might consider himself a passive ally of those who supported such segregation elsewhere than in his home state of Alaska. Humphrey could not command how

Bartlett would vote. He could and did command that Bartlett cast a publicly visible vote, that he accept personal responsibility in deciding whether to support or oppose this social practice, this oppression of blacks. Humphrey used his authority as presiding officer of the Senate so that Bartlett clearly understood the personal moral significance of his vote, a conflict between justice and a highway, between remaining in the Senate and being a senator.

Bartlett never learned whether he would be reelected in 1970 or whether he would have benefited from Senator Russell's support. He had a sudden heart attack and died in December 1968.

Defeat of the filibuster had a further impact on me. During the Senate vote, I sat in the gallery next to Clarence Mitchell Jr., the chief legislative lobbyist for the NAACP. I had never been directly introduced to Mitchell but knew him because he had attended all the morning strategy sessions in Phil Hart's Senate office. Seated in the gallery during the cloture vote, I was so gripped by the drama unfolding on the Senate floor that I took no notice of who sat next to whom. But when the Senate voted cloture and the chamber erupted in cheers, Mitchell and I looked directly at one another for the first time—me, the twenty-eight-year-old staffer, and him, probably in his early fifties. We were both crying, we hesitated a moment, and then we embraced.

We then walked together out of the Senate building toward Mitchell's office on New Jersey Avenue and my home beyond, on F Street, S.E. As we walked, Mitchell told me that his grandfather had been a slave and that he would have been proud of this country for finally keeping its promise and proud of him for the work he had done in bringing about this new guarantee of emancipation. And I told him of my grandfather who had escaped the Russian army and threats of pogroms to find freedom in this country, and how proud he would have been of this country and of me for my small supporting role. At his office, Mitchell and I didn't embrace again; I, at least, was too shy. Instead we shook hands, and I continued toward home. On that precious day, our nation's commitment to democratic principle was a living truth.

NOTES

Foreword

1. R. A. Burt, *Withholding Nutrition and Mistrusting Nurturance: The Vocabulary of* In re Conroy, 2 Issues in Law & Medicine 317, 329 (1987).
2. Alexander M. Bickel, *The Supreme Court and the Idea of Progress* (Yale Univ. Press, 1978) (1970) at pp. 91–92.
3. *Id.* at 239.
4. Owen M. Fiss, *The Odd Couple*, 125 Yale L.J. 796 (2016) (available at http://www.yalelawjournal.org/tribute/the-odd-couple).
5. Robert C. Post, *Remarks for Robert Burt*, 125 Yale L.J. 796 (2016) (available at http://www.yalelawjournal.org/tribute/remarks-for-robert-burt).

Introduction

1. See the collection of tributes to Professor Burt that were given at his memorial service at Yale Law School on November 1, 2015, published in 125 Yale L.J. 796 (2016).
2. 347 U.S. 483 (1954).
3. 304 U.S. 144 (1938).
4. United States v. Vuitch, 402 U.S. 62 (1971); Roe v. Wade, 410 U.S. 113 (1973).
5. 347 U.S. 483 (1954).
6. 349 U.S. 294 (1955).
7. Owen M. Fiss, *The Odd Couple*, 125 Yale L.J. 801 (2016).
8. Id. at 805–6.
9. The Court, arguably uncharacteristically, promoted further deliberative process in a collection of cases regarding religious objections by nonprofit organizations to providing their employees with contraception coverage under the Affordable Care Act. In *Zubik v. Burwell*, 578 U.S. ___ (2016) (slip opinion), the court issued a *per curiam* order in which it remanded the disputes to the Circuit Courts of Appeals and stated that "the parties on remand should be afforded an opportunity to arrive at an approach going forward that accommodates" the petitioners' religious exercise and the government's interest in ensuring that women receive the insurance coverage mandated by the act.

Chapter 1. A Living Truth

1. The mimeographed class materials were subsequently published. See Joseph Goldstein & Jay Katz, *The Family and the Law* (New York: Free Press, 1965) p. 9 & n. 1.
2. Id. at 189–90.
3. Id. at 556.
4. Id. at 557.
5. Id. at 113.
6. This thin, rationalistic conception of law is not restricted to English thinking or to the time when I studied there. For example, it lies beneath the core proposition of the modern Law and Economics movement that, for purposes of evaluating legal regulations, it is appropriate and even necessary to assume that all individual subjects of regulations are rational actors pursuing their chosen preferences. Even the contemporary critics of this premise, who cite the irrational convictions that typically guide personal choice, still hold firm to their conviction that these irrationalities can be readily identified and rationally manipulated by these critics using their own rational capacities to purposefully influence the choices of less self-consciously aware subjects. This thin rationality is also visible in the work of contemporary moral philosophers—for example, Martha Nussbaum, who correctly sees the wrongful revulsion in popular stereotypes toward LGBTQ people but imagines that this deeply irrational degradation can readily be dissolved by rational correctives. See *From Disgust to Humanity: Sexual Orientation and Constitutional Law* (New York: Oxford Univ. Press, 2010).
7. 304 U.S. 144 (1938).
8. Nebbia v. New York, 291 U.S. 502 (1934); National Labor Relations Board v. Jones & Laughlin Steel Corp., 301 U.S. 1 (1937).
9. Brown v. Board of Education, Order for Reargument, 345 U.S. 972 (1953).
10. Quoted in Richard Kluger, *Simple Justice: The History of "Brown v. Board of Education" and Black America's Struggle for Equality* (New York: Knopf, 1976) at p. 643.
11. Grutter v. Bollinger, 539 U.S. 306 (2003).
12. Frontiero v. Richardson, 411 U.S. 677 (1973).
13. Cleburne v. Cleburne Living Center, 473 U.S. 432 (198).

Chapter 2. Judicial Power to Command

1. I previously published an account of these events. See *Law Touched Our Hearts: A Generation Remembers Brown v. Board of Education* (M. Robinson & R. Bonnie, eds.) (Nashville, Tenn.: Vanderbilt Univ. Press, 2007).

2. See Charles Black, *The Unfinished Business of the Warren Court*, 46 Wash. L. Rev. 3, 22 (1970); Louis Lusky, *The Stereotype: Hard Core of Racism*, 13 Buff. L. Rev. 450, 457 (1963).
3. See Gerald N. Rosenberg, *The Hollow Hope: Can Courts Bring About Social Change?* (Chicago: Univ. of Chicago Press, 2008).

Chapter 3. All That Is Solid

1. Dred Scott v. Sandford, 60 U.S. 393, 410 (1857).
2. See, e.g., David Brion Davis, *The Problem of Slavery in Western Culture* (Oxford: Oxford Univ. Press, 1988).
3. Bernard Bailyn, *The Ideological Origins of the American Revolution* (Cambridge, Mass.: Harvard Univ. Press, 1967) at pp. ix, 102, 107, 11, 119–20, 122, 125–26.
4. *Taxation No Tyranny*, in *The Works of Samuel Johnson* 14:93 (Troy, N.Y.: Paffreats, 1913).
5. Edmund S. Morgan, *American Freedom American Slavery: The Ordeal of Colonial Virginia* (New York: W. W. Norton, 1975). See David Brion Davis's elaboration of this idea, that "the whites' projection on blacks of unwanted animal traits and attributes highlighted the blacks' supposed incapacity for freedom" and that "blacks represented and sometimes absorbed the finitude, imperfections, sensuality, self-mockery, and depravity of human nature, thereby amplifying the opposite qualities in the white race." *The Problem of Slavery in the Age of Emancipation* (New York: Knopf, 2014) at pp. 13, 42.
6. See David E. Stannard, *American Holocaust: The Conquest of the New World* (Oxford: Oxford Univ. Press, 1992) pp. 105–9.
7. See David Brion Davis, *Inhuman Bondage: The Rise and Fall of Slavery in the New World* (Oxford: Oxford Univ. Press, 2006) p. 144.
8. Id. at 152. Thus Vermont outlawed slavery in its 1777 Constitution; Pennsylvania enacted gradual emancipation in 1780, as did Connecticut and Rhode Island in 1784, New York in 1799, and New Jersey in 1804. In Massachusetts, emancipation was achieved by judicial ruling in 1783. See id. at xii–xiv.
9. "[T]he 1780s witnessed a great upsurge of anti-slavery sentiment in the upper South as well as in the North. . . . [I]n 1782 Virginia passed a law that eased and even encouraged private manumissions. In 1784 the Continental Congress came within one vote of passing Jefferson's bill that purported to exclude slavery from the *entire* trans-Appalachian territory [including what would become] Alabama, Mississippi . . . Kentucky and

Ohio. . . . Before the American Revolution the status [of free blacks] had been ambiguous, and the number of free blacks was insignificant. By 1810, however, as a result of the emancipation that had accompanied and followed the Revolution, there were approximately one hundred thousand free blacks and mulattoes in the Southern states." Id. at 154, 204.

10. Robert A. Burt, *The Constitution in Conflict* (Cambridge, Mass.: Harvard Univ. Press, 1992) at pp. 155–57.

11. As Carl Becker classically observed, the American Revolutionary War for "home rule" was a temporary lull in the domestic struggle over "who should rule at home." *The History of Political Parties in the Province of New York, 1760–1776* (Madison: Univ. of Wisconsin Press, 1909) at p. 22.

12. Adrienne Koch, *Madison's "Advice to My Country"* (Princeton: Princeton Univ. Press, 1966) p. 137.

13. Joel Williamson, *The Crucible of Race: Black-White Relations in the American South since Emancipation* (Oxford: Oxford Univ. Press, 1984) at pp. 15–16.

14. "[After 1810, legislators in the Upper South] tightened restrictions on private acts of freeing slaves . . . A rash of new laws, similar to the later Black Codes of Reconstruction, reduced free blacks almost to the status of slaves without masters. The new laws regulated their freedom of movement, forbade them to associate with slaves, subjected them to surveillance and discipline by whites, denied them the legal right to testify in court against whites, required them to work at approved jobs, and threatened them with penal labor if not actual reenslavement. . . . The intense and even worsening racism from Virginia to New England presented an ominous message with respect to a postemancipation America." Davis, *Inhuman Bondage, supra* n. 7, at p. 204. In 1806, the Virginia legislature specified that any subsequently freed slave in the state after manumission would forfeit "his or her right to freedom . . . and may be apprehended and sold by the overseers of the poor." This law was, however, only sporadically enforced; in 1837, in apparent recognition of this fact, the legislature provided that slaves freed after 1806 could remain in the state only after specific judicial certification of their "peaceable, orderly and industrious" character. Paul Finkleman, The Law of Freedom and Bondage (New York: Oceana Publications, 1986) pp. 114–15; Benjamin Klebaner, *American Manumission Laws and the Responsibility for Supporting Slaves*, 63 Va. Mag. Hist. and Biography 443, 449 (1955).

15. See Burt, *supra* n. 10, at pp. 155–59 and sources cited there.

16. Edmund S. Morgan, *American Slavery American Freedom: The Ordeal of Colonial Virginia* (New York: W. W. Norton, 1975) at p. 386.

17. See Sean Wilentz, *The Rise of American Democracy: Jefferson to Lincoln* (New York: W. W. Norton, 2005) at p. 516; Gerald Leonard, *The Invention of Party Politics: Federalism, Popular Sovereignty, and Constitutional Development in Jacksonian Illinois* (Chapel Hill: Univ. of North Carolina Press, 2002).

18. Alexis de Tocqueville, *Democracy in America* (J. Mayer ed., Garden City, N.Y.: Anchor Books, 1969) at pp. 246–47.

19. James McPherson, *Commentary on "A Census-Based Count of the Civil War Dead,"* Civil War History 57, no. 4 (2011) p. 310.

20. J. David Hacker, *A Census-Based Count of the Civil War Dead*, Civil War History 57, no. 4 (2011) at p. 308.

21. Id. at p. 313.

22. Williamson, *supra* n. 13, at p. 306.

23. "One of the most striking aspects about the lynching phenomenon was . . . the suddenness of its appearance in and after 1889 as a distinctly interracial happening in the South. . . . The cold statistics hardly begin to capture the emotional heat generated by the crises of sex and race in the South in the early 1890s." Id. at 184–85.

24. See sources cited in *Lawrence v. Texas*, 539 U.S. 558, 568–69 (2003).

25. Ariella Dubler, *Wifely Behavior: A Legal History of Acting Married*, 100 Colum. L. Rev. 957, 970 (2000).

26. Michael Grossberg, *Balancing Acts: Crisis, Change, and Continuity in American Family Law, 1890–1990*, 28 Ind. L. Rev. 273, 278–80 (1995).

27. See, e.g., Buck v. Bell, 274 U.S. 200 (1927).

28. Nicola Beisel, *Imperiled Innocents: Anthony Comstock and Family Reproduction in Victorian America* (1997) at pp. 36–37.

29. James C. Mohr, *Abortion in America: The Origins and Evolution of National Policy, 1800–1900* (1978) at p. 200.

30. President Ulysses S. Grant, State of the Union address (December 4, 1871) (available at htt///www.thisnation.com/library/sotu/1871ug.html).

31. See Late Corp. of the Church of Jesus Christ of Latter-day Saints v. United States, 136 U.S. 1 (1890).

32. At this same time, state regulatory ambitions dramatically increased over a wide range of social activities beyond sexual conduct. See Robert Wiebe, *The Search for Order, 1877–1920* (New York: Hill & Wang, 1967).

33. See generally C. Vann Woodward, *The Strange Career of Jim Crow* (New York: Galaxy Books, 1957).

34. See Henry Adams's observation that as "a young man [he had] helped to waste five or ten thousand million dollars and a million lives . . . to enforce unity and uniformity on people who objected to it . . . [and by 1867] in view of the late civil war, [he] had doubts of his own on the facts

of moral evolution." *The Education of Henry Adams* (New York: Modern Library, 1951 ed.) pp. 226, 229.

35. See Frank Rich, *Who Was JFK?* NY Rev. Books, February 20, 2014, at p. 22: "Up until now, if there's been one unifying article of faith about the assassination [of President Kennedy], it's that the country changed irrevocably thereafter—ultimately for better or for worse (depending on your political outlook). It's a defining motif of our culture. . . ."

36. According to the Pew Forum on Religion & Public Life, 51.3 percent of the American population in 2007 was Protestant, while 23.9 percent was Catholic and 1.7 percent was Jewish. religions.pewforum.org/reports.

37. Karl Marx and Friedrich Engels, *The Communist Manifesto* (David McLellan, ed., Oxford: Oxford University Press, 1992) at p. 6.

38. Prigg v. Pennsylvania, 41 U.S. 539 (1842).

39. Dred Scott v. Sandford, *supra* n. 1.

40. Civil Rights Cases, 109 U.S. 3 (1883).

41. Plessy v. Ferguson, 163 U.S. 537 (1896).

42. Williams v. Mississippi, 170 U.S. 213 (1898).

43. See James Kainen, *The Historical Framework for Reviving Constitutional Protection for Property and Contract Rights*, 79 Cornell L. Rev. 87 (1993).

44. West Coast Hotel v. Parrish, 300 U.S. 379 (1937); National Labor Relations Board v. Jones & Laughlin Steel Corp., 301 U.S.1 (1937).

45. The Court's prolonged hostility to governmental regulation of capitalist enterprise dated from the mid-1880s. See, e.g., In re Debs, 158 U.S.564 (1895). Nonetheless, this persistent judicial inclination was generally known as the *Lochner* era, so named for *Lochner v. New York*, 198 U.S. 45 (1905), which overturned a state law regulating wages and employment hours for bakers.

46. Finley Peter Dunne, *The Supreme Court's Decisions*, in *Mr. Dooley's Opinions* (New York: R. H. Russell, 1901) at p. 26.

47. 304 U.S. 144 (1938).

48. 310 U.S. 586 (1940).

49. 310 U.S. at 595.

50. 310 U.S. at 598–600.

51. Jones v. City of Opelika, 316 U.S. 584, 623–24 (1942).

52. 319 U.S. 624, 641 (1943).

53. Missouri ex rel. Gaines v. Canada, 305 U.S. 337 (1938).

54. Morgan v. Virginia, 328 U.S. 373 (1946).

55. Smith v. Allright, 321 U.S. 649 (1944).

56. Shelley v. Kraemer, 334 U.S. 1 (1948).

57. Sweatt v. Painter, 339 U.S. 629 (1950); McLaurin v. Oklahoma State Regents, 339 U.S. 637 (195).

Chapter 4. *This Word "Reason"*

1. See, e.g., Antonio Damasio, *Self Comes to Mind: Constructing the Conscious Brain* (New York: Vintage Books, 2010) at pp. 184–86.

2. See Mary Douglas, *Purity and Danger: An Analysis of Concepts of Pollution and Taboo* (New York: Routledge & Kegan Paul, 1966), final chapter, entitled *The System Shattered and Renewed.*

3. Thomas Hobbes, *Leviathan* (Edwin Curley, ed.) (Indianapolis: Hackett, 1994) at p. 9. Hobbes does not claim that this distinction comes naturally to all people or even to most. He continues, "The most difficult discerning of a man's dream from his waking thoughts is . . . when by some accident we observe not that we have slept, which is easy to happen to a man full of fearful thoughts, and whose conscience is much troubled, and that sleepeth without the circumstances of going to bed, or putting off his clothes, as one that noddeth in a chair." Id. at p. 10.

4. See Sigmund Freud, *Analysis Terminable and Interminable*, Int. J. Psycho-Anal. (1937), 18:373–405; and the edited final sentence of *Civilization and Its Discontents*, regarding the eternal struggle between Eros and Thanatos: with who knows what result? Sigmund Freud, *Civilization and Its Discontents* (New York: W. W. Norton, 1962) at p. 92.

5. Eric Kandel, *The Age of Insight* (New York: Random House, 2012) p. 462.

6. For a further example, see Stanislas Dehaene, *Reading in the Brain: The New Science of How We Read* (New York: Penguin Books, 2009) at pp. 92–93 ("[C]onscious reflection is blind to the true complexity of work recognition. Reading is not a direct and effortless process. Rather, it relies on an entire series of unconscious operations. . . . The entire visual word recognition process, from retinal processing to the highest level of abstraction and invariance, thus unfolds automatically, in less than one-fifth of a second, without any conscious examination.")

7. Kandel, supra n. 5, at p. 465.

8. Ibid.

9. William Faulkner, *Requiem for a Nun* (New York: Random House, 1951) at p. 92.

10. See Jonathan Lear, *Love and Its Place in Nature: A Philosophic Interpretation of Freudian Psychoanalysis* (New York: Farrar, Straus & Giroux, 1990) at pp. 217–18, 221.

11. Sigmund Freud, *New Introductory Lectures on Psycho-Analysis*, volume XXII, p. 80. See also Freud, *The Ego and the Id*, volume XIX, p. 56.

12. Hans W. Loewald, *Psychoanalysis and the History of the Individual* (New Haven: Yale Univ. Press, 1978) at pp. 11, 18–19.

13. Freud, *Civilization and Its Discontents* (New York: W. W. Norton, 1961) p. 15. Freud's account mirrors Aristophanes's myth in Plato's *Symposium* that humans originate as round two-headed eight-limbed creatures, are split in half immediately after birth, and spend their lives searching for fusion with their originally separated half. This is the same instinctual understanding of the conclusion drawn in Genesis after Eve's emergence from Adam's rib: "Thus does a man leave his father and his mother and cling to his wife." This impulse for recapture of boundless selves also lies behind Freud's observation about love as a normal psychosis—that the emotion is regularly experienced as the dissolution of boundaries between lover and beloved. See id. at pp. 12–13 ("Normally, there is nothing of which we are more certain than the feeling of our self, of our own ego. This ego appears to us as something autonomous and unitary, marked off distinctly from everything else.... [S]uch an appearance is deceptive.... [T]oward the outside ... the ego seems to maintain clear and sharp lines of demarcation. There is only one state—admittedly an unusual state, but not one that can be stigmatized as pathological—in which it does not do this. At the height of being in love the boundary between ego and object threatens to melt away. Against all the evidence of his senses, a man who is in love declares that 'I' and 'you' are one, and is prepared to behave as if it were a fact.") Recent neurological studies have confirmed the existence of an infantile sense of boundless connection to others through newborns' imitation of facial expressions. This apparently innate imitative capacity provides "evidence of a primary intersubjectivity [in infants] that precedes the development of the capacity to entertain beliefs about other minds." Paul B. Armstrong, *How Literature Plays with the Brain: The Neuroscience of Reading and Art* (Baltimore: Johns Hopkins Univ. Press 2013) at p. 168.

14. See Armstrong, id., at pp. 41–42: "The brain is [less like a high-speed computer and] more like a fluid, immensely complex, reciprocally interactive network of parallel-processing operations. As Dehaene observes, '... All the brain regions operate simultaneously and in tandem, and their messages constantly crisscross each other.... [T]he brain is an ensemble of simultaneously firing neurons that interact multidirectionally (bottom up, top-down, back and forth).... No one is in charge, the system has no center, and the work gets done all the more effectively because it is distributed and interactively processed....' [The brain] interactions are neither exclusively top-down nor exclusively bottom-up ... but both down and up, back and forth, across disparate regions of the brain, reciprocally, multidirectionally, in millisecond interactions beneath conscious awareness. They are not governed by a central controller—a little man in the

machine—but are complexly linked parallel processes that are organized as well as fluid, structured as well as open, patterned as well as variable."

15. The sociobiologist Edward O. Wilson characterizes this sought-for independent "self" as a "confabulation." Thus he observes, "Conscious mental life is built entirely from confabulation. It is a constant review of stories experienced in the past and competing stories invented for the future. . . . [W]hat if anything in the manifold activities of the brain could possibly pull away from the brain's machinery in order to create scenarios and make decisions of its own? The answer is of course the self. And what would that be? And where is it? The self cannot exist as a paranormal being living on its own within the brain. It is instead the central dramatic character of the confabulated scenarios. In these stories it is always on center stage, if not as a participant then as observer and commentator, because that is where all of the sensory information arrives and is integrated. . . . The self, despite the illusion of its independence created in the scenarios, is part of the anatomy and physiology of the body." *The Meaning of Human Existence* (New York: Liveright, 2014) at pp. 167–69.

16. Freud, supra n. 13, at 18.

17. Modern neurological observation confirms Freud's hypothesis about the indestructability of memory. See Armstrong, supra n. 13, at p. 73: "Confronted with novelty or anomaly, an interpreter does not erase his or her brain's habitual patterns of response and start over again from scratch but, rather, revises and extends the familiar to accommodate the unfamiliar."

18. Until very recently, this capacity for self-consciousness was believed to be unique to human beings. There is now considerable evidence that some other animals—elephants, chimpanzees, dolphins, and whales—are able to recognize mirror images of themselves as such. Some researchers deduce that this capability implies self-consciousness in these animals, at least in rudimentary forms. James Gorman, *The Humanity of Nonhumans*, N.Y. Times, December 10, 2013, p. D1. Interestingly, other species, including monkeys, dogs, and cats, apparently have no cognitive capacity to recognize mirror images of themselves. Stuart Firestein, *Ignorance: How It Drives Science* (Oxford: Oxford Univ. Press, 2012) pp. 101–6.

19. Charles Taylor, *Sources of the Self: The Making of the Modern Identity* (Cambridge, Mass.: Harvard Univ. Press, 1989) at pp. 175–76.

20. See also Alfred I. Tauber, *Requiem for the Ego: Freud and the Origins of Postmodernism* (Stanford: Stanford Univ. Press, 2013), quoting Ludwig Wittgenstein at pp. 156, 173 (dismissing "an authoritative self-conscious ego" and identifying "'bad grammar' of which the most glaring is the

representation of oneself to oneself as an object, entity or circumscribed ego"), Martin Heidegger at p. 109 ("Dasein . . . is in contrast to the process of objectificating one that requires a subject to assume a perspective of, a distance from, the object of experience"), and Jacques Lacan at p. 130 ("[N]o stable identity as such exists in the Lacanian construct").

21. Id. at p. 315.

22. On the extensive debate among philosophers about the relationship of first-person and third-person perspectives in understanding consciousness, see Daniel C. Dennet, *Sweet Dreams: Philosophical Obstacles to a Science of Consciousness* (Cambridge, Mass.: MIT Press, 2005) pp. 144–51.

23. Shaun Gallagher & Dan Zahavi, *The Phenomenological Mind: An Introduction to Philosophy* (New York: Routledge, 2008), at pp. 202–4.

24. Armstrong, supra n. 13, at pp. 127–28.

25. Erving Goffman, *Behavior in Public Places: Notes on the Social Organization of Gatherings* (New York: Free Press, 1963), *Relations in Public: Microstudies of the Public Order* (New York: Basic Books, 1971).

26. Goffman, *Relations in Public*, supra n. 25, at p. 32 & n. 6.

27. Goffman, *Behavior in Public Places*, supra n. 25, at p. 84.

28. The psychiatrist and psychoanalyst Otto Kernberg has identified the mechanism as "clinically extremely useful" and has described its two related aspects, "projective identification" and "projection": [In] projective identification . . . the subject projects intolerable intrapsychic experiences onto an object [i.e., another person], maintains empathy with what he projects, tries to control the object in a continuing effort to defend against the intolerable experience, and, unconsciously, in actual interaction with the object, leads the object to experience what has been projected onto him. Projection, a more mature form of defense, consists of first repressing the intolerable experience, then projecting the experience onto the object, and finally separating or distancing oneself from the object to fortify the defensive effort. Otto F. Kernberg, *Projection and Projective Identification: Developmental and Clinical Aspects*, J. Am. Psychoanal. Ass'n. (1987), 35:795, 796.

29. Second Annual Message, December 6, 1830, 2 *Messages and Papers of the Presidents* at 521.

30. Michael Paul Rogin, *Ronald Reagan, the Movie, and Other Episodes in Political Demonology* (Berkeley: Univ. of California Press, 1987) at p. 154.

31. Alexis de Tocqueville, *Democracy in America* (J. Mayer ed., Garden City, N.Y.: Anchor Books, 1969) at p. 508.

32. See Donald Moss, *On Hating in the First Person Plural: Thinking Psychoanalytically about Racism, Homophobia, and Misogyny*, 49 J. Amer. Psychoanalytic Ass'n 1315 (2001).

33. As the cultural historian David Nirenberg has observed, "[W]e remain heavily dependent on certain tools of perception and conception that our cultural and biological heritages have taught us are useful. These tools . . . are powerful precisely because they reduce complexity to intelligibility by projecting our mental concepts onto the world." At the same time, in his exploration of cultural views of Jews and Judaism from earliest to modern times, Nirenberg's basic "project . . . [is to] encourage reflection about [whether or the extent to which] our 'projective behavior' . . . might generate 'pathological' fantasies of Judaism." To this end, he observes, "Clearly we do not want our decisions about the world to be made in the grips of fantasy or pathology. But how can we tell whether we are being adequately reflective in our 'projective behavior,' that is, in our deployment of our concepts into and onto the world, in order to make sense of it?" David Nirenberg, *Anti-Judaism: The Western Tradition* (New York: W. W. Norton, 2013) at pp. 463–64, 466, 468.

Chapter 5. The Healthiest Possible Soul

1. Annual Message to Congress, December 2, 1862.
2. *Mary Chesnut's Civil War* (New Haven: Yale Univ. Press, 1981) (C. Vann Woodward, ed.) pp. 198–99.
3. Alexis de Tocqueville, *Democracy in America* (J. Mayer ed., Garden City, N.Y.: Anchor Books, 1969) at p. 358.
4. Hans W. Loewald, *On the Therapeutic Action of Psychoanalysis*, in *Papers on Psychoanalysis* (New Haven: Yale Univ. Press, 1980) at p. 254.
5. Loewald, *Psychoanalysis as an Art*, in id. at p. 363.
6. Otto F. Kernberg, *Aggression in Personality Disorders and Perversions* (New Haven: Yale Univ. Press, 1992) p. 159.
7. *Gorgias*, in *The Collected Dialogues of Plato* (E. Hamilton & H. Cairns, eds.) (New York: Bollingen Foundation, 1981) (W. D. Woodhead, trans.) at p. 306.
8. Id. chapter 3, at p. 307.
9. Hans W. Loewald, *Psychoanalysis and the History of the Individual* (New Haven: Yale Univ. Press, 1978) at p. 21.
10. See Alfred I. Tauber, *Requiem for the Ego: Freud and the Origins of Postmodernism* (Stanford: Stanford Univ. Press, 2013) at p. 199: "To understand Freud's enterprise and its importance, we must distinguish both his error and his achievement. . . . [T]he error begins with the psychoanalytic depiction of the ego. Despite recognizing the ego's destabilization by unconscious elements and the resulting compromise of autonomy and self-direction, Freud held on to the claim of the rational agent to engage that unruly interpsychic presence."

Chapter 6. *The Democratic Path*

1. 163 U.S. 537 (1896).

2. This conceptualization was implicit in the Supreme Court's fallacious assumption in *Plessy v. Ferguson* that race segregation was "a badge of inferiority" only because "the colored race chose to put that construction on it." 163 U.S. (1896) at p. 551. Herbert Wechsler explicitly embraced this fallacy in his charge that *Brown* violated white peoples' freedom of association. *Toward Neutral Principles of Constitutional Law*, 73 Harv. L. Rev. 1, 34 (1959). See Charles Black's rejoinder in *The Lawfulness of the Segregation Decisions*, 69 Yale. L.J. 423 (1960).

3. The Court subsequently enunciated a new jurisprudential ruling that justified no more than prospective application of new-found constitutional entitlements; but in this event, the newly proclaimed rights would at least benefit the immediate complainants. See *Lemon v. Kurtzman*, 411 U.S. 192 (1973); *City of Phoenix v. Kolodziejski*, 399 U.S. 204 (1970).

4. Brown II, 349 U.S. 294 (1955).

5. 358 U.S. 1 (1958).

6. Quoted in Ed Cray, *Chief Justice: A Biography of Earl Warren* (New York: Simon & Schuster, 1997) at p. 292.

7. Memorandum from Justice Tom Clark, cited in Dennis J. Hutchinson, *Unanimity and Desegregation: Decisionmaking in the Supreme Court, 1948–1958*, 68 Georgetown L.J. 1 (1980).

8. Robert Dahl, *Preface to Democratic Theory* (Chicago: Univ. of Chicago Press, 1956) at p. 90.

9. See Owen M. Fiss, *Groups and the Equal Protection Clause*, 5 J. Philosophy & Public Affairs 107 (1976).

10. See generally Richard Hofstadter, *The Idea of a Party System: The Rise of Legitimate Opposition in the United States, 1780–1840* (Berkeley: Univ. of California Press, 1969).

11. Pamela C. Corley, Amy Steigerwalt & Artemus Ward, *The Puzzle of Unanimity: Consensus on the United States Supreme Court* (Stanford: Stanford Univ. Press, 2013) at p. 97. See also Cornell Clayton & Howard Gillman, *Supreme Court Decision-Making: New Institutional Approaches* (Chicago: Univ. of Chicago Press, 1999) at p. 93: In the nineteenth and early twentieth centuries . . . the justices tended to conform to the will of the majority [on the Court] and to refrain from publishing their differences. Justices Oliver Wendell Holmes and Louis D. Brandeis [were considered] "the great dissenters." Yet, according to Brandeis, "Holmes was reluctant to [dissent in subsequent and similar cases] again, after he had once had his say on a subject." In contrast,

Justices Hugo L. Black and William O. Douglas, among others, noted every dissent.

12. See Lee Epstein, William M. Landes & Richard A. Posner, *Are Even Unanimous Decisions in the United States Supreme Court Ideological?* 106 Northwestern L. Rev. 699 (2012).

13. Richard A. Posner, *The Federal Courts: Challenge and Reform* (Cambridge, Mass.: Harvard Univ. Press, 1996) at p. 359.

14. Unanimity failed in a race segregation case for the first time since 1940 in *Keyes v. School District No.1*, 413 U.S. 189 (1973), when Justices Lewis Powell and William Rehnquist dissented; both had been appointed by President Richard Nixon in 1971.

15. Earl Warren, *The Memoirs of Chief Justice Earl Warren* (New York: Madison Books, 1977) at p. 285.

16. Hutchinson, supra n. 7, at nn. 322–23; Richard Kluger, *Simple Justice: The History of "Brown v. Board of Education" and Black America's Struggle for Equality* (New York: Knopf, 1976) at p. 694.

17. Planned Parenthood of S. E. Pennsylvania v. Casey, 505 U.S. 833, 867 (1992) (plurality opinion).

18. National Labor Relations Board v. Canning 573 U.S. ___ (decided June 26, 2014), slip opinion at pages 10, 12, 13, 16, 28, and 47, concurring opinion of Justice Scalia.

19. King v. Burwell, dissenting opinion of Scalia, J., 576 U.S. ___ (2015), slip opinion at pp. 1, 7, 8, 12.

20. Obergefell v. Hodges, 576 U.S. ___ (2015), dissenting opinion of Scalia, J.

21. Chief Justice Roberts and Justices Thomas and Alito joined Justice Scalia in his opinion in *Canning*, Thomas and Alito joined him in *King*, and Thomas alone joined him in *Obergefell* (though Roberts and Alito also dissented in that case).

22. See, e.g., Nate Cohn, *Polarization: It's Everywhere*, N.Y. Times, June 12, 2014, p. A3. ("[P]artisan and ideological animosity is dividing American society. . . . The urban-rural divide is at the heart of the polarization of Congress. There would be many more competitive districts if Democrats and Republicans were more dispersed across the country, as they were for most of the middle of the 20th century. Geographic polarization means that there are few areas where is it even possible to draw a district full of persuadable voters.")

Chapter 7. Enslaving Criminals

1. See Orlando Patterson, *Slavery and Social Death* (Cambridge, Mass.: Harvard Univ. Press), 1985.

2. In re Kemmler, 136 U.S. 436 (1890).
3. Powell v. Alabama, 287 U.S. 45 (1932).
4. Avery v. Georgia, 345 U.S. 559 (1953).
5. 391 U.S. 510 (1968).
6. 398 U.S. 262 (1970).
7. Evan J. Mandery, *A Wild Justice: The Death and Resurrection of Capital Punishment in America* (New York: W. W. Norton, 2013) at p. 37.
8. Id. at p. 91.
9. 402 U.S. 183 (1971).
10. Furman v. Georgia, 408 U.S. 238 (1972).
11. William Brennan, *Constitutional Adjudication and the Death Penalty: A View from the Court*, 100 Harv. L. Rev. 313, 323 (1986).
12. See Mandery, *supra* n. 8, at p. 142.
13. Barefoot v. Estelle, 463 U.S. 880, 916 (1983).
14. Barclay v. Florida, 463 U.S. 939, 991 (1983).
15. California v. Ramos 463 U.S. 992, 1029 (1983).
16. Callins v. Collins, 510 U.S. 1141 (1994).
17. Mandery, *supra* n. 8, at p. 418.
18. Coker v. Georgia, 433 U.S. 584 (1977).
19. Enmund v. Florida, 458 U.S. 782 (1982).
20. Lockett v. Ohio, 438 U.S. 586 (1978).
21. Gardner v. Florida, 430 U.S. 349 (1977).
22. Richard Weisberg, *Deregulating Death*, 1983 Sup. Ct. Rev. 305, at n. 1.
23. 408 U.S. 238 at 316.
24. See Robert A. Burt, *Death Is That Man Taking Names* (Berkeley: Univ. of California Press, 2004).
25. Barefoot v. Estelle, 463 U.S. 880 (1983).
26. 469 U.S. 412 (1985).
27. Barefoot v. Estelle, 463 U.S. 880, 915 (1983) (dissenting opinion).
28. Jack Greenberg, *Capital Punishment as a System*, 91 Yale L.J. 908, 917–18 (1982).
29. Coleman v. Balkcom, 451 U.S. 949, 957, 959 (1981) (dissent from denial of certiorari).
30. Strickland v. Washington, 466 U.S. 668, 689 (1984) ("Judicial scrutiny of counsel's performance must be highly deferential.").
31. In re Winship, 397 U.S. 358 (1970).
32. 476 U.S. 162, 178 (1986).
33. 481 U.S. 279 (1987).
34. McQuiggin v. Perkins, 133 S.Ct. 1924 (2013).
35. See Amnesty International, *Death Penalty and Innocence* (2014) (available at AmnestyUSA.org).

36. Glossip v. Gross, 135 S.Ct. 2726 (2015).
37. Erica Goode, *Incarceration Rates for Blacks Haven Fallen Sharply, Report Shows*, N.Y. Times, February 28, 2013, p. A12.
38. See the Canadian Supreme Court ruling in 2002 that denial of voting rights for convicted felons serving sentences of more than two years' confinement was inconsistent with the Charter of Rights. Sauvé v. Canada (Chief Electoral Officer) 2002 SCC 68.
39. Tamara Rice Lave, *Only Yesterday: The Rise and Fall of Twentieth Century Sexual Pyschopath Laws*, 69 Louisiana L. Rev. 549, 590 (2009).
40. Cross v. Harris, 418 F.2d 1095, 1107 (D.C. Cir., 1969).
41. Specht v. Patterson, 386 U.S. 605 (1967).
42. Lave, *supra* n. 39, at p. 591.
43. Rachel Aviv, *The Science of Sex Abuse*, New Yorker, January 14, 2013, p. 39.
44. Id. at p. 41.
45. Kansas v. Hendricks, 521 U.S. 346 (1997).
46. See Robert A. Burt, *Promises to Keep, Miles to Go: Mental Health Law Since 1972*, in *The Evolution of Mental Health Law* (Lynda E. Frost & Richard J. Bonnie, eds.) (Washington, D.C.: American Psychological Ass'n, 2001) pp. 11–30.
47. Elliot S. Valenstein, *Great and Desperate Cures: The Rise and Decline of Psychosurgery and Other Radical Treatments for Mental Illness* (New York: Basic Books, 1986) pp. 3–6.
48. See Kaimowitz v. Dep't of Mental Health (Mich. Cir. Ct., Wayne County, July 10, 1973); Robert A. Burt, *Why We Should Keep Prisoners from the Doctors: Reflections on the Detroit Psychosurgery Case*, 5 Hasting Center Report 25–35 (1975).
49. So the Supreme Court has held since *Gideon v. Wainright*, 372 US. 335 (1963).

Chapter 8. Respecting Same-Sex Relations

1. 478 U.S. 186 (1986).
2. 478 U.S. at 197.
3. 539 U.S. 558 (2003).
4. 539 U.S. at 605 (Scalia, J., dissenting).
5. Id. at 578.
6. Id. at 574.
7. Id. at 577.
8. See Reva Siegel, *Dignity and the Politics of Protection*, 117 Yale L.J. 1694 (2008).
9. Goodridge v. Dep't of Public Health, 798 N.E.2d 941, 948–49 (2003).

10. Baker v. Vermont, 744 A.2d 864 (VT, 1999).
11. Bahr v. Lewin, 852 P.2d 44 (HW 1993).
12. Hernandez v. Robles, 855 N.E.2d 1 (NY 2006).
13. In re Marriage Cases, 183 P.3d 384 (CA 2008).
14. Strauss v. Horton, 207 P.3d 48 (2009).
15. See the cases cited id. at p. 60.
16. See later in this chapter for the interaction between state and federal courts.
17. Perry v. Brown, 671 F.3d 1052 (9th Cir. 2012).
18. Hollingsworth v. Perry, 570 U.S. (2013).
19. 133 S.Ct. 2675 (2013).
20. Obergefell v. Hodges, 576 U.S. ___ (2015), slip opinion.
21. See Appendices A and B in Obergefell v. Hodges, 576 U.S. ___ (2015), slip opinion at pp. 34–35.
22. Alexander M. Bickel, *The Least Dangerous Branch: The Supreme Court at the Bar of Politics* (Indianapolis: Bobbs-Merrill, 1962) at pp. 143–56.
23. See Smelt v. County of Orange, 447 F.3d 673, 686 (9th Cir.) *cert. denied* 127 S.Ct. 396 (2006).
24. Cruzan v. Director, Missouri Dep't of Health, 407 U.S. 261, 279 (1990).
25. Hall v. Florida, 572 U.S. ___ (May 27, 2014), slip opinion at p. 12.
26. Roper v. Simmons, 543 U.S. 551, 564–65 (2005).
27. In his majority opinion for the Court in *Obergefell*, Justice Kennedy explicitly recited the extensive state legislative action, state and federal litigation, referenda, and general public debate that had occurred regarding same-sex marriage since 2003. He did not clearly explore the relevance of this "ongoing dialogue" for the Court's ultimate finding of a constitutional right, though he lightly alluded to the "enhanced understanding of the issues" that resulted from this deliberative process as "an understanding reflected in the arguments now presented as a matter of constitutional law." Obergefell v. Hodges, slip opinion at pp. 10, 23–24.
28. Cooper v. Aaron, 358 U.S. 1, 20 (1958).

Chapter 9. Abortion

1. 402 U.S. 62 (1971).
2. See Reva Siegel, *She the People: The Nineteenth Amendment, Sex Equality, Federalism and the Family*, 115 Harv. L. Rev. 947 (2002).
3. 410 U.S. 113 (1973).
4. Id. at p. 163.
5. See Planned Parenthood of Central Missouri v. Danforth, 428 U.S. 52 (1976).

6. See the sources cited in Geoffrey R. Stone et al., *Constitutional Law* (6th ed.) (Austin: Wolters Kluwer, 2009) at pp. 851–52.

7. 277 U.S. 438, 478 (1928) (Brandeis, J., dissenting).

8. Dred Scott v. Sandford, 60 U.S. 393 (1857).

9. 163 U.S. 537 (1896).

10. "If the two races are to meet upon terms of social equality, it must be the result of natural affinities, a mutual appreciation of each other's merits, and a voluntary consent of individuals." Plessy v. Ferguson, 163 U.S. 537, 551 (1896).

11. See Lochner v. New York, 198 U.S. 45 (1905).

12. John Stuart Mill, *On Liberty* (Dover Thrift ed.) (Mineola, N.Y.: Dover, 2002) at p. 22.

13. See Editorial, *Real Goal of Abortion "Limits": Bans*, N.Y. Times, May 11, 2014, p. 12. (Regarding state laws enacted in Mississippi and Texas and near passage in Alabama, Louisiana, Oklahoma, and Wisconsin.)

14. In *Planned Parenthood of Southeastern Pennsylvania v. Casey*, 505 U.S. 833 (1992), four justices announced their willingness to overrule *Roe:* Chief Justice Rehnquist and Justice White (both of whom had originally dissented in *Roe*) and Justices Scalia and Thomas. The first three are no longer on the Court, but Justice Thomas remains and has been joined by Chief Justice Roberts and Justice Alito, who appear likely to support overrule.

15. See Mary Ziegler, *After Roe: The Lost History of the Abortion Debate* (Cambridge, Mass.: Harvard Univ. Press, 2015) pp. 131, 153, 215.

16. Sociologist Kristin Luker reported that between 1968 and 1972, after enactment of the new law, abortions performed in California "increased by 2000 *percent. . . .* [B]y late 1970, of all women who applied for an abortion, 99.2 percent were granted one. By 1971 abortion was as frequent as it would ever become in California," even after *Roe v. Wade.* Kristin Luker, *Abortion and the Politics of Motherhood* (Berkeley: Univ. of California Press, 1984) (emphasis in original) at p. 94.

17. Id. at pp. 88–90.

18. See Susan Harding, *The Book of Jerry Falwell* (Princeton: Princeton Univ. Press, 2000).

19. Shapiro v. Thompson, 394 U.S. 618 (1969).

Chapter 10. Race Relations

1. See Dennis J Hutchinson, *Unanimity and Desegregation: Decisionmaking in the Supreme Court, 1948–1958*, 68 Georgetown L.J. 1 (1980).

2. Griffin v. County School Board, 377 U.S. 218 (1964).

3. Green v. County School Board, 391 U.S. 430 (1968).

4. Swann v. Charlotte-Mecklenburg Board of Education, 402 U.S. 1 (1971).
5. 413 U.S. 189 (1973).
6. Texas Dep't of Housing & Community Affairs v. Inclusive Communities Project Inc., 576 U.S. ___ (2015).
7. Parents Involved in Community Schools v. Seattle School District No. 1, 551 U.S. 701 (2007).
8. See Schuette v. Coalition to Defend Affirmative Action, Integration and Immigration Rights and Fight for Equality By Any Means Necessary (BAMN), 572 U.S. ___ (2014), where the Court upheld a state constitutional amendment, enacted by referendum that banned use of racial preferences in admissions to state universities. The Court upheld voter preference and did not itself ban affirmative action programs, but the undertone to this effect was nonetheless discernible. See Chief Justice John Roberts's facile observation "The way to stop discrimination on the basis of race is to stop discriminating on the basis of race." Parents Involved in Community Schools vs. Seattle School District Number 1, 551 U.S. 701, 748 (2007). Compare Justice Sonya Sotomayor's rejoinder in *Schuette* to Roberts's observation, supra: "In my colleagues' view, examining the racial impact of legislation only perpetuates racial discrimination. This refusal to accept the stark reality that race matters is regrettable. The way to stop discrimination based on race is to speak openly and candidly on the subject of race, and to apply the Constitution with eyes open to the unfortunate effects of centuries of race discrimination." Slip opinion at p. 46.
9. Board of Education v. Spangler, 427 U.S. 424 (1976); Board of Education of Oklahoma City Public Schools v. Dowell, 498 U.S. 237 (1991); Freeman v. Pitts, 503 U.S. 467 (1992). See also Shelby County, Alabama v. Holder, 1335 S.Ct. 2612, 2619 (2013) (overturning section 4 of the Voting Rights Act of 1965 on the ground that it "imposes current burdens [on states based on past discriminatory conduct, but cannot be justified] by current need.").

INDEX

Aaron, Cooper v. (1958), 18–20, 90, 91–94, 111
abolition of slavery, 1, 31, 32, 47, 187n8
abortion, xii, xxii, 157–69; acrimonious debate over, 41, 42, 165; church-state relations and, 166; clinics, restrictions on, 165; constitutional amendment proposal on, 167; doctors as decision makers, 36, 41–42, 158; free choice statutes, states with, 166; harm principle and, 162; history of U.S. restrictions on, 36; moment of conception as creating separate human being, 162–63; poverty and welfare assistance for, 169; privacy rights of women and, 158–60, 162–64, 169; pro-life statutes, states with, 167, 201n13; residency requirements in state laws, 168–69; subordination of women and, 157, 163, 165; Supreme Court justices' positions on, 165, 167, 168; Supreme Court's role in creating polarizing issue of, 158, 167, 169; vagueness of state statutes, 157, 167. See also *Roe v. Wade*
abstention doctrine, 153–54
Adam and Eve, 192n13
Adams, Henry, 189–90n34
Affordable Care Act (2010), 185n9

African Americans: assaults in Southern states on, 41; categorical distinction to demean as inferior to whites, 37–39, 81, 97, 105, 161, 187n5; compared to homosexuals' treatment by Court, 135–36; election of Obama as first African American president, 45; fear of black male sexuality, 34–35, 189n23; Fourteenth Amendment and, 29; free blacks in pre-Civil War era, 32, 188n9, 188n14; incarcerated black men, disproportionate number of, 128–29; lynchings of, 189n23; migration to Northern cities, 39; military service in World War II by, 39; miscegenation laws, invalidation of, 135–37; race-based sentencing in death penalty cases, 119–21; residential discrimination against, 180; as suspect class, 15; voting rights of, 47. See also *Brown v. Board of Education*; Civil Rights Acts; Jim Crow regime; *Plessy v. Ferguson*; race relations; school desegregation; slavery; Voting Rights Act
Age of Jackson. *See* Jackson, Andrew
Alabama: condemning *Brown I* decision, 91; pro-life laws in, 201n13

Alaska: abortion and free choice in,
166; Civil Rights Act (1968) and,
xxiii, 183
Alito, Samuel, 197n21, 201n14
anti-Semitism, 23–25
Aristophanes, 191–92n13
Arkansas, condemning *Brown I*
decision, 91
Armstrong, Paul B., xx, 63, 192n14,
193n17
Articles of Confederation, 31

Baars, Bernard, xx, 56
BAMN, Schuette v. (2014), 202n8
*Barnette, West Virginia Board of
Education v.* (1943), 48–49
Bartlett, Bob, 181–84
Bazelon, David L., 130
Becker, Carl, 188n11
Beverley Beach, Maryland, racial
policies of, 23–25
Bickel, Alexander M., viii, 97, 153
Bishop, Maxwell v. (1970), 106–7
Black, Hugo L., 48, 106, 197n11
Black Codes of Reconstruction,
188n14. *See also* Jim Crow regime
Blackmun, Harry, 107, 112–13, 122, 158
blacks. *See* African Americans; race
relations
Blackstone, William, 138
Boies, David, 146
Bowers v. Hardwick (1986), 137, 138
Brandeis, Louis D., 159, 196n11
Brennan, William, 108–11, 113–14,
123, 126
Breyer, Stephen, 125–26, 176
Brown, Jerry, 146
Brown v. Board of Education (*Brown I*
1954): accusatory implications of,
170–71; *Cooper's* reaffirmation of,

18–19, 90, 91–94; Court
conferences prior to voting on,
99–100; Court view of Jim Crow
system in, xxii, 14, 170;
diminished promise of, xvi;
egalitarianism of Court's role in,
85–88; Eisenhower's overstepping
with Warren when case pending,
91, 136; enforcement powers of
Court and, 25–26, 90–91; as
harbinger of protection for the
vulnerable, 11, 12; Little Rock
school board's implementation,
17–18; *Loving* and, 135–36;
Marshall (Thurgood) as chief
counsel in, 15; NAACP Legal
Defense Fund role in, 107;
psychological harm inflicted on
black children by public school
segregation, 81, 86–87; right to be
left alone and, 160; Silver Spring,
Maryland, schools and, 21–23;
Southern states' resistance to, 91,
170; Wechsler on violation of
whites' right to freedom of
association, 196n2
Brown v. Board of Education (*Brown
II* 1955), xxii; analogy to
psychotherapist's "holding space"
to allow for reflective
deliberation, 89, 95; defensible
decision based on democratic
theory, 88; delay by court instead
of ordering immediate
compliance, xxii, 25–26, 87–88,
136, 152, 169, 170; dilemma of
coercive force and, 90; Faubus's
challenge to, 92, 94; later Court
repudiating delay, 171; open to
range of remedies and

Declaration of Independence, 28
Defense of Marriage Act (DOMA),
146–48
Dehaene, Stanislas, 192n14; *Reading
in the Brain*, 191n6
Delaware, same-sex marriage in, 151
democratic values, xiii, 17, 179–80;
majority rule and, 96, 97. *See also*
equality; oppression of
subordinate groups; protection of
the vulnerable; respect
Dennet, Daniel C., 194n22
Denver school board case (*Keyes v.
School District No. 1* [1973]), 171–72,
197n14
dignity: core indignity of slavery,
156; invasion of privacy and, 139;
pregnant woman's and fetus's
status in debate over, 163–64; as
relational concept, 159–60;
Supreme Court's recognition of
human right to, 135, 140
disabled persons: disability rights
movement, 29; special protection
of, 16
discrimination. *See* African
Americans; Civil Rights Acts;
equality; homosexuality and
same-sex relationships; race
relations
disruptions: Footnote Four's
promise to protect the weak
against the strong and, 14, 19;
hierarchic eras' need to subjugate,
27, 37–38; loss of faith in
traditional caretakers as result of,
41–42, 46; major wars and
economic disasters connected to,
33, 34, 37, 43–44, 46;
psychological effects of, 40, 51–52,

71, 78; social solidarity in face of,
46; undermining confidence of
oppressors, 27, 38, 44, 71. *See also*
emancipation periods
dissent, in democratic theory, 98
District of Columbia: abortion
statute, 157–58; same-sex marriage
in, 151
doctors as decision makers in
abortion cases, 36, 41–42, 158
DOMA (Defense of Marriage Act),
146–48
domestic law. *See* family law
"don't ask, don't tell" rule, 151–52
Douglas, William O., 48, 108, 110,
197n11
Dred Scott v. Sandford (1857), 1,
28–29, 30, 97, 105, 160, 161
due process, 3, 109, 126, 130

economic regulation: capitalism vs.
labor, 40, 47, 162, 190n45;
economic liberty cases, 161; in
Lochner era, 11, 190n36. *See also*
New Deal legislation
effective assistance of counsel, 118,
133
egalitarianism: Age of Jackson and,
32; California supreme court in
dealing with gay rights and
same-sex marriage, 144–45;
Footnote Four of *Carolene
Products Co.* and, 17, 84, 97, 178;
litigation as effective method to
achieve, xxiv, 145–47;
postindependence generation
and, 31; psychological basis for,
82–83; Socrates in dialogue with
Callicles, 82–84; Supreme Court
and, 85–88, 93–94, 140, 149

Eighth Amendment, 108–9, 125, 127
Eisenhower, Dwight, 18, 90–91, 136
elections. *See* voting rights
Ely, John Hart, 96, 97; *Democracy and Distrust*, 17
emancipation periods: alternating with repression periods, ix, 27–28, 30, 37–38, 43–44, 130, 175, 179; Civil War and, 33; contemporary emancipatory impulse, duration of, 45–46; identification of three such periods, 28; protests of subjugated groups and, 29; same-sex marriage cases and, 143; Supreme Court's role in, 46–47
empathy, xi, xii; democratic values and, 179–80; developing empathic identification between previously warring parties, 75, 179; oppressors feeling unaccustomed kinship with oppressed, 44–45; projection as basis for, 68; in same-sex marriage rulings, 148; social solidarity in face of disrupted external order and, 46; in Socrates's relationship with Callicles, 72; therapist's display of, 75
English law, 4, 11, 186n6
equality: as constitutional norm, 87, 156; Court's role to protect, 13; effort needed to reach with adversaries, xii, 17, 19, 96, 178, 201n10; favoritism in American law toward rich and powerful, 12; judicial role to apply metric of equality, 178; majority rule and, 96; pregnant woman's and fetus's status with claims to, 163–64; as relational concept, 159. *See also*

specific vulnerable groups (e.g., African Americans, women, etc.)
equal protection: abortion restrictions and, 159, 169; equal respect and, 16; interpretivism and, 3; *Loving* and, 136; privileges and immunities to all citizens, 127; role of judiciary in achieving, 178–80

Fair Housing law (1968), xxii, 170, 180–81
family law, 5–12; best interests of child, 8; common-law marriage, 35; discussion of case in psychoanalytic terms, 5–10; marriage laws and licensing, 35–36; miscegenation laws, invalidation of, 135–37
Faubus, Orval, 18, 92, 94–95, 136
Faulkner, William, 56
feminism, 157. *See also* women
Fifteenth Amendment, 47
Fifth Amendment, 3, 109, 126–27
Firestein, Stuart, 193n18
First Amendment, 48
first-person vs. third-person perspectives, 62, 194n22
Fiss, Owen, xii, xxiv
flag salute case (1940), 47–49
Footnote Four of *Carolene Products Co.*: affirmative obligation of Court to safeguard minorities, xx, 13–16, 170; *Barnette* and, 48–49; denial of respect to blacks as wrong inflicted by racially segregated schools, 81; dissenters as problem for, 98; egalitarian

Hawaii: abortion and free choice in, 166; constitutional amendment in, 143; same-sex marriage approved by legislature in, 151; Supreme Court on same-sex marriage in, 141, 147

Heidegger, Martin, 193–94n20

Hobbes, Thomas, xx, 53, 58, 169; *Leviathan*, 52, 191n3

Hodges, Obergefell v. (2015), xiv, 12, 137, 150–52, 155, 197n21, 200n27

"holding space" in law and psychology, 73, 76–77, 89, 95

Hollingsworth v. Perry (2013), 155

Holmes, Oliver Wendell, 139, 196n11

homosexuality and same-sex relationships, x, xiv, xxi–xxii, 3, 5, 135–56; avoidance of litigation by LGBTQ people, 154; civil unions, 141, 142, 143–44, 151; compared to blacks' treatment by Court, 135; as criminal offense, 137–38; degradation of, 35, 37, 135, 137; gay protests, 29; invasion of privacy and privacy issues, 139, 140; military participation and repeal of "don't ask, don't tell" rule, 151–52; reevaluation of status of, 41; silence of Court from 2003 to 2015, 154–55. *See also* same-sex marriage

Humphrey, Hubert, 180–84

Iacobucci, Frank, viii, xvii

Illinois, same-sex marriage in, 151

interdisciplinary approach to law, vii, xxiii, 5

interpersonal relationships and the law, vii, xxiv, 4

interpretivism, 3–4

invasion of privacy: homosexual relations and, 139, 140; women's rights, 158–60, 162–64, 169

"invisible hand," 19

Iowa, same-sex marriage in, 144

Jackson, Andrew: genocide policy toward Native Americans, 32; projection by, 66–67; rigid views in reaction to post-Revolutionary War emancipations, 43; universal white suffrage and, 33

Jackson, Robert, 48

Javits, Jacob, 180

Jefferson, Thomas, 43, 187–88n9

Jehovah's Witness flag salute case (1940), 47–49

Jews, exclusion of, 23–25

Jim Crow regime: devalued status of blacks in, 97; forced compliance, inability to remedy through greater force, 89–90; miscegenation laws, 135–36; replacement for slavery, 28, 188n14; social relations between black and whites, regulation of, 37; Supreme Court's challenge to, 49, 85–87; Supreme Court's discomfort with in 1930s and 1940s, 106; Supreme Court's failure to protect blacks from, 13. *See also Plessy v. Ferguson*; "separate but equal"

Johnson, Lyndon, 181

Johnson, Samuel, 30

judicial activism, Nixon's opposition to, 108

judicial deference, 13

judicial power and role of judiciary, xix–xx; allowing conflicting parties to work out their differences, vii, xiii, xxiv, 88–89, 94, 95–96, 169; benefits of passage of time in decision making vs. sudden announcement of Court direction, 111–12, 153–55; command that oppression is evil, effect of, 67–68; conventional application of metric of equality, xxiv, 178; expectation of judge that his judgment will be accepted by parties, 82; imposing rules as self-defeating, x, xii; school desegregation and, 21–26; supervision of parties' engagement in interactive process to achieve equality, 178. See also *Brown II*; Footnote Four of *Carolene Products Co.*; personal attitudes of judges; protection of the vulnerable; similarities between litigation and psychotherapy
just vs. unjust wars, 90
juvenile exemption in death penalty cases, 121

Kandel, Eric, 55
Kansas, civil commitment of sexual offenders in, 131
Katz, Jay, vii, 5–11, 186n1
Kemp, McCleskey v. (1987), 120–21, 123
Kennedy, Anthony, 100, 101, 139, 148–49, 200n27
Kennedy, John F., assassination of, 40, 190n35
Kennedy, Robert, assassination of, 40–41

Kennedy, Ted, 180
Kernberg, Otto, 194n28
Keyes v. School District No. 1 (1973), 171–72, 197n14
King, Martin Luther, Jr., assassination of, 40
King v. Burwell (2015), 197n21

Lacan, Jacques, 194n20
La Rochefoucauld, François de, 94, 131
Lawrence v. Texas (2003), 138–41, 148–49
Legal Defense Fund (LDF), 15, 107, 119–20
legislative logrolling, 97
Lesser v. Lesser (pseudonyms in family law case), 5–12
LGBTQ people. *See* homosexuality and same-sex relationships; same-sex marriage
liberty's protection as goal of Supreme Court, 12–13, 14
Libet, Benjamin, xx, 54–55
life sentences without possibility of parole, 129, 133
Lincoln, Abraham, 1, 22, 33, 41, 69
Little Rock, Arkansas, school board's implementation of *Brown I*, 17–18, 92
Lochner era, 11, 190n36
Lockhart v. McCree (1986), 118–19, 120–21
Loewald, Hans, ix, xx, 57, 70–71, 76
loss of faith in traditional caretakers, 41–42, 46
Louisiana: condemning *Brown I* decision, 91; pro-life laws in, 201n13
Loving v. Virginia (1967), 135–37

respect: acceptance of separate and merged selves to promote, 68; democracy, requirement of, xii, 126; equal respect between opposing parties, xxiv, 16, 76, 169, 179; failure to achieve goal of, in either litigation or therapy, 80; gays' right to, 152, 155–56; judge and therapist both seeking as outcome to conflict, 79, 179; as key to protection of minority, xxiv; lack of respect among Supreme Court justices, 100–101

Revolutionary War, xx, 30–32, 188n11; period following, characterized as emancipatory, 28, 40, 45; slaveholders analogizing British treatment of them to slavery, 30; social ordering after, considered stable, 33; subjugatory relationships with black slaves and Native Americans as troubling to colonists during, 31

Rhode Island: emancipation in, 187n8; same-sex marriage in, 151

Rich, Frank, 190n35

right to die, 154

ripeness, 153–54

Roberts, John, 197n21, 201n14, 202n8

Roe v. Wade (1973), 100, 158–59, 165–67; *Brown* lesson ignored in, 169; likelihood of Supreme Court overruling, 165, 167, 168, 201n14

Rogin, Michael Paul, 66

Romney, Mitt, 142

rootlessness of American experience, 66–67

rules of etiquette masking aggression and psychic incoherence, 63–65, 75

Russell, Richard, 182, 184

same-sex marriage, xii, xiii, xxi, 3; certiorari denied by Supreme Court (2014 cases), 149–50, 155; constitutional right to, 137; dissents' focus on Court usurping legislative domain, 155; Scalia dissent, 101, 138–40; special protection of gay and lesbian rights, 16; split among the states over, 149; unlikely acceptance of in 1960s, 137; *Windsor* case (2013), 147–49, 154. *See also* homosexuality and same-sex relationships

Scalia, Antonin, 100–101, 126, 138–40, 197n21, 201n14

school desegregation, xx–xxi, 11, 21–26, 170–71. See also *Brown v. Board of Education*

Schuette v. BAMN (2014), 202n8

Schwarzenegger, Arnold, 146

scientific progress, and ability to control social conduct, 132

Seattle School District Number 1, Parents Involved in Community Schools v. (2007), 202n8

semi-suspect class, women as, 15–16

Senate filibuster rules, 91, 171, 180–84

sentencing. *See* death penalty cases; prisons and prisoners

"separate but equal," 14, 49, 86. See also *Plessy v. Ferguson*

World War II: blacks' military service in, 39; period following, characterized as emancipatory, 28, 39, 45–46; social effect of, 40

Yale Law School, xix, xxiv; Burt as student at, 4–11

Zubik v. Burwell (2016), 185n9